THROUGH INDIAN EYES

The Native Experience in Books for Children

By Beverly Slapin and Doris Seale

New Society Publishers

Philadelphia, PA   Gabriola Island, BC

Inquiries regarding requests to reprint all or part of *Through Indian Eyes: The Native Experience in Books for Children* should be addressed to:

New Society Publishers
4527 Springfield Avenue
Philadelphia, PA 19143

ISBN USA 0-86571-212-3 Hardcover
ISBN USA 0-86571-213-1 Paperback
ISBN CAN 1-55092-164-9 Hardcover
ISBN CAN 1-55092-165-7 Paperback

Printed in the United States of America on partially recycled paper by Capital City Press of Montpelier, Vermont.

Cover design by Sharol Graves.
Book design by Martin Kelley.

To order directly from the publisher, add $2.50 to the price for the first copy, 75¢ each additional. Send check or money order to:

New Society Publishers
4527 Springfield Avenue
Philadelphia, PA 19143
In Canada, contact:
New Society Publishers/New Catalyst
PO Box 189
Gabriola Island, BC VOR 1XO

New Society Publishers is a project of the New Society Educational Foundation, a nonprofit, tax-exempt, public foundation. Opinions expressed in this book do not necessarily represent positions of the New Society Educational Foundation.

Through Indian Eyes was originally published by Oyate.

Oyate is a group of Native Elders, artists, activists, educators, and writers who, from increasing concern for the future of our children, have come together to bring the real histories of the indigenous peoples of this continent to the attention of all Americans. Our purpose is to deal with issues of cultural and historical bias as they affect the lives of all our children. Our work includes evaluation of texts and resource books as well as fiction, workshops to help educators deal in a positive way with the literature about American Indians, and the distribution of children's books written and illustrated by Native people. For our own children, whose needs are great, our intent is that they may know what they came from, who they are, and that their lives need not be such as they are now. Oyate is a non-profit organization. Write for a list of our materials:

Oyate
2702 Mathews Street
Berkeley, CA 94702

Dedications

To Billy Joe Wahpepah; may your spirit soar with the Eagles. Go well.

And "E'he!" to my cohort, Doris, for her warmth, humor, and hard work; and for keeping me "on task" and reminding me of the necessity of this project.

And, of course, to Carlos.

—B.S.

This writing is for my People. I dedicate it to: Beth Brant; Ruth Charnes; Joan Lester; Linda, Melvin and Darius Coombs; to Giny, sister of my spirit and my blood; to Anthony and his mother; to Cení, Mashammoquet, Sokenunese, Althnageebah and Sepeyeonkqua; to Brian and Louise.

And to Beverly, for caring.

And always and forever, Tom.

—D.S

This edition of *Through Indian Eyes* is dedicated to all the sisters and brothers who have died in the cause and those who still survive in the belly of the beast.

Camilla

Who stands beside you?
Run fast
My girl,
Run
Into the dawn,
Run
To the rising sun
Run
East.

We will shape
You
Into beauty.
With the water
Of life
We will make
You strong.
With pollen
You will be blessed.
In beauty
Will it be
Finished.

Preface to the Third Edition

When we first talked about doing this book, it was going to be "just a couple articles and a few book reviews." That went by the board almost immediately, but it was not until the first edition was actually published, that we began to realize just how much was out there. Native people from all over North America wrote and telephoned with support and suggestions: "Do you know about this?" or "Have you heard about...?" We received books, from small publishers, for the most part, who are doing wonderful things, working with Native writers, many of whom are so gifted that they would be famous, if they were not Indians.

The truth is, *Through Indian Eyes* is a book that wanted to be born. Through it all, we have been guided. When a thing was needed, it came. From the work of the contributors, freely given and gladly received, to the new friendships made, the gifts to us have been beyond reckoning. To all of you, we say, with gratitude, this would have been much less without you.

It is a way of the People, not to take something away without giving something back. We know, because we have been told, that we have spoiled some people's favorite books forever. For that, we are sorry. But we also know that in the end, for the sake of all our children, it is better to tell the truth. Our hope is, for those whose illusions we have destroyed, that they will find something better here to take their place.

Doris Seale
Beverly Slapin

October 1990

Acknowlegements

We gratefully acknowledge and thank the authors, poets, and the following presses for their permission to reprint the essays and poetry noted below.

alive now! September-October 1987 for Awiakta's "The Real Thing."

Association on American Indian Affairs for Mary Gloyne Byler's "American Indian Authors for Young Readers: A Selected Bibliography," 1973.

Blue Cloud Quarterly Press for Mary TallMountain's "The Last Wolf," "Indian Blood," "Good Grease," from *There is No Word for Goodbye*, 1982.

Corridors, vol. 3, no. 1, spring 1982, for Beth Brant's "Ride the Turtle's Back."

Council on Interracial Books for Children, for Michael A. Dorris' "Why I'm Not Thankful for Thanksgiving," from *Bulletin*, vol. 9, no. 7, 1978.

Fireweed, A Feminist Quarterly, for Marilou Awiakta's "What the Choctaw Woman Said," Chrystos' "Interview With the Social Worker," Lenore Keeshig-Tobias' "Those Anthropologists," Winter 1986.

Greenfield Review Press for Paula Gunn Allen's "Kopis'taya (A Gathering of Spirits)," Diane Burns' "Sure You Can Ask Me a Personal Question," Ted D. Palmanteer's "Granma's Words," from *Songs From This Earth on Turtle's Back, Contemporary American Indian Poetry*, edited by Joseph Bruchac, 1983; Louis (Littlecoon) Oliver's "The Stout of Heart," from *Caught in a Willow Net*, 1983; Linda Hogan's "Calling Myself Home" from *Calling Myself Home*, 1978.

IKON, for Beth Brant's "Grandmothers of a New World," Winter/Spring 1987-88.

Malki Museum Press for Wendy Rose's "I expected my skin and my blood to ripen" and "Three Thousand Dollar Death Song," from *Lost Copper*, 1980.

National Storytelling Journal, Spring 1987, for Joseph Bruchac's "Storytelling and the Sacred: On the Uses of Native American Stories."

Neek for Nora Dauenhauer's "Seal Pups," "Kelp," "Rookery," and "Genocide."

Orion Nature Quarterly, 1987, for Joseph Bruchac's "Thanking the Birds."

Rounds, Cross Cultural Communications, 1982, for Gogisgi's "Ayohu Kanogisdi (Death Song)."

Scarecrow Press, for Michael A. Dorris' "I Is Not for Indian," from *American Indian Stereotypes in the World of Children*, edited by Arlene B. Hirschfelder, 1982.

Sonoma State University, for Marilou Awiakta's "When Earth Becomes an 'It'," from *Sonoma Mandala*, 1989–90.

Tennessee Conservationist, for Marilou Awiakta's "Dying Back," January/February 1987.

University of Tennessee Press, for Marilou Awiakta's "Out of Ashes Peace Will Rise," from her essay, "Daydreaming Primal Space" in *The Poetics of Appalachian Space*, edited by Parks Lanier, 1991.

West End Press, for Jimmie Durham's "Columbus Day," "Geronimo Loved Children," "Mouse Blessings," "Resistance in 1951," "Teachings of My Grandmother," "Trees Dance," "Where He Said Where He Was," from *Columbus Day*, 1983; Luci Tapahonso's "All I Want," "For Misty Starting School," "A Spring Poem," "Yes, It Was My Grandmother," from *A Breeze Swept Through*, 1987.

Table of Contents

List of Illustrations

Contributors to this Project

Editing	Doris Seale, Beverly Slapin
Art	Hooty Croy, Annie Esposito, John Kahionhes Fadden, Sharol Graves
Essays	Beth Brant, Joseph Bruchac, Mary Gloyne Byler, Michael A. Dorris, Rosemary Gonzales, Lenore Keeshig-Tobias, Cení Myles, Doris Seale, Beverly Slapin
Poems	Paula Gunn Allen, Awiakta, Beth Brant, Diane Burns, Chrystos, Nora Dauenhauer, Jimmie Durham, Gogisgi, Linda Hogan, Lenore Keeshig-Tobias, Louis (Littlecoon) Oliver, Ted D. Palmanteer, Wendy Rose, Doris Seale, Mary TallMountain, Luci Tapahonso

Introduction

Like many others outside of the Native world, I grew up with the prevailing stereotypes of the People. I learned that "Indians" whoop and holler and run around in little more than war paint and feathers, brandishing tomahawks and dancing on one leg; they scalp, torture and menace innocent settlers; they beat on tom- toms and live in "teepees"; their language consists mainly of raising one hand shoulder-high and grunting "how" or "ugh!"; and they are not women, men, and babies, but "squaws," "braves," and "papooses." Then, as now, "Indians" jumped out from comic books, greeting cards, games and toys, food packages, advertisements, movies, and TV. I can still see, in my mind's eye, images of "Indians" attacking stagecoaches and covered wagons (and in my childhood nightmares, attacking *me*). The only "Indians" I remember fondly were Princess Summerfall Winterspring, whom I dearly loved, and Chief Thunderthud ("How! Kowabunga!"), both of whom hung out with Howdy Doody and Buffalo Bob Smith.

As I grew older, a burgeoning social activism was nurtured by the stories my mother and grandma told me about the Holocaust, which wiped out much of my family, and of the heroic Warsaw Ghetto revolt. (Along with the "Indian" nightmares, I often woke up in a cold sweat after dreaming that the Nazis were coming to get me).

My father's father was a Bolshevik organizer in one of the shtetles of Czarist Russia, and one day, the Cossacks grabbed him up and tossed him into exile, where he later died. (During many of the times that I was banished to my room for one offense or another, I imagined that I was in Siberia, where I would surely freeze to death.) Of course, I never met my grandfather, but my mother says I had "blood of that nature," that, as a young child, I was always talking about justice and fairness. But I still watched TV, and, as a child influenced by this dominant culture, I absorbed all of the racist images society fed me.

Little has changed for children since my childhood. Some children who go back on their promises are called "Indian givers." "Ten Little Indians" is still a popular counting song. Non-Native children still dress as "Indians" for Halloween. Around Thanksgiving, teachers all over the United States routinely trim their bulletin boards with befeathered "Indians," and girls and boys take part in school pageants, dressed in makeshift "headdresses" and Indian "costumes." And books about Native peoples are still written, published, and promoted, by outsiders.

About four years ago, an Ojibway friend and I had an impassioned argument with a school librarian. We wanted to clear the shelves of books that demean and stereotype Native peoples, and to replace them with accurate, exciting, life-affirming books written by the people they portray. The librarian brushed us off, and that argument was followed by letters, meetings with the principal, meetings with the administration, fiery speeches at school board meetings, and, finally, locking the offending books in a closet. The shelves were temporarily cleared, and we had a short-lived victory.

It still goes on, in the same old way, and for the same old reasons: to justify the land grab by the United States of Native lands. As Robert B. Moore and Arlene B. Hirschfelder note,

> Children's books are not merely frivolous "entertainment." They are part of a society's general culture. U.S. culture is white-dominated and racist. Children's books in the U.S. reflect our society, while at the same time reinforcing and perpetuating its racism. The ideology of racism against Native Americans developed in colonial times to justify the physical destruction of Native peoples and nations, in order for Europeans to take over their lands. The ideology was later refined to justify the genocidal policies and the treaty abrogations of the U.S., as land continued to be taken away.
>
> The struggle of Native nations to regain their sovereignty, independence and self-determination against the encroachment of the U.S. is as real today as it was in the past... the "energy crisis" has put a premium on the...coal, gas, oil, uranium—which abound on the remaining reservation and treaty land of Native nations today. The desire of expanding urban populations...for land and water is continuing the historical abuse of Native nations' rights and property. Meanwhile, across the country, Native peoples are increasing their struggles to regain treaty lands and rights illegally taken away from them.[1]

Few Native writers and artists are being published by mainstream presses, and few children have even a passing knowledge of the real histories and cultures of Native peoples. Names like Alcatraz, Wounded Knee, Big Mountain, Anna Mae Aquash, Sarah Bad Heart Bull, Dennis Banks, Wilma Mankiller, Leonard Peltier, Bill Wahpepah, Roberta Blackgoat, the American Indian Movement, Women of All Red Nations—are rarely mentioned in the history or social studies texts, and if they are, they are given little credibility and short shrift.

So, while non-Native children, now as then, continue to "play Indian," the People's rights are still being eroded by the U.S. government, and the People's children are still being assaulted by the media and denied access to their cultures.

But times change, and with them, their demands. It is no longer acceptable for our children—both Native and non-Native—to be hurt by racist ideologies which justify and perpetuate oppression. It is imperative that, if our children are to grow up to create a more equitable, bias-free society, they must be carefully nurtured now.

It was with this idea that this book is intended and offered.

Recently, there has been an upsurge in the move toward teaching from what has been called "multicultural literature." But what *is* multicultural literature? It seems to be one of those all-encompassing terms, meaning all things to all people. A friend, a primary school teacher, asked me for my thoughts about a "multicultural" book list she was working on. There were three categories: African-American, Asian-American, and Native American. All of the books on the African-American list were written by African-American authors; all of the books on the Asian-American list were written by Asian-American authors; and all of the books on the Native American list were written by—did you guess?—whites. Variations of this story are often shared among Native people, who, time and again, have to explain to well-meaning educators why a "multicultural" list of books written by whites is not "multicultural." It is, if I may coin a term, "unicultural," as Eurocentric as *Dick and Jane*, and to be relegated to the same trash heap.

True multicultural literature, as a friend explains it, is a "gathering of mythos and tales of various cultures of the world representing the experiences of indigenous peoples...it is a gift of traditional peoples handed down—a sharing of stories, songs, dances—told to help each generation, like an original seed passed on."[2] That is multicultural literature.

A note on the use of names: In the minds of the People, none of the terms "Native American," "Indian," or "American Indian" is more acceptable; nevertheless, most People just call themselves "Indians" when speaking among themselves or with non-Native people.

All of these terms are, to say the least, inaccurate, since "Indians" were named for a geographical mistake almost 500 years ago. (And, as the old joke goes, "It's a good thing Columbus didn't think he had found Turkey.")

Every Nation has a name for itself. Generally, these names are some version of "the People," or, the People of a specific place, e.g., Dawn People, or People of the First Light, for those who live nearest to the eastern ocean. Some Nations, such as the Dakota, also have several divisions , so that one might, with complete accuracy, refer to oneself as Santee, Dakota, or Sioux. Most of the names by which Native people are commonly known today came from those given to them by enemies, and roughly translated and distorted by European conquerors and settlers. In this book, we will use these names interchangeably, as do the People themselves, with preference given to

their traditional ones. None of these is necessarily more "right" than any other; some prefer one, some another.

Contributors here do not claim to speak for all of the People, or even for all people of their respective Nations. They wish to share with you their different perspectives, as Native people, and as individuals. If some of them seem angry, consider that:

American Indian unemployment is higher than 70%; that the average annual income of an American Indian family is less than $2,000 in a country where the official poverty level is $6,000 annual income; that approximately 30% of all Indian women have been sterilized [most without their consent or knowledge—ed.]; that three out of five Indian children die in the first year after birth; that 70% of all Indian people suffer from malnutrition; that Indian people are imprisoned ten times more than whites; that the FBI has admitted to terrorist tactics against the American Indian Movement; that Indian people are losing their land base at a rate of 45,000 acres a year every year in this century; that more than one-third of all Indian children are removed from their families and cultures; that the average education of an Indian is five years; that most Indian people on reservations have no electricity, plumbing, or adequate housing; that the Bureau of Indian Affairs totally controls the affairs of Indian people, with an annual budget of more than $1 billion; that Indian land is being destroyed by coal strip-mining; that most Indian land is being leased by the government to multi-national corporations and white ranchers; that Indian people have spent huge amounts of time and money attempting to seek redress through the U.S. courts and are only imprisoned, repressed or assassinated for their efforts; and all of this according to the U.S. government's own conservative statistics—

This tragic situation is growing steadily worse, even though we presented these statistics to the Human Rights Commission's 34th session, at which Mr. Mezvinsky stated that Indian people were "free to criticize"—

Under the circumstances, that is like saying that Indian people are free to scream under torture.[3]

We hope readers will not take the anger personally: no one of us individually caused the horrendous conditions that assault the People today, but, at the same time, we bear the collective responsibility for correcting it. As my friend Awiakta has said, "In the fullness of time, we will create a new harmony for all of our peoples."

It would be presumptuous to think that a book of this limited scope would correct a problem that has taken centuries to produce, but we hope it will be considered as a contribution toward the goal.

Any effort that has to do with multicultural issues requires much time and energy and hard work, many hearts, and many minds. The end result of such a collaboration is a strengthened perspective.

Doris and I are indebted to the following people and organizations for their help and support during these four years: contributors Beth Brant, Joe Bruchac, Mary Gloyne Byler, Hooty Croy, Michael Dorris, Rosemary Gonzales, Sharol Graves, Kahionhes, Lenore Keeshig-Tobias, and Ceni Myles; poets Paula Gunn Allen, Awiakta, Diane Burns, Chrystos, Nora Dauenhauer, Jimmie Durham, Gogisgi, Louis (Littlecoon) Oliver, Ted D. Palmanteer, Wendy Rose, Mary TallMountain, and Luci Tapahonso. Judy Calder, Andrea Carmen, Téveia Clarke, Mary Jean Robertson, and Tawna Sanchez brought to this project insight and clarity (not to mention some hilarious stories) about Native issues. Ruth Charnes gave us patience, input, and critical suggestions. Lyn and Chuck Reese, and David Albert, Barbara Hirshkowitz, and

Ellen Sawislak at New Society Publishers contributed their technical expertise and generous assistance. And I thank Akwesasne Notes, the American Indian Movement, the International Indian Treaty Council, and Women of all Red Nations, for putting up with my seemingly endless questions.

I am singularly grateful to this project for the many wonderful friends who were given to me: my *comadre*, sister, and kindred spirit, Doris, for the poems in the mail, and secret jokes and stories we continue to share; my long-distance pal, Awiakta, who persistently maintains that my "verve and gumption" are the "warp and woof of my bein'" (I'm not sure what that means, but I think it's a compliment); my teachers Téveia Clarke and Mary TallMountain, who appear limitless in their patience and humor; and, finally, "Ish," Hooty, Bia, Nilak, Yvonne, Johnelle, Rosie, Bev, Kathleen, Bernadette, Dennis, June, Gina, Carol, and Anna, all of whom I probably never would have gotten to know but for this project.

I am a much different person than I was when we began this. Over the past four years, I have begun to have a different sense of things. I talk differently—more slowly, more thoughtfully, instead of blurting out whatever comes to mind. I think differently—weighing alternatives and meanings. My sense of humor is different—I laugh more easily, and find outrageously funny things which, a few years ago, I would have cringed at. And even my writing has changed—I often tell stories to make a point. When I am in an argument, I listen to the other side, pause, state my point, listen, pause, restate my words. I am probably just as quick to anger, but slower in showing it. What else? I choose my battles more carefully. I ask for advice more easily. I think I've even become more intuitive, less inclined to seek reasons for everything. I acknowledge and laugh at my mistakes, knowing that they will probably be followed by much good-natured teasing.

This book has been for us a gift, a blessing, an honoring. We—Doris and I—are grateful to have had the opportunity to work on it.

We hope this book is useful. Compiling it was a work of love.

A final word: There are people at the administration level of the school district—who shall, for the time being, remain nameless—who cross the street when they are lucky enough to see me coming before I see them. Since I now have a reputation as a "pain-in-the-neck social activist parent," I wear it proudly. I have no intention of taking it off.

Beverly Slapin
August 1990

Footnotes

1. "Feathers, Tomahawks and Tipis: A Study of Stereotyped 'Indian' Imagery in Children's Picture Books" by Robert B. Moore and Arlene B. Hirschfelder, from *Unlearning "Indian" Stereotypes* by the Council on Interracial Books for Children, New York, 1977. Reprinted with permission from the Council and the authors.
2. These are the words of a Choppunish friend, Téveia Clarke.
3. This is an excerpt from the response of Jimmie Durham, a delegate of the International Indian Treaty Council to the United Nations, to the U.S. government's response to Durham's report to the United Nations Economic and Social Council Commission on Human Rights, held in Geneva in 1979. From Jimmie Durham's book, *Columbus Day*, (Minneapolis: West End Press, 1983). Reprinted with permission of the publisher.

The Bloody Trail of Columbus Day
Beverly Slapin and Doris Seale

On October 12, 1992 there were two celebrations. One was for the 500th anniversary of Christopher Columbus' "discovery of America," and the United States, Spain, the Vatican, and many other European and Latin American governments sponsored the event. The other was the commemoration of 500 years of indigenous resistance to genocide and colonialism in the western hemisphere, and organizations of indigenous peoples throughout the hemisphere celebrated this event.

When Christopher Columbus landed here, he found the Arawak and Taino peoples he encountered remarkable (by European standards, anyway) for their gentleness, their hospitality, their generosity, their belief in sharing. Some modern theoreticians propose that Columbus called these people "indios," not because he thought he had found India, but because he felt them to be "people of god."

"They are a gentle and comely people," he wrote. "They are so naive and so free with their possessions that no one who has not witnessed them would believe it. When you ask for something they have, they never say no. To the contrary, they offer to share with anyone...They brought us parrots and balls of cotton and spears and many other things, which they exchanged for the glass beads and hawks' bells. They willingly traded everything they owned..."

Columbus, however, did not let his admiration for these "gentle and comely people" prevent him from taking many of them back to Spain in chains. "With fifty men," he wrote, "we could subjugate them all and make them do whatever we want." And that's what he did. He set in motion what Bartolomé de las Casas, a friar who fought for half a centruy to save the People from the conquistadores, called "the beginning of the bloody trail of conquest across the Americas."

Columbus wasn't nearly the first to land here, only one of the first to exploit the land and its people. He built Puerto de Navidad, the first European military base in the western hemisphere. From Puerto de Navidad, in Haiti, Columbus' men roamed the island in gangs, looking for gold and committing brutalities of every sort, taking women and children as slaves for sex and labor. In 1495, he and his men rounded up some 1,500 Arawak women, men, and children, and selected the fittest 500 to load onto ships. Some 200 died en route to Spain, and the remaining 300, upon arrival, were put up for sale by an archdeacon. Most of them died in captivity.

There was organized resistance to colonialism, even then. Virtually the entire island rose up in revolt, but the people's bows and arrows and fishbone-tipped spears (which were the only weapons they had ever needed) were no match for the crossbows, knives, artillery, cavalry, and dogs of the conquistadores, and the people were quickly defeated. All prisoners were hanged or burned to death. And many of those who survived the cold steel succumbed to the germ warfare of European diseases.

Terrorized and demoralized, the People were subjected to the payment of a tribute: people over 14 years of age were forced to pay enough gold to fill a hawk's bell measure every three months—or be killed by having their hands cut off. In despair, with no gold left, the people fled their homes for the mountains, leaving their crops unplanted, preferring to starve to death. Most of those trying to get to the mountains were hunted down with dogs and killed, as an example to the others. One by one, all of the indigenous leaders were tortured, impaled, hanged, burned at the stake. Then the mass suicides began, as Arawak people killed themselves with casava poison.

The people continued to fall victim to the conquistadores' greed and lust—and Christian piety. De las Casas reports how the Spanish constructed low, wide gallows on which they strung up the people, their feet almost touching the ground. Then they put burning green wood at their feet. Thirteen Arawak people were hanged each time, de las Casas said, "in memory of Our Redeemer and His twelve Apostles."

The people died, as they lived, with great dignity. Hatuey, a Taino leader, fled with his people from Haiti to Cuba. With the Spaniards right behind, the people did a mock dance of worship before a basket of gold, and then heaved it into the river. Captured, tied to a stake, and ordered to be burned alive, Hatuey was offered eternal life in heaven if he recanted. He asked the friar if all Spaniards went to heaven, and when the friar answered that only the good ones did, Hatuey replied, "The best are good for nothing, and I will not go where there is a chance of meeting one of them. I would prefer then to go to hell."

The conquest of the islands—Haiti, Cuba, Puerto Rico, Jamaica, the Antilles, the Bahamas—and the slaughter of their people raged on. Millions of good and true people died like flies, from exhaustion, torture, famine, and disease.

The Arawak people and the Taino people are all but gone. But the struggle continues. Today, indigenous peoples in these continents are still battling for land, independence, and self-determination. From Big Mountain to Akwesasne to the Black Hills to Guatemala to the Amazon rainforest, Native peoples are fighting for the right to live on their land, to speak their languages, to practice their religions, to govern themselves, to live with dignity and in harmony with nature. They are fighting a bloodline that runs from Columbus all the way to Arco, Exxon, Peabody, General Electric, and all the other conquistadores that continue to pillage and plunder the people and the land.

And the beginning of this struggle is what was commemorated on October 12, 1992.

Sources:

Columbus, Christopher, *Journal of the First Voyage to America*. Completed in 1493, first published in 1924. Salem, NH: Ayer & Co., 1972.

Curl, John, *Columbus in the Bay of Pigs*. (Homeward Press, P.O. Box 2307, Berkeley, CA 94702).

De las Casas, Bartolomé, *Historia de las Indias (History of the Indies)*. Completed in 1559, first published in 1875. New York: Harper & Row, 1971.

Koning, Hans, *Columbus: His Enterprise*. New York: Monthly Review Press, 1976.

Williams, Eric, *From Columbus to Castro: The History of the Caribbean*. New York: Random House, 1970.

Zinn, Howard, *A People's History of the United States*. New York: Harper & Row, 1980.

"Let us put our minds together and see what life we will make for our children." [1]
Doris Seale

The town I mostly grew up in was big enough to have a Carnegie library, one of those squat, blood-red brick buildings, and it was the treasure house of my childhood. I don't remember how old I was when I discovered the Laura Ingalls Wilder books, but I was intrigued by them, and showed them to my Dad. Someway, I couldn't say just how he worked it, we didn't take any of them home that day.

A few years ago, tired of hearing, "What do you *mean* you haven't read the Wilder books?!" and still curious, I opened one and found out why my Dad didn't check them out for me. In *Little House on the Prairie*, for example, on page 137:

> The naked wild men stood by the fireplace...Laura smelled a horrible bad smell...Their faces were bold and fierce. [2]

And so on. Many years stand between the nowday me and the round little girl with braids who, when this sort of thing came up in the classroom, used to sit, with dry mouth and pounding heart, head down, *praying* that nobody would look at her. But the feeling is the same. The heart begins to pound, the mouth goes dry. Only now, the emotion is not sick shame, but rage.

On the whole, people who work with children do believe that what kids read, or have read to them, *does* affect them. It is the premise on which those of us who are teachers and librarians have based our lives. Volumes have been written on the subject.

Back in the late sixties, as one result of the Black civil rights movement, there began to be a new idea about children and books. This idea was that, not only did racially biased reading give children horrible ideas about what other people were like; it might also not be good for the children of the *other* people to be wounded in their sense of self by the things they read in books. It began to be suggested, even in the professional literature, that maybe *all* children had a right to books in which portrayal of those similar to themselves would not give them feelings of shame and worthlessness.

But this idea was not very well received by the children's literature establishment. Editorial positions were taken. Articles were written. And there were letters, lots of letters. What they all said, in one way or another, was that, just because a few people were personally offended by them, did not give us the right to deprive children of such classic treasures as *Doctor Doolittle, The Five Chinese Brothers, Little Black Sambo*, to name just a few. Some of the more intellectualized responses were gracefully written. Nat Hentoff, in an article for *School Library Journal*, quoted an unnamed "internationally renowned writer for children," who said,

> Of course, we should all be more tender and understanding toward the aged and we should work to shrive ourselves of racism and sexism, but when you impose guidelines…on…writing…you're limiting the ability to imagine. To write according to such guidelines is to take the life out of what you do. Also the complexity, the ambivalence. And thereby, the young reader gets none of the wonders and unpredictabilities of living.[3]

As though deleting biases from children's books would somehow destroy the literary quality—or is a "sense of the wonders and unpredictabilities of living" something to be reserved for children of the white upper and middle classes?

On June 28, 1972, the Board of Directors of the Children's Services Division of the American Library Association, in response to "increasing concerns about the contents of communications media and their potential effect on children,"[4] had adopted a statement on Reevaluation of Children's Materials. It was intended as a "support to intelligent collection building," and said in part,

> When it is not clear from the context that the material belongs to a past era, when it…fosters…concepts which are now deemed to be false or degrading, then despite the title's prestige, the librarian should question the validity of its continued inclusion in the library collection.[5]

This statement was immediately attacked by ALA's Intellectual Freedom Committee, on the grounds that it "presents serious conflicts with the Library Bill of Rights." By November, the Board was "reviewing" the statement, and "developing further clarification and explanation where it might be appropriate."[6] And that was pretty much the end of that. By the late seventies, a label had been found for those who spoke out against all biases in books written for children: we had become the "censorship of the left." No further consideration needed.

For those of us whose work gives them responsibility for what goes into children's minds, however, it should not be a dead issue. For those who are not members of white society, it isn't. In some ways, there has been change. Black children now have available to them beautifully written, beautifully illustrated work done by gifted writers and artists, praise be. Not enough yet, but it's out there. Some white illustrators are very careful to produce multi-ethnic pictures. I have noticed one thing about these, though: they never include a Native American child.

As a children's librarian, it is my obligation to see that the collection contains balance, that the Children's Room be a place where all children will feel welcome, and comfortable. As a Native woman, it doesn't seem to me a lot to ask that the books written about Indians be honest, if nothing else. This is not so simple as it sounds. Very few non-Native writers have bothered to acquire the knowledge to produce meaningful work about our history, culture and lives— although this ignorance does not stop them from doing the books, *and getting published*…. In fact, Indians are the only Americans whose history has been set down almost exclusively by those who are not members of the group about which they are writing.

The American literary establishment may pay lip service to ideas of cultural pluralism, but it is nonetheless subject to the same biases that afflict society as a whole.

Educated people are likely to have acquired most of their attitudes toward Indians from the writings of anthropologists, for whom Native societies are considered worthy of study insofar as they have preserved aspects of pre-conquest cultures. For them, contemporary Indians are, by and large, degenerate survivors of a more glorious past. The idea that such people may have meaningful contributions to make to the literature, is one that is received with scorn. At the same time, to be educated is to somehow become less "Indian"; to be successful is to find oneself dismissed as no longer "authentic." This double bind is the result of a compelling need, even among members of the intelligentsia, to be able to regard us as inferior. I think that there is a great unconscious fear at the bottom of white America's soul—if it has one—that a "civilization" built on slavery and genocide might be rotten at the core. When Native peoples are allowed to speak of their history and their lives, it will be to tell the truth. And what will white America tell its children, then?

Balancing my concerns against the needs of assignment-driven children, who are going to be in trouble with their teachers if they don't come back with a certain book, raises, always, the question of which is worse: a book that lies, or no book. Later, I will be discussing a number of titles; first, I would like to share with you some of the reasons I have come to believe that not having *any* book to hand a child is better than giving her one filled with misrepresentations, or outright lies.

My work environment is one that would probably be considered intellectual, and my co-workers, educated and intelligent people. Most of them are dedicated, and sincere in their belief in the importance of making the written word available to all, without let or hindrance. From time to time, adult services staff will give me something on Indians to look at for accuracy, and such. This day, it is a novel based on the Hopi migrations. When I tell them that I don't think much of it, and besides, this particular author has been ripping off other people's cultures for years, someone says, *"But the only person who will know it's inauthentic is you, so does it really make any difference?"* On another day, some of my colleagues find it hilarious that a book on the arts and crafts of the Americas contains instructions on how to shrink a human head, and even funnier that I get mad.

Later, at lunch in the staffroom, there is discussion about a member of senior personnel, who has managed to irritate almost everyone. The conversation goes as follows: *"Say, Doris, isn't there some old Indian torture where they tie a wet thong around someone's neck and let it shrink?"* At which point, I lose it completely, and say, *"No, that's not the way we did it."* And of course, they are all agog to get the inside dope, straight from the Indian's mouth, so I say, *"Well, you take a strip of rawhide, see, and get it good and wet. Then you tie it around your captive's head, as tight as you can get it. Then you stake him out in the sun until the hide shrinks and his skull splits and his brains pop out. That's how we did it."* With that one remark, I managed to set Native-white relations in the library back by about 300 years. My only regret, upon later—and calmer—reflection, was at the realization that most of them probably believed me.

Every Thanksgiving, I am asked to come and be Indian-show-and-tell in the public schools. Rarely, a teacher will want her class to learn something real about Native peoples. Generally, the interest is on the level of the woman who thought it would be lovely if I could just come and tell her class "how Indians sat in a circle and talked to rocks."

All of this is nickle-and-dime stuff, the sort of average, everyday insensitivity that all people of color in the United States learn to deal with. It illustrates a point, however: Native Americans are no more, now, thought of as human beings, on the same level as members of white society, than at any other time in the last 500 years. Ignorance on the part of the non-Native population, about our history, cultures, and lives, remains near-total. The images of Indians found in children's literature have always reflected that ignorance; they have not changed appreciably over the last 40 years.

In 1941, Walter D. Edmonds received the Newbery Medal, awarded for "one of the most distinguished contributions to American literature for children," for *The Matchlock Gun*. The book has been reprinted 25 times since then, and is currently available. The writing is vivid, richly evocative. The story is ominous, filled with foreboding, and fear of the Indians, who, we know, are going to come. The illustrations are luminous, and they show Indians, one behind the other, hunched over, menace on two feet; dancing around the leaping flames of burning cabins, always in darkness, always terrifying.

> There were five of them, dark shapes on the road, coming from the brick house. They hardly looked like men, the way they moved. They were trotting, stooped over, first one and then another coming up like dogs sifting up to the scent of food.[7]

No reason is given for the Native attack on this decent and appealing little family, which makes it all the more horrible, all the more savage.

In 1984, *War Clouds in the West: Indians and Cavalry, 1860–1890*, was published. The author is a specialist in modern British history, and "intellectual and social history." The book is dedicated to the "peaceful folk, who tried to find a better way," whatever that may mean. In it, Indians go on the warpath, warriors are "braves," women are beasts of burden.

> The Plains Indian was a fearsome warrior. He hunted to live, but he lived to fight. War was his favorite pastime, his greatest joy and pleasure...To him, peace and not war was unnatural.

And,

> Captured white men were never spared. It was the custom of the Plains Indians to torture prisoners to death. Braves expected such treatment at enemy hands. They had spent most of their lives thinking about it, and preparing for it... Plains men had a saying, repeated again and again in wartime: "When fighting Indians, keep the last bullet for yourself."[8]

(Of this book, School Library Journal said, "These people [are] described with sympathy and understanding"[9] and compared *War Clouds in the West* favorably with *Bury My Heart at Wounded Knee*.)

In recent years, some attempts have been made to counter these appalling stereotypes. The cure has frequently been almost as bad as the disease. The flip side of the savage and brutal, tomahawk-wielding collector of scalps, is the Noble Redman, living a primitive, beautiful-but-doomed existence, in tune with Nature, who could track a fly across the ceiling in the dark. He is Good, because he helps white people. Alas, Uncas is alive and well and living in children's books. A corollary is the Vanishing Indian: members—and few at that—of a conquered people, incapable of adapting to a sophisticated, superior technological society. Modern Indians are known to have lost their traditions and cultures, to be living in squalor, drinking away their welfare checks. On the other hand, those Native people who have become educated, particularly if they do not live on reservations, are known not to be "real" Indians. A relatively recent one, that is especially popular with the so-called "New Age" people, is the wise shamans, who have retained occult knowledge, which they are now ready to share with white society, in order to save it from itself.

All of these, of course, are gross distortions. Romanticizing Indians may be potentially less inimical to our continued existence, but it is no less insulting to people who want only to be seen as real. Dehumanization of Indians remains good coin of the realm, because it is as useful today as it has ever been.

Of course, it has always been a matter of economics...

By 1492, the European continent had become overpopulated and had gone a long way toward depleting its resources. When the Romans left Britain, for example, two-thirds of the land had been deforested. The age of sail took care of most of the rest of it.[10] So, two whole new continents for the taking was a gift, with only one minor problem: there were already people living here. And even Columbus admitted that the Natives were a "gentle and comely people"—although it did not prevent him from sending many of them back to Spain in chains.

But the invaders had a hunger. Being a godly people, they felt some need to justify their land grab. And so was born the myth of the treacherous and immoral savage, who deserved no consideration from decent and civilized folk. It was a concept written into the 18th Century colonists' Declaration of Independence. In the words of Thomas Jefferson, "He (the British monarch) has excited domestic Insurrections amongst us, and has endeavored to bring on the Inhabitants of our Frontiers, the merciless Savages, whose known Rule of Warfare, is an undistinguished Destruction, of all Ages, Sexes, and Conditions."

One hundred years ago, the Seventh Cavalry of the United States Army shot down some 200 Lakota—men, women, and children—near a creek called Wounded Knee. It was winter. The people were cold and hungry. They had been harried from place to place. And they had been promised that they would be safe, if they "came in." This has been called the last battle of the Indian Wars. Some of the soldiers received the Congressional Medal of Honor for their efforts. From that time, Indians have been relegated to some of the most infertile and inhospitable areas of their original territories. Some, of course, were removed from their homelands forever. Unfortunately, some of those lands considered unusable by the white man, have turned out to contain rich mineral deposits. So it has not ended...

In the Big Mountain Joint Land Use Area, Hopi and Diné (Navajo) people have been set against each other by a government responding to pressures from mining interests. "Geologists for Peabody Coal estimate that the area around Big Mountain (a sacred Diné landmark that lies in the center of the disputed terrain) known as Black Mesa, is perched above 600 million tons of coal deposits, worth about $9 billion...There is also an undetermined amount of uranium, oil and other valuable minerals..."[11] The Northern Cheyenne are sitting on one of the largest remaining coal deposits in the Western hemisphere, and so are faced with yet another struggle to preserve their lands.[12] Plains peoples must fight ranchers to retain their water rights, and Akwesasne must deal with some of the worst industrial pollution in the country.

A 1985 magazine article detailed the conflict over hunting rights between Anishinabes and whites in Wisconsin. As with salmon fishing on the Pacific coast, the contention was that the Indians were spoiling it for the white "sportsmen." "It's open season on Indians," declared an unofficial notice at a local courthouse, with a "bag limit of ten per day."[13]

In recent years, an assortment of Native Rights groups has managed to win financial compensation for a few territories irretrievably lost. They are still working for the people at Big Mountain, for the Black Hills, and in many other areas. Such efforts are invariably met with hostility. An editorial in the Indiana Gazette in May 1986, for example, said:

> The present generation of Americans owes the present generation of Indians neither money, guilt, nor special sympathy. Some contemporary Americans have created a cottage industry of making American children feel bad about their past by fabricating and distorting American history. The myth fed to many children these days is that the American Indian was a utopian individual who lived in perfect peace and harmony until the bad old white man came along...That is stuff and nonsense. The American Indian lived in a savage stone age culture and needed no lessons from Europeans in cruelty, torture and killing...when the Indians came howling down and murdered women and children...they sealed their own fate...we should eliminate any special status granted to Indians...we should end this nonsense of special privileges.[14]

As long as we have anything, it seems, some white man is going to want it. And, just so long, will it be to the best interests of American society to preserve the accepted images of Indians. And that long, the Indians portrayed in books written for children will be racist stereotypes.

Are you tired of hearing it, from one "minority" or another? Does it make any difference, a few people arguing over the content of some children's books? After all, while the stereotypes may be exaggerations, don't they have some basis in fact? No, I promise you, they do not.

You know us only as enemies. Believing that it is important to know how to die well, is *not* the same as being in love with war.

That is not an accusation that can be made with justice against *Native* Americans. And, indeed, life on reservations can be without blessing, but that is not the fault of the people who live there. It has happened as a result of deliberate national policy. It happens, in part, because people have grown up believing the monster stories. What we let our children read about Indians may matter more now than at any other time in our history.

It should matter to you for two reasons. First, if the people of this Earth do not learn to care for each other, there will be no tomorrow—for anyone. Second, the child who is taught to feel hate or contempt for those who seem different from herself, will be less than a whole human being because of it. For us, it is, as it has always been, a matter of life and death. Today, unemployment on many reservations is at 80%, with per capita income of less than $2,000 a year. Health care is minimal, even for those who can get to a hospital or medical center. Native people who live in cities are rarely hired for anything but the most menial and low-paying jobs. Infant mortality is high. In a nation already appalled at the high rate of suicide among teenagers, the rate for young Native Americans is more than twice the national average. Life expectancy is less than 50 years. Insurmountable obstacles are put in the way of Native children, in the pursuit of even a secondary education. Those who *do* make it, *and* retain their identity, are not necessarily the most gifted, but the strongest, both physically and psychologically. Indians have been exterminated, allocated, reorganized, relocated and terminated. And we still survive. Native peoples have resisted, both actively and passively. That so many of us have managed to survive, even to become educated, is no tribute to the American system, but to those traditions we are supposed to have lost, and to the strength of our spirit.

But it is always at a cost. The child who is taught to believe that she is but a few generations removed from a state of bloody savagery, that her people are helpless anachronisms incapable of surviving in a "civilized" world, is wounded and warped in her sense of self, in a way that may never be completely remedied. Some, of course, have been destroyed as human beings. And we are human. This is all real. The lies that are told are about real people. We are alive. We love each other. We cry when our children die. Just like you.

Oh, yes, it matters now. Past politeness, beyond objectivity.

In 1972, Molly Cone wrote a book based on news reports from the West coast, about the death by drowning of an Indian teenager.[15] He had been, by all accounts, a boy of some promise. His clothes were found, neatly folded, on the porch of a nearby house. In one pocket, was a flyer for an Indian Law Day program. On the back of it, he had written this:

> I wanna be an Indian
> I wanna be red
> I wanna be free
> Or I wanna be dead.

What if he had been *your* child?

Footnotes

1. Tatanka Iotanka (Sitting Bull).
2. Wilder, Laura Ingalls, *Little House on the Prairie*. First published 1935; Harper & Row, 1971, p. 137.
3. Hentoff, Nat, "Any Writer Who Follows Anyone Else's Guidelines Ought to Be in Advertising." *School Library Journal*, November 1977, p. 28.
4. *Top of the News*, November 1972, p. 5.
5. Ibid.
6. Ibid.
7. Edmonds, Walter D., *The Matchlock Gun*. Dodd, Mead, 1941, p. 39.
8. Marrin, Albert, *War Clouds in the West: Indians and Cavalrymen, 1860-1890*. Atheneum, 1984, pp. 27 and 39.
9. *School Library Journal*, March 1985.
10. Ehrlich, Anne and Paul, *Earth*. Franklin Watts, 1987.
11. *Boston Sunday Globe*, July 26, 1987, p. 71.
12. A detailed account of this situation may be found in Ashabranner, Brent, *Morning Star, Black Sun: The Northern Cheyenne Indians and America's Energy Crisis*. Dodd, Mead, 1982.
13. "Open Season on Indians," *Newsweek*, September 30, 1985.
14. *Indiana Gazette*, May 1986.
15. Cone, Molly, *Number Four*. Houghton Mifflin, 1972.

Why I'm Not Thankful for Thanksgiving
Michael A. Dorris

In preparing this essay on stereotyping and Native American children, I did not concern myself with overt or intentional racism. Native American young people, particularly in certain geographical areas, are often prey to racial epithets and slurs—and to physical abuse—just by being who they are. No amount of "consciousness-raising" will solve this problem; it must be put down with force and determination.
—*M.D.*

Native Americans have more than one thing *not* to be thankful about on Thanksgiving. Pilgrim Day, and its antecedent feast Halloween, represent the annual twin peaks of Indian stereotyping. From early October through the end of November, "cute little Indians" abound on greeting cards, advertising posters, in costumes, and school projects. Like stock characters from a vaudeville repertoire, they dutifully march out of the folk-cultural attic (and right down Madison Avenue!) *ugh*ing and *wah-wah-wah*ing, smeared with lipstick and rouged; decked out in an assortment of "Indian suits" composed of everything from old clothes to fringed paper bags, little trick-or-treaters and school pageant extras mindlessly sport and cavort.

Considering that virtually none of the standard fare surrounding either Halloween or Thanksgiving contains an ounce of authenticity, historical accuracy, or cross-cultural perception, why is it so apparently ingrained? Is it necessary to the American psyche to perpetually exploit and debase its victims in order to justify its history? And do Native Americans have to reconcile themselves to forever putting up with such exhibitions of puerile ethnocentrism?

Being a parent is never uncomplicated. One is compelled, through one's children, to re-experience vicariously the unfolding complexities of growing up, of coping with the uncomprehended expectations of an apparently intransigent and unaffectable world, of carving a niche of personality and point of view amidst the abundance of pressures and demands which seem to explode from all directions. Most people spend a good part of their lives in search of the ephemeral ideal often termed "identity," but never is the quest more arduous and more precarious—and more crucial—than in the so-called "formative years."

One would like, of course, to spare offspring some of the pains and frustrations necessarily involved in maturation and self-realization, without depriving them of the fulfillments, discoveries and excitements which are also part of the process. In many arenas, little or no parental control is—or should be—possible. Learning, particularly about self, is a struggle, but with security, support, and love it has extraordinary and marvelously unique possibilities. As parents, our lot is often to watch and worry and cheer and commiserate, curbing throughout our impulse to intervene. The world of children interacting with children is in large part off-limits.

Passivity ends, however, with relation to those adult-manufactured and therefore wholly gratuitous problems with which our children are often confronted. We naturally rise against the greed of panderers of debilitating junk foods; we reject dangerous toys, however cleverly advertised; and we make strict laws to protect against reckless motorists. We dutifully strap our children into seatbelts, keep toxic substances out of reach, and keep a wary eye for the molesting or abusive stranger.

With so many blatant dangers to counter, perhaps it is unavoidable that some of the more subtle and insidious perils to child welfare are often permitted to pass. The deficiencies of our own attitudes and training may be allowed to shower upon our children, thus insuring their continuation, unchallenged, into yet another generation. Much of what we impart is unconscious, and we can only strive to heighten our own awareness and thereby circumvent a repetition *ad infinitum* of the "sins of the fathers" (and mothers).

And of course we all make the effort to do this, to one degree or another. It is therefore especially intolerable when we observe other adults witlessly, maliciously, and occasionally innocently, burdening our children with their own unexamined mental junk. Each of us has undoubtedly amassed a whole repertoire of examples of such negative influences, ranked in hierarchy of infamy according to our own values and perspectives. Even with the inauguration of certain broad controls, Saturday morning cartoon audiences are still too often invited to witness and approve violence, cruelty, racism, sexism, ageism, and a plethora of other endemic social vices.

Attitudes pertinent to "racial" or "sex-role" identity are among the most potentially hazardous, for these can easily be internalized—particularly by the "minority" child. Such internalized attitudes profoundly affect self-concept, behavior, aspiration, and confidence. They can inhibit a child before he or she has learned to define personal talents, limits or objectives, and tend to regularly become self-fulfilling prophesies. Young people who are informed that they are going to be underachievers do underachieve with painful regularity.

The progeny of each oppressed group are saddled with their own specialized set of debilitating—and to parents, infuriating—stereotypes. As the father of three Native American children, aged ten, six, and three, I am particularly attuned (but not resigned) to that huge store of folk Americana presuming to have to do with "Indian lore." From the "One little, two little..." messages of nursery school, to the ersatz pageantry of boy scout/campfire girl mumbo jumbo, precious, ridiculous and irritating "Indians" are forever popping up.

Consider for a moment the underlying meanings of some of the supposedly innocuous linguistic stand-bys: "Indian givers" take back what they have sneakily bestowed in much the same way that "Indian summer" deceives the gullible flower bud. Unruly children are termed "wild Indians" and a local bank is named "Indian Head" (would you open an account at a "Jew's hand," "Negro ear" or "Italian toe" branch?). Ordinary citizens rarely walk "Indian file" when about their business, yet countless athletic teams, when seeking emblems of savagery and bloodthirstiness, see fit to title themselves "warriors," "braves," "redskin" and the like.

On another level, children wearing "Indian suits," playing "cowboys and Indians" (or, in the case of organizations like the Y-Indian Guides, Y-Indian Maidens and Y-Indian Princesses, simply "Indians") or scratching their fingers with pocket knives (the better to cement a friendship) are encouraged to shriek, ululate, speak in staccato and ungrammatical utterances (or, conversely, in sickeningly flowery metaphor)—thus presumably emulating "Indians." With depressing predictability, my children have been variously invited to "dress up and dance," portray Squanto (Pocahontas is waiting in the wings: my daughter is only three), and "tell a myth."

Not surprisingly, they have at times evidenced some unwillingness to identify, and thus cast their lot, with the "Indians" which bombard them on every front. My younger son has lately taken to commenting "Look at the Indians!" when he comes across Ricardo Montalban, Jeff Chandler or the improbable Joey Bishop in a vintage TV western. Society is teaching him that "Indians" exist only in an ethnographic frieze, decorative and slightly titillatingly menacing. They invariably wear feathers, never crack a smile (though an occasional leer is permissible under certain conditions), and think about little besides the good old days. Quite naturally, it does not occur to my son that he and these curious and exotic creatures are expected to present a common front—until one of his first grade classmates, garbed in the favorite costume of Halloween (ah, the permutations of burlap!) or smarting from an ecology commercial, asks him how to shoot a bow, skin a hamster or endure a scrape without a tear. The society image is at the same time too demanding and too limiting a model.

As a parent, what does one do? All efficacy is lost if one is perceived and categorized by school officials as a hyper-sensitive crank, reacting with horror to every "I-is-for-Indian" picture book. To be effective, one must appear to be super-reasonable, drawing sympathetic teachers and vice-principals into an alliance of the enlightened to beat back the attacks of the flat-earthers. In such a pose, one may find oneself engaged in an apparently persuasive discussion with a school librarian regarding a book titled something like *Vicious Red Men of the Plains* ("Why, it's set here for 20 years and nobody ever noticed that it portrayed all Indi...uh, Native Americans, as homicidal maniacs!"), while at the same time observing in silence a poster on the wall about "Contributions of the Indians" (heavy on corn and canoes, short on astronomy and medicine).

Priorities must be set. One might elect to let the infrequent coloring book page pass uncontested in favor of mounting the battlements against the visitation of a traveling Indianophile group proposing a "playlet" on "Indians of New Hampshire." These possibly well intentioned theatricals, routinely headed by someone called "Princess Snowflake" or "Chief Bob," are among the more objectionable "learning aids" and should be avoided at all costs. It must somehow be communicated to educators that *no* information about Native peoples is truly preferable to a reiteration of the same old stereotypes, particularly in the early grades.

A year ago my older son brought home a program printed by his school; on the second page was an illustration of the "First Thanksgiving," with a caption which read in part: "They served pumpkins and turkeys and corn and squash. The Indians had never seen such a feast!" On the contrary! The *Pilgrims* had literally never seen "such a feast," since all foods mentioned are exclusively indigenous to the Americas and had been provided, or so legend has it, *by* the local tribe.

Thanksgiving could be a time for appreciating Native American peoples as they were and as they are, not as either the Pilgrims or their descendant bureaucrats might wish them to be. If there *was* really a Plymouth Thanksgiving dinner, with Native Americans in attendance as either guests or hosts, then the event was rare indeed. Pilgrims generally considered Indians to be devils in disguise, and treated them as such.

And if those hypothetical Indians participating in that hypothetical feast thought that all was well and were thankful in the expectation of a peaceful future, they were sadly mistaken. In the ensuing months and years, they would die from European diseases, suffer the theft of their lands and property and the near-eradication of their religion and their language, and be driven to the brink of extinction. Thanksgiving, like much of American history, is complex, multi-faceted, and will not bear too close a scrutiny without revealing a less than heroic aspect. Knowing the truth about Thanksgiving, both its proud and its shameful motivations and history, might well benefit contemporary children. But the glib retelling of an ethnocentric and self-serving falsehood does not do one any good.

Parents' major responsibility, of course, resides in the home. From the earliest possible age, children must be made aware that many people are wrong-headed about not only Native Americans, but about cultural pluralism in general. Children must be encouraged to articulate any questions they might have about "other" people, and "minority" children must be given ways in which to insulate themselves from real or implied insults, epithets, slights or stereotypes. "Survival humor" must be developed and positive models must, consciously and unconsciously, be available and obvious. Sadly, children must learn *not* to trust uncritically.

Protecting children from racism is every bit as important as insuring that they avoid playing with electrical sockets. Poison is poison, and ingrained oppressive cultural attitudes are at least as hard to antidote, once implanted, as are imbibed cleaning fluids. No one gains by allowing an inequitable and discriminatory status quo to persist. It's worth being a pain in the neck about.

Notes from an Indian Teacher
Rosemary Gonzales

I am sitting at a desk at the back of my classroom. My teacher hands out papers, and tells us to fill them out if we are Indian, or "part Indian." I take the paper automatically, without question, fill it out, and hand it in. I am confused and embarrassed, but I accept it with a fourth grader's acceptance of adults' purposeless rules. The only reason given is that the school is "counting Indians"....

At college, I become more aware. I attend social studies workshops sponsored by Native people. The things they talk about bring back family memories. There is some comfort in that my values come from "somewhere," they have roots. The natural intuitive gifts we have, the perception of "nature," the spiritual ties, all seem to be "right" now....

I finish a unit on "racism and Native Americans" for an education class, and receive a low grade because my project is called "inappropriate subject material" to be taught to children. I am outraged. My classmates treat my anger and insight with pity; I know they see me as having emotional problems, or, at best, as being politically extreme....

Years later, I come to get my older son at his daycare. I am very tired. It is one day after another of many pre-Thanksgiving hooplas. My son is in the back, reading, not participating in the class art project. I look over at it, and tears sting my eyes—the children are creating masks of "Indian" faces. I look at my son, brown, beautiful, and alone, and I want to protect him from the whole racist world and the destruction of our values, of our People. On the way home, we talk about it briefly. I lay my hand on his shoulder, and then let it go....

The next day, I pick up my younger son at his school, and see another "art" project—paper plates with "Indian" braids and faces. I feel overwhelmed at what my children have to endure. I speak to the teacher, who stares at me blankly, uncomprehending. "I didn't mean to offend anyone," she says, and besides, the pictures are not of Indians, but of "Native Americans." I take my son by the hand and walk out. At home, I tell him that he does not look like those paper plates. I hold him up to the mirror. I say, "Our people are beautiful...."

At a school in which I teach, a colleague asks me "what I am" because of my last name and appearance, I suppose. The discussion involves more people, and I am uncomfortable. After a while, I tell them I am Native. They question "how much" and inquire whether I am "legally" Indian. As with so many times, I feel my anger rise up through my chest and burn on my face.

"Would you like a blood test, to measure a percentage," I ask. The conversation abruptly stops. After our meeting, I tell my colleague why I am offended. She bursts into tears, and the others come to her defense....

Together with a friend, at about Thanksgiving time, I remove a bunch of racist books from the school library and stack them in my classroom. We read every book. We mark every racist line. We consult with other Native people. We prepare a detailed report and distribute it to teachers, the librarian, the principal. We argue with them, again and again. I am reprimanded for being "unprofessional." We invite Native leaders to talk with the children and staff at school, hoping to educate them with truth instead of lies. But the lies surface in the children's questions, and I become sick, and I become saddened....

At another school, at Halloween, children are dressed as goblins, pirates, animals, monsters. The school principal asks me how I like her costume. She is dressed as an "Indian Princess." "I'm a Native American," she says....

I watch a Thanksgiving assembly. The children, dressed in paper-feather headdresses, sing "Ten Little Indians." The audience applauds. I stay in the back, pacing quietly, shocked. After the performance, I ask to organize the next Thanksgiving assembly, working with the same teacher who thinks that children singing "Ten Little Indians" is cute....

As a teacher, I find lies about my People everywhere. I attempt to teach truth to my children, so they, in turn, may teach their children. I feel out of place, most of the time, because of the ignorance of many. But I do what I must in my way to change the education of our children so that they may make realistic choices with real information about real People.

I have become tired and sad, however, because of the injustice of having to do it all, and the bombardment of racism in our children's minds. It is not their fault, of course, but it is a real tool of oppression for all—and a denial of richness, wisdom, health and harmonious life which is available to everyone.

There is comfort, sometimes, as I sit out at night, remembering my Grandmother's wisdom. "The trees are very protective of People," she said, "and when you cannot hold yourself up any longer, they will do it for you. It is a purpose of the Creator."

"I" Is Not for Indian
Michael A. Dorris

"I" isn't for Indian; it is often for Ignorance. In the Never-Never land of glib stereotypes and caricature, the rich histories, cultures, and the contemporary complexities of the indigenous, diverse peoples of the Western Hemisphere are obscured, misrepresented, and rendered trivial. Native Americans appear not as human beings but as whooping, silly, one-dimensional cartoons. On occasion they are presented as marauding, blood-thirsty savages, bogeys from the nightmares of "pioneers" who invaded their lands and feared for the consequences. At other times they seem preconcupiscent angels, pure of heart, mindlessly ecological, brave and true. And worst of all, they are often merely cute, the special property of small children.

It's an easy way to dismiss an unproud history. A society that chooses to make a running joke of its victims embalms both its conscience and its obligations, relegating a tragic chronology of culture contact to ersatz mythology. It's hard to take seriously, to empathize with, a group of people portrayed as speaking ungrammatical language, as dressing in Halloween costumes, as acting "wild," as being undependable in their promises or gifts. Frozen in a kind of pejorative past tense, these make-believe Indians are not allowed to change or in any other way be like *real* people. They are denied the dignity and dynamism of their history, the validity of their myriad and major contributions to modern society, the distinctiveness of their multiple ethnicities.

It's a shame. To deprive our children (who grow up to become no less deprived adults) access to the wealth and sophistication of traditional Native American societies is indefensible. Among the several hundred separate cultures of North America alone, comprising as they did between 12 and 20 million people in 1491, there existed a pluralism of societal experimentation and worldview unimagined by the melting pot theorists. Every known form of political system was practiced, from democracy to theocracy to communism to hereditary leadership.

In the vast majority of these societies, power and decision-making rested with both women and men. Most Native peoples were village-based agriculturists, not "roaming hunters." A wide variety of sciences—astronomy, agronomy, medicine, mathematics, geology, meteorology, and taxonomy, to name only a few—were highly developed and practiced. A wealth of spiritual and philosophical beliefs flourished. A tolerance for individual difference, either within one's own culture or in another society altogether, was the norm. Literature, music, dance, and art found widely divergent and brilliant expression. And yet this treasure trove of experience and intelligence, perfected over tens of thousands of years' residence on this continent, is allowed to be eclipsed by racist drivel.

Real American history, abounding with confusion, misunderstanding, exploitation, good people and bad ones, cultural chauvinism and hard-won insight, contains lessons that vitally need to be learned, not forgotten or whitewashed. We, as a people, must not make the same mistakes again in other dealings with new societies that seem to be initially either strange or unfathomable to us.

Some readers may find individual instances of stereotyping to be inoffensive, and individually they may be. Taken out of the general context, objection to a particular toy or school symbol or nursery rhyme might seem to be a case of over-sensitivity. "Where's your sense of humor?" they may ask. "Aren't all groups satirized or emblemized? Irish-Americans are proud of the Fighting Irish of Notre Dame! What's wrong with exhorting little boys to want to be brave and stoic? Can't you take a joke?"

No. It's no joke when a dominant group, with a sorry history of oppression towards its minorities, expropriates a shallow version of a subordinate, relatively powerless group

and promulgates that imagery as valid. This realization may come slowly, but it can come. Even the most hearty enthusiast can probably comprehend today the tastelessness of little Black jockey statues in front of a house or the rolling-eyed parody of minstrel-show revelry. Even the most oblivious observer cannot help but see the danger inherent in early Nazi caricatures of Jewish people or Gypsies. Italian anti-defamation leagues are strong in their censure of media gangsters with Sicilian names. For most of us the Polish joke is at least suspect.

So why should standards of respect and restraint differ when it comes to Indians? Are Native people less worthy of serious consideration, less contemporary, less complicated? Is it any less demeaning or ridiculous to portray every Indian with feathers than it would be to present every Afro-American with a spear or every Hispanic with a sombrero?

Indian tribes in the United States are self-governing, political entities, many of them rich in natural resources and all of them rich in human potential. For far too long they have been denied their legitimate place, their own voice, the public awareness of their diverse heritage. Let "I" be for something else.

Two Plus Two or Why Indians Flunk

Beverly Slapin

All right, class, let's see who knows what two plus two is. Yes, Doris?

I have a question. Two plus two what?

Two plus two anything.

I don't understand.

OK, Doris, I'll explain it to you. You have two apples and you get two more. How many do you have?

Where would I get two more?

From a tree.

Why would I pick two apples if I already have two?

Never mind, you have two apples and someone gives you two more.

Why would someone give me two more, if she could give them to someone who's hungry?

Doris, it's just an example.

An example of what?

Let's try again—you have two apples and you find two more. Now how many do you have?

Who lost them?

YOU HAVE TWO PLUS TWO APPLES!!!! HOW MANY DO YOU HAVE ALL TOGETHER????

Well, if I ate one, and gave away the other three, I'd have none left, but I could always get some more if I got hungry from that tree you were talking about before.

Doris, this is your last chance—you have two, uh, buffalo, and you get two more. Now how many do you have?

It depends. How many are cows and how many are bulls, and is any of the cows pregnant?

It's hopeless! You Indians have absolutely no grasp of abstractions!

Huh?

Sun Dance

The Bull,
They say,
Tatanka Iotanka,
Gave
One hundred pieces of skin
That time
When we danced,
Before the Greasy Grass.
Eagles rode the wind,
Eagle-bone whistle,
Stained with paint
And blood.

Now
Those who are not
The People
Wear
The Thunderbird
On silver chains
And bola ties.
They demonstrate
That they have won
The heavy-headed grasses
Nodding in the sun,
The Eagle's sweet, two-bladed cry—
Everything.

Be careful.

Maybe the Thunderbird will think you call his name,
And come across the hills before the driving rain,
Wakan,
And tear you into little pieces
To feed His children
And the waiting Mother Earth.

Poetry

Poetry is an important form of expression for Native people, particularly for writers working now. It is a way of being able to make the words of an alien language speak for us. The English language—even for those of us for whom it is our only language—expresses itself in ways that are completely at odds with Native thought patterns. It is both too precise and too general.

The English language has its own beauty, in the hands of those who love it, and many of the People use it with skill and grace. That is because, for us, words and the ways in which they are put together, are of vital importance. We learn early that the whiteman distrusts silence. Many of us, as a sort of protective coloration, learn to babble with the best of them. Our true bent, however, is to be wary of words, and to treat them with respect.

Words weave a pattern. So do our lives. With poetry, the two may come together, and we may say what our lives mean. In spite of all that has been done to warp and distort it, our words may still help us to work out the destiny that was ours from the beginning. Reading their poetry is a good way—if you will let yourselves—to know the heart of a People.

Good Grease

The hunters went out with guns
at dawn.
We had no meat in the village,
no food for the tribe and the dogs.
No caribou in the caches.

All day we waited.
At last
As darkness hung at the river
we children saw them far away.
Yes! They were carrying caribou!
We jumped and shouted!

By the fires that night
we feasted.
The old ones clucked,
sucking and smacking,
sopping the juices with sourdough bread.
The grease would warm us
when hungry winter howled.

Grease was beautiful,
oozing,
dripping and running down our chins,
brown hands shining with grease.
We talk of it
when we see each other
far from home.

Remember the marrow
sweet in the bones?
We grabbed for them like candy.
Good.
Gooooood.

Good grease.

— Mary TallMountain

I expected my skin and my blood to ripen

When the blizzard subsided four days later (after the Wounded Knee Massacre), a burial party was sent to Wounded Knee. A long trench was dug. Many of the bodies were stripped by whites who went out in order to get the Ghost Shirts and other accoutrements the Indians wore...the frozen bodies were thrown into the trench stiff and naked...only a handful of items remain in private hands...exposure to snow has stiffened the leggings and moccasins, and all the objects show the effects of age and long use...(Items are pictured for sale that were gathered at the site of the massacre:) Moccasins at $140, hide scraper at $350, buckskin shirt at $1200, woman's leggings at $275, bone breastplate, at $1000.

—Kenneth Canfield, 1977 Plains Indian Art Auction Catalog

I expected my skin
and my blood to ripen
not be ripped from my bones;
like fallen fruit
I am peeled, tasted, discarded.
My seeds open
and have no future.
Now there has been no past.
My own body gave up the beads,
my own hands gave the babies away
to be strung on bayonets,
to be counted one by one
like rosary-stones and then
tossed to the side of life
as if the pain of their birthing
had never been.
My feet were frozen to the leather,
pried apart, left behind—bits of flesh
on the moccasins, bits of paper deerhide
on the bones. My back was stripped of its cover,
its quilling intact; it was torn,
was taken away. My leggings were taken
like in a rape and shriveled
to the size of stick figures
like they had never felt the push

of my strong woman's body
walking in the hills.
It was my own baby
whose cradleboard I held—
would've put her in my mouth like a snake
if I could, would've turned her
into a bush or rock if there'd been magic enough
to work such changes. Not enough magic
to stop the bullets, not enough magic
to stop the scientists, not enough magic
to stop the money. Now our ghosts dance
a new dance, pushing from their hearts
a new song.

— Wendy Rose

Kopis'taya (a Gathering of Spirits)

Because we live in the browning season
the heavy air blocking our breath,
and in this time when living
is only survival, we doubt the voices
that come shadowed on the air,
that weave within our brains
certain thoughts, a motion that is soft,
imperceptible, a twilight rain,
soft feather's fall, a small body
dropping into its nest, rustling, murmuring,
settling in for the night.

Because we live in the hardedged season,
where plastic brittle and gleaming shines
and in this space that is cornered and angled,
we do not notice wet, moist, the significant
drops falling in perfect spheres
that are the certain measures of our minds;
almost invisible, those tears,
soft as dew, fragile, that cling to leaves,
petals, roots, gentle and sure,
every morning.
We are the women of daylight; of clocks and steel
foundries, of drugstores and streetlights,
of superhighways that slice our days in two,
Wrapped around in glass and steel we ride
our lives; behind dark glasses we hide our eyes,
our thoughts, shaded, seem obscure, smoke
fills our minds, whisky husks our songs,
polyester cuts our bodies from our breath,
our feet from the welcoming stones of earth,
Our dreams are pale memories of themselves,
and nagging doubt is the false measure of our days.

Even so, the spirit voices are singing,
their thoughts are dancing in the dirty air.
Their feet touch the cement, the asphalt
delighting, still they weave dreams upon our
shadowed skulls, if we could listen.
If we could hear.

— Paula Gunn Allen

Columbus Day

In school I was taught the names
Columbus, Cortez, and Pizarro and
A dozen other filthy murderers.
A bloodline all the way to General Miles,
Daniel Boone and General Eisenhower.

No one mentioned the names
Of even a few of the victims.
But don't you remember Chaske, whose spine
Was crushed so quickly by Mr. Pizarro's boot?
What words did he cry into the dust?

What was the familiar name
Of that young girl who danced so gracefully
That everyone in the village sang with her—
Before Cortez' sword hacked off her arms
As she protested the burning of her sweetheart?

That young man's name was Many Deeds,
And he had been a leader of a band of fighters
Called the Redstick Hummingbirds, who slowed
The march of Cortez' army with only a few
Spears and stones which now lay still
In the mountains and remember.

Greenrock Woman was the name
Of that old lady who walked right up
And spat in Columbus' face. We
Must remember that, and remember
Laughing Otter the Taino who tried to stop
Columbus and was taken away as a slave.
We never saw him again.

In school I learned of heroic discoveries
Made by liars and crooks. The courage
Of millions of sweet and true people
Was not commemorated.

Let us then declare a holiday
For ourselves, and make a parade that begins
With Columbus' victims and continues
Even to our grandchildren who will be named
In their honor.

Because isn't it true that even the summer
Grass here in this land whispers those names,
And every creek has accepted the responsibility
Of singing those names? And nothing can stop
The wind from howling those names around
The corners of the school.

Why else would the birds sing
So much sweeter here than in other lands?

— Jimmy Durham

The Real Thing

"We're the most exclusive
Indian shop in New York City.
We only sell *the real thing*."
Coyote-smooth, the man
lured a covey of customers
to where he held up a weaving
three feet by two.
"This rug is genuine Navajo.
You know it by the tiny flaw
they always leave
to let the evil spirit out."
"Ah..." sighed the covey
and leaned closer.

Behind them a buckshot laugh
exploded
     scattered thoughts
   turned heads
toward a black-haired
four-square woman.
"I *am* Navajo," she said.
"My family makes rugs.
When I was a child
I herded our sheep,
helped Mother clean the wool.
Grandma spun and wove it.
We don't leave a flaw
'to let the evil spirit out.'
We leave it to show
what's made by humans
can't be perfect.
Only the Great Spirit
makes perfect things."

The covey stared
    blank
  silent
then closed back
to their smooth comfort—
"As I was saying...
This rug is genuine Navajo.
You know it by the tiny flaw
they always leave
to let the evil spirit out."

— **Marilou Awiakta**

For Misty Starting School

help her
my shiny-haired child
laboriously tying her shoes
she's a mere child of 4.

she starts school today
smiling shyly
pink heart-shaped earrings
long black hair

we pause outside the house and pray
a pinch of pollen for you starting school
and you, the older sister
and you, father of bright-eyed daughters.
with this pollen, we pray
you will learn easily
in this new place
you will laugh and share
loving people other than us.
guide her now. guide us now.
we tell her at school
sprinkle cornmeal here
by the door of your classroom.
she takes some and looks at me
then lets it fall to the threshold.
to help my teacher, mommy?
she asks

yes, to help your teacher
to help you
to help us as we leave her now.
oh, be gentle with her
feelings, thoughts and trust.

i tell them again:
remember now, my clear-eyed daughters
remember now, where this pollen
                where this cornmeal is from
                remember now, you are no different
see how it sparkles
feel this silky powder
it leaves a fine trail skyward
as it falls
blessing us
strengthening us.

remember now, you are no different
                blessing us
                leaving us.

— Lucy Tapahonso

Granma's Words

"When you are
ill at ease in
heart,
take a walk.

Do anything
that has to
be done.
Walk
it out.

Walk alone,
in the hills
in the mountains.

Be strong
in the heart,
nothing lasts
forever.

— **Ted D. Palmanteer**

Ride the Turtle's Back

A woman grows hard and skinny.
She squeezes into small corners.
Her quick eyes uncover dust and cobwebs.
She reaches out
for flint and sparks fly in the air.
Flames turned loose on fields
burn down to the bare seeds
we planted deep.

The corn is white and sweet.
Under its pale, perfect kernels
a rotting cob is betrayal
and it lies in our bloated stomachs.

I lie in Grandmother's bed
and dream the earth into a turtle.
She carries us slowly across the universe.
The sun warms us.
At night the stars do tricks.
The moon caresses us.

We are listening for the sounds of food.

Mother is giving birth, Grandmother says.
Corn whispers.
The earth groans with labor
turning corn yellow in the sun.

I lie in Grandmother's bed

We listen.

We listen.

— Beth Brant

Teachings of My Grandmother

In a magazine too expensive to buy I read about
How, with scientific devices of great complexity,
U.S. scientists have discovered that if a rat
Is placed in a cage in which it has previously
Been given an electrical shock, it starts crying.

I told my grandmother about that and she said,
"We probably knew that would be true."

In another magazine I read about a man who spent
Twenty years of his life studying why birds sing.
He made thousands of tape recordings, mechanical singing
Devices, and artificial birds. He also killed many birds
To study them, and put others in cages so they
Wouldn't fly away during experiments.
In the end he learned that birds sing to communicate
To each other, and that each bird has its own song
Besides the regular communication songs.

I told my grandmother about that and she said,
"Twenty years! How did he support his family, then?"
I explained that the government and the university
Paid him to do that.

She said, "We probably knew that would be true."

— Jimmie Durham

Yes, It Was My Grandmother

Yes, it was my grandmother
who trained wild horses for pleasure and pay.
People knew of her, saying:
>   She knows how to handle them.
>   Horses obey that woman.

She worked,
skirts flying, hair tied securely in the wind and dust.
She rode those animals hard and was thrown,
time and time again.
She worked until they were meek
and wanting to please.
>   She came home at dusk,
>   tired and dusty,
>   smelling of sweat and horses.

She couldn't cook,
my father said smiling,
your grandmother hated to cook.

>   Oh Grandmother,
>   who freed me from cooking.
>   Grandmother, you must have made sure
>   I met a man who would not share the kitchen.

>   I am small like you and
>   do not protect my careless hair
>   from wind or rain—it tangles often,
>   Grandma, and it is wild and untrained.

— Lucy Tapahonso

All I Want

All I want is the bread to turn out like hers just once
        brown crust
        soft, airy insides
        rich and round
that is all.
So I ask her: How many cups?
        Ah yaa ah, she says,
        tossing flour and salt into a large silver bowl.
        I don't measure with cups.
        I just know by my hands.
        just a little like this is right, see?
        You young people always ask
        those kinds of questions,
        she says,
thrusting her arms into the dough
and turning it over and over again.
The table trembles with her movements.
I watch silently and this coffee is good,
           strong and fresh.
        Outside, her son is chopping wood,
        his body an intense arc.
        The dull rhythm of winter
        is the swinging of the axe
        and the noise of children squeezing in
        with the small sighs of wind
        through the edges of the windows.

She pats and tosses it furiously
shaping balls of warm, soft dough.
        There, we'll let it rise,
        she says, sitting down now.
        We drink coffee and there is nothing
        like the warm smell of bread rising
        on windy, woodchopping afternoons.

— Luci Tapahonso

The Stout of Heart

On the trail of tears my people
Struggled against mighty odds
as they pushed through snow—waist deep
      temperature below freezing
      feet wrapped in rags—frayed
      and torn blankets on their backs;
—no children—they died from starvation.
They possessed one bag of cornmeal
      that could not feed them all.

Three young scouts—miles ahead
      blazing a trail
weak from lack of nourishment
      but stout of heart.
They found a log cabin—blue smoke
      spiraling from its chimney.
No tracks or sign of habitation,
      just the smoke.

They opened the snow-locked door
      very slowly—looked inside.
On the floor, three sick white men
—a foul stench engulfed the scouts.
The leader jumped back—shouting:
      "Leche kaka!"

Great fear shook them for an instant,
      but very calmly the leader spoke:
      "We cannot take this evil to our people,
      enough have died."
They parted from each other—
      stripped themselves bare
      to die in the snow.

Leche kaka: smallpox

— Louis (Littlecoon) Oliver

Geronimo Loved Children

Looking at old photographs of Geronimo
I always get the feeling that he is going to shoot
The photographer.

Hey   Desert Hawk.   Son of a stone and cactus.
Coyote's brother   Tecolote's teacher.
Hey   you old geezer   stop faking like a jackrabbit—
We know you're not dead.

Geronimo had many children
Geronimo always took time to talk to children
Geronimo loved children
Geronimo cried for his children
Geronimo saw many hungry children
Geronimo saw many soldier-killed children
Geronimo saw all the children
Geronimo fought for his children

Hey   old road-runner   They whisper in the camps.
They sing of how you ride the dry wind.

Geronimo   Listen   Someone is taking our children.
Brave and sacred old scrap of leather
Are you going to shoot or not?

The eyes of young men
The tears of mothers
Show your wolf spirit

Don't try to fool me   old man
I see your defiant laugh
In the crouched legs of our Puma-Warriors.
And I see your wind-hand turning the children
Toward the sun.

Are you going to shoot or not?

— Jimmie Durham

Where He Said Where He Was

He sent them a message,
He said you send someone to come get me here.
I am going to stay here in these hills
In these woods.
They know me here
They agree with me
And I agree with them.
I am going to stay here
By this creek now,
Where my ancestors laugh in the water.
These dogwood tree brothers
And all of these brothers
And little mothers here
They want me here.

If you want me you send someone here
To get me.

— Jimmie Durham

Resistance in 1951

In a tar-paper shack in that thin desert
Which lies between each town and the prairies
He sat on a bed where his brothers and sisters
Were sleeping.

He wanted to go outside and piss
But he listened to his father and his mother talking.

His father was scheming one of those plans
Warriors of this century dream up:

"Look at my hands, woman. I can't work that job
Tomorrow. My fingers won't even bend anymore.
Where will we get food? Look, if I was
In jail the county would feed you and the kids."

His mother was crying very quietly because the kids
Were asleep. His mother was crying the next
Week when they came and said that his father
Was in jail for forging a check and getting drunk.

He listened to the welfare agent explain
To his mother that she had certainly picked
The wrong man as father for those poor children.

Just a drunken Indian who stole.
"Don't worry, we'll keep him a long time so
He won't bother you anymore. Find yourself
A responsible man."

— Jimmie Durham

Kelp

Ribbons of iodine
unrolled by the hands
of the waves.

Rookery

Under its brown fur
the beach twitches with life.

Voices

We sound like crying bullheads
when we sing
our songs.

Granddaughters dancing,
blossoms
swaying in the wind.

Genocide

Picketing the Eskimo
Whaling Commission
an over-fed English girl
stands with a sign
"Let the Whales Live."

— Nora Dauenhauer

What the Choctaw Woman Said

My husband is an alcoholic.
He went to the Veterans' Hospital and said,
"My spirit is sick. I am dying."
They said, "You need tests. Go to the lab."
He came home.

Later he went back and told them again,
"My spirit is sick. I am dying."
"You need meaningful work," they said.
"Go to the social worker."
He came home.

The last time he went they
sent him to a psychiatrist.
When my husband told him, "My spirit is
sick. I am dying," the psychiatrist
said, "What do you mean by 'spirit'?"

My husband came home. He'll never go back.
My only hope is to get him to a medicine man
but the great ones are in the West.
I don't have the money to take him.

The trouble is, most people look down on
us and our culture. It's harder on a man.
It kills his pride. For a woman it's not
as bad. We have to make sure the children
survive, no matter what.

If I stay with my husband, the children will
get sick in their spirits. They may die.
I have to leave him.

— **Marilou Awiakta**

Indian Blood

On the stage I stumbled,
my fur boot caught
on a slivered board.
Rustle of stealthy giggles.

Beendaaga' made of velvet
crusted with crystal beads
hung from brilliant tassels of wool,
wet from my sweat.

Children's faces stared.
I felt their flowing force.
Did I crouch like *goh*
in the curious quiet?

They butted to the stage,
darting questions; pointing.
        Do you live in an igloo?
        Hah! You eat blubber!

Hemmed in by ringlets of brass,
grass-pale eyes,
the fur of *daghooda-aak*
trembled.

Late in the night
I bit my hand until it was
pierced
with moons of dark
Indian blood.

beendaaga'	*mittens*
goh	*rabbit*
daghooda-aak	*caribou parka*

— **Mary TallMountain**

Those Anthropologists

Those anthropologists,
sociologists and
historians who
poke at our bones,
our social systems
and past events
try to tell us
who we are.

When we don't read
their book
they think we are
rejecting
our heritage.

So, they feel
sorry for us
and write
more books
for themselves.

— Lenore Keeshig-Tobias

Interview with The Social Worker

It all started because I gave her my best chair with the black velvet
   cushion
embroidered with red roses & she sat in it like it was a disease
She said how can you live like this
I said how can you live like that
she said don't get smart with me
I said I'm always smart I have too many brains
it's not my fault genetics
she said I don't think you're eligible
I said I'm still unmarried she said
that has nothing to do with it I think
I am through here
I said I'll never let you through here
not if I have anything to say about it

                                                 — Chrystos

Now That They Know
I'm an Indian (sorry, Will)

Nothing of her
But doth change
Into Something
Dark
And Strange....

— Doris Seale

Sure You Can Ask Me a Personal Question

How do you do?
           No, I am not Chinese.
No, not Spanish.
           No, I am American Indi—uh, Native American.
No, not from India.
           No, not Apache.
No, not Navajo.
           No, not Sioux.
No, we are not extinct.
           Yes, Indin.
Oh?
           So that's where you got those high cheekbones.
Your great grandmother, huh?
           An Indian Princess, huh?
Hair down to there?
           Let me guess. Cherokee?
Oh, so you've had an Indian friend?
           That close?
Oh, so you've had an Indian lover?
           That tight?
Oh, so you've had an Indian servant?
           That much?
Yeah, it was awful what you guys did to us.
           It's real decent of you to apologize.
No, I don't know where you can get peyote.
           No, I don't know where you can get Navajo rugs real cheap.
No, I didn't make this. I bought it at Bloomingdale's.
           Thank you. I like your hair too.
I don't know if anyone knows whether or not Cher is really Indian.
           No, I didn't make it rain tonight.
Yeah. Uh-huh. Spirituality.
           Uh-huh. Yeah. Spirituality. Uh-huh. Mother
Earth. Yeah. Uh-huh. Uh-huh. Spirituality.
           No, I didn't major in archery.
Yeah, a lot of us drink too much.
           Some of us can't drink enough.
This ain't no stoic look.
           This is my face.

— **Diane Burns**

Three Thousand Dollar Death Song

Nineteen American Indian Skeletons from Nevada...valued at $3000...
—Museum invoice, 1975

Is it in cold hard cash? the kind
that dusts the insides of men's pockets
lying silver-polished surface along the cloth.
Or in bills? papering the wallets of they
who thread the night with dark words. Or
checks? paper promises weighing the same
as words spoken once on the other side
of the grown grass and dammed rivers
of history. However it goes, it goes
Through my body it goes
assessing each nerve, running its edges
along my arteries, planning ahead
for whose hands will rip me
into pieces of dusty red paper,
whose hands will smooth or smatter me
into traces of rubble. Invoiced now,
it's official how our bones are valued
that stretch out pointing to sunrise
or are flexed into one last foetal bend,
that are removed and tossed about,
catalogued, numbered with black ink
on newly-white foreheads.
As we were formed to the white soldier's voice,
so we explode under white students' hands.
Death is a long trail of days
in our fleshless prison.

From this distant point we watch our bones
auctioned with our careful beadwork.
our quilled medicine bundles, even the bridles
of our shot-down horses. You: who have
priced us, you who have removed us: at what cost?
What price the pits where our bones share
a single bit of memory, how one century
turns our dead into specimens, our history
into dust, our survivors into clowns.

Our memory might be catching, you know;
picture the mortars, the arrowheads, the labrets
shaking off their labels like bears
suddenly awake to find the seasons have ended
while they slept. Watch them touch each other,
measure reality, march out the museum door!
Watch as they lift their faces
and smell about for us; watch our bones rise
to meet them and mount the horses once again!
The cost, then, will be paid
for our sweetgrass-smelling having-been
in clam shell beads and steatite,
dentalia and woodpecker scalp, turquoise
and copper, blood and oil, coal
and uranium, children, a universe
of stolen things.

— **Wendy Rose**

Mouse Blessings

There is a mouse in my kitchen.
A good, brave, wild animal
Who races back and forth
From one chairlegs forest to another
In broad daylight,
Counting coup on the world.

Brave from hunger, or because of hungry babies,
Or maybe just a free animal mouse
In a city she did not choose.
Her name is Laughing Bread-Stealer.

Grandmother! Thank you for sending mouse
Who gives her blessing
By stealing my bread so bravely.

— Jimmie Durham

A Spring Poem
Song for Misty and Lori

feel good about yourself
        early in the morning
        you can hear the birds chirping, whistling
        right there   right there in the yard
                listen to them   see how
                light they are hopping about

they know the spirits are here
early in the morning before sunrise
in the gray light   the spirits hover about
                go out and welcome them
                savor the morning air
                savor the stillness of little bird noises

they wait for you: the spirits of your grandpa acoma
                the spirits of your uncles
                the spirits of relatives you never knew
                they know you   they marvelled at your birth
                they wait for you saying: come out
                greet us, our little ones
                come out, we want to see you again
they hover waiting in front of the house
by the doors, above the windows
they are waiting to give us their blessing
        waiting to give us their protection

go out and receive them: the good spirits in the gentle-bird morning
they hover singing, dancing in the clean morning air
they are singing   they are singing.

— Luci Tapahonso

Trees Dance

Sky dances
Willows dance like women
Dance like snakes,
Willows dance before the mirror
Fish dance in the mirror.   Turtles dance
Oaks dance like bears,
Clouds sing   like skybears,
Pines dance,
They are stars

Storm has come here
To kill the grubs,
To kill worms

Seeds dance
Water dances—
It is proud skyhorses.

The corn will grow and dance with us.

Lances of storms are with us.
New plants grow
New things ride this way.
Sky dances

— Jimmie Durham

Dying Back

On the mountain
the standing people are dying back—
hemlock, spruce and pine
turn brown in the head.
The hardwood shrivels in new leaf.
Unnatural death
from acid greed
that takes the form of rain
and fog and cloud.

In the valley
the walking people are blank-eyed.
Elders mouth vacant thought.
Youth grow spindly, wan
from sap too drugged to rise.
Pushers drain it off—
sap is gold to them.
The walking people are dying back
as all species do
that kill their own seed.

— Marilou Awiakta

When Earth Becomes an "It"

When the people call Earth "Mother,"
they take with love
and with love give back
so that all may live.

When the people call Earth "it,"
they use her
consume her strength.
Then the people die.

Already the sun is hot
out of season.
Our mother's breast
is going dry.
She is taking all green
into her heart
and will not turn back
until we call her
by her name.

— **Marilou Awiakta**

The Last Wolf

the last wolf hurried toward me
through the ruined city
and I heard his baying echoes
down the steep smashed warrens
of Montgomery Street and past
the few ruby-crowned highrises
left standing
their lighted elevators useless.

passing the flicking red and green
of traffic signals
baying his way eastward
in the mystery of his wild loping gait
closer the sounds in the deadly night
through clutter and rubble of quiet blocks

I heard his voice ascending the hill
and at last his low whine as he came
floor by empty floor to the room
where I sat
in my narrow bed looking west, waiting
I heard him snuffle at the door and
I watched
he trotted across the floor

he laid his long gray muzzle
on the spare white spread
and his eyes burned yellow
his small dotted eyebrows quivered

Yes, I said.
I know what they have done.

— Mary TallMountain

Calling Myself Home

There were old women
who lived on amber.
Their dark hands
laced the shells of turtles
together, pebbles inside
and they danced
with rattles strong on their legs.

There is a dry river
between them and us.
Its banks divide up our land.
Its bed was the road
I walked to return.

We are plodding creatures
like the turtle
born of an old people.
We are nearly stone
turning slow as the earth.
Our mountains are underground
they are so old.

This land is the house
we have always lived in.
The women,
their bones are holding up the earth.
The red tail of a hawk
cuts open the sky
and the sun
brings their faces back
with the new grass.

Dust from yarrow
is in the air,
the yellow sun.
Insects are clicking again.

I came back to say good-bye
to the turtle
to those bones
to the shells locked together
on his back,
gold atoms dancing underground.

— Linda Hogan

Out of Ashes Peace Will Rise

Survival Chant

Our courage is our memory:

Out of ashes
peace will rise
if the people
are resolute.
If we are not resolute
we will vanish
and out of ashes
peace will rise.

In the Four Directions—
Out of ashes, peace will rise.
Out of ashes, peace will rise.
Out of ashes, peace will rise.
Out of ashes, peace will rise.

Our courage is our memory.

— Marilou Awiakta

(First stanza: Leader. Second stanza: All. Facing each of the Four Directions in turn, with arms raised, palms toward the sky, and ending with hands clasped to heart—the source of memory—for the last line.)

Ayohu Kanogisdi /Death Song

aya ahaniquo
I am here only

usdi nahiyu
a little while

ayagʋgeyu
I have loved

ulihelisdi elohi
the joy of the earth

osiyo ayohu
hello death

— Gogisgi

Fiery Red
Cení Myles

Narissa Morgan walks out of the library in her pea-coat pulled up high, with a cup of decaffeinated coffee. It's windy, yet she stands in the brisk cold. Five minutes is all that she can stand, without her contorted spine beginning to ache. She sits on the library steps and mulls over her warm coffee. Narissa notices the autumn leaves scattered on the soft ground and closes her eyes to breathe in the cold air through her nose. Mmm, she could detect the smell of an old wood-burning stove, just like Mom's.

"Mom, I don't *want* to comb out my hair."

"Do it!"

"But Mom, it's all tangled and it's going to hurt!"

"Do what I *told* you!"

"No,....Bitch!"

"*What?!!!*"

It all comes back to her: Narissa was eight years old when she called her Mom a bitch. As heavy as her Mom was, she still could chase Narissa around that old wood stove, carrying a huge old wooden hairbrush.

She laughs to herself. Yep, Mom chased her around that wood stove about two and a half times before catching her by the hair.

God, Narissa could still feel the stinging of the brush on her legs.

Those were the good ole days before her life became chaotic at age nine. Her Mom had died of polio, the night before she was to be taken to the hospital. Since her father was an alcoholic, she was taken to an all-girls boarding school. Her two baby sisters were too young to go, so they were given to a foster family.

Boarding school was a miserable experience. The teachers tried to indoctrinate her into thinking she would never amount to anything (for four reasons): she was Indian, poor, and non-Christian; and her father was the town drunk. Plus, none of the white kids wanted to associate with Narissa because they thought she was *too dark*. The Black kids didn't want to associate with her either because they thought she was *too light*.

Narissa could recall one clear image, of her sitting at a wooden desk with an inkwell.

"Narissa, did you do your homework?"

"No," she mumbled.

"*What? I can't hear you.*"

"*No!!!*" Narissa screamed.

"Come up here, right this instant, before I snatch you!"

Narissa could remember walking slowly to Mrs. Jones' desk; all eyes were on her.

"Put your hands out."

Mrs. Jones pulled out her infamous metal-tipped ruler. As soon as she thrust her hand down with the ruler, Narissa quickly pulled *her* hand out of the way; causing Mrs. Jones to hit her own flabby thigh.

"*Owwwww!!!*" she screamed, "For this you will go to bed two hours early this evening—and without any supper!"

Those sonsofbitches, she thought. They treated her like shit. The entire faculty thought she would wind up on a reservation, both toothless and penniless.

Until she was a senior in high school, this life continued. Then her guidance counselor, Mr. Mahue, called her into his office. "Sit down, I have the results of your SATs."

"Oh."

"You received a 300 on the math section," then he paused for about five minutes. "Oh, and you received an 800 on the verbal section."

What seemed a lifetime for Mr. Mahue to tell Narissa, was her four-year scholarship to attend Simmons College in Boston.

College life wasn't much better; except here none of the faculty paid her any mind. As far as they were concerned, she wasn't going anywhere. She graduated, then went to work as an aide at a public library. She stayed with that library and eventually became the executive director of Children's Services.

Narissa doesn't have any real regrets, except for not having the chance to get to know her mom or dad. Her dad was a whole different story. No, not really—he too was suffering from an illness, alcoholism. It just happened—her mom happened to die before her dad did when she was 15 years old.

The more Narissa thinks about her past, the more she feels a void in her life. She wanted her parents to have seen her graduate from college…Narissa knows they would've been proud. But most of all, she wanted a family to spend the holidays with. It was so lonely for her when the holidays came around…

The only other feelings she has are anger and happiness. She is still angry, years later, at those teachers who predicted she'd starve on a reservation. *They would shit in their pants*, Narissa thinks, if they knew what her life was like now.

Narissa is content with her life now. She enjoys her high-paying job with two things she loves—kids and books. She has strong ties with her younger sisters, Ginny and Diane. She enjoys the company of her many Native friends—friends who accept her for who she is, a strong compassionate woman; friends who aren't concerned that she is *too light* or *too dark*.

Narissa looks at her watch. Shit, her coffee break is over. She dumps her coffee on the ground and pulls the pea-coat over her rather large body. She slowly stands up and trudges down the ramp to the Children's Room. Before she enters, she takes one more deep breath of the same wood-burning smell. Just like home, she thinks, and walks in with her head held high.

Thanking the Birds
Native American Upbringing and the Natural World
Joseph Bruchac

One day, some 30 years ago, Swift Eagle, an Apache man, visited some friends on the Onondaga reservation in central New York. While he was out walking, he heard the sounds of boys playing in the bushes.

"There's another one. Shoot it!" said one of the boys.

When he pushed through the brush to see what was happening, he found that they had been shooting small birds with a BB gun. They had already killed a chickadee, a robin, and several blackbirds. The boys looked up at him, uncertain what he was going to do or say.

There are several things that a non-Indian bird lover might have done: given a stern lecture on the evil of killing birds; threatened to tell the boys' parents on them for doing something they had been told not to do; or even spanked them. Swift Eagle, however, did something else.

"Ah," he said, "I see you have been hunting. Pick up your game and come with me."

He led the boys to a place where they could make a fire and cook the birds. He made sure they said a thank-you to the spirits of the birds before eating them, and as they ate, he told stories. It was important, he said, to be thankful to the birds for the gifts of their songs, their feathers, and their bodies as food. The last thing he said to them they never forgot—for it was one of those boys who told me this story many years later:

"You know, our Creator gave the gift of life to everything that is alive. Life is a very sacred thing. But our Creator knows that we have to eat to stay alive. That is why it is permitted to hunt to feed ourselves and our people. So I understand that you boys must have been very, very hungry to kill those little birds."

I have always liked that story, for it illustrates several things. Although there was a wide range of customs, lifeways, and languages—in pre-Columbian times, more than 400 different languages were spoken on the North American continent—many close similarities existed among virtually all of the Native American peoples. Thus, ideas held by an Apache from the Southwest fitted into the lives and traditions of Onondagas in the Northeast.

One of these ideas, expressed in Swift Eagle's words to the boys, was the continent-wide belief that people depended on the natural world for survival, on the one hand, and had to respect it and remain in right relationship with it on the other. A friend of mine of Cherokee descent, Norman Russell, is a poet and botanist and author of a book entitled *Introduction to Plant Science: A Humanistic and Ecological Approach.* "Ecological balance," he said to me, "is nothing new for the Native American. It was their way of life."

Particularly Indian, too, is Swift Eagle's method of dealing with children who had done something incorrect, or out of balance. The Apache's gentleness calls to mind, for instance, what was said about children by Handsome Lake, the Seneca Iroquois visionary of the early 1800s. His body of teachings, which is called in English, "The Good Message," was the basis of a revival of the spirit and strength of the Iroquois at a time when alcohol and loss of land seemed to be leading them toward destruction as a people. He is still regarded by the Iroquois as a prophet whose words were given him by the Creator, and "The Good Message" is still memorized and spoken in their longhouses in New York State and Canada. It covers many subjects and takes several days to recite.

One of its sections deals with children. "Talk slowly and kindly to children," Handsome Lake says. "Never punish them unjustly."

His words are echoed by Indians of other nations. "Someone who strikes a child," a Kwakiutl woodcarver from the Pacific Northwest said, "has to be a great coward. Children are so much smaller than adults." "My father never struck me," my own Abenaki grandfather said. "Instead, he would just talk to me." Though it probably did happen from time to time, corporal punishment of children was the exception rather than the rule among American Indian people of the past, and this largely remains true today.

As the anecdote about Swift Eagle shows, children were taught the values of their culture through example and stories. Instead of scolding or lecturing them, Swift Eagle showed the boys how to build a fire and cook the game they had shot, giving the songbirds the same respect he would have given a rabbit or deer.

He told stories that pointed out the value of those birds as living beings. The ritual activity of making the fire, thanking the spirits of the birds, hearing the stories, and then eating the game they had killed taught the boys more than a hundred stern lectures would have done, and the lesson stayed with them all their lives.

Western education today tends to be didactic. Children are told—in books, lectures, film strips, and movies—*about* things, but rarely do them, experience them. Adults then test the children by having them answer questions about what they have "learned."

There is good reason for this method, of course. The world our children must know about is much too broad to allow them to learn everything through a hands-on approach. However, as many educators have observed, the result of such a method is too often learning that is more a conditioned reflex than a true understanding. Furthermore, the artificial divisions among fields of study—with natural sciences alone being divided into botany, zoology, geology, astronomy, and hundreds of other areas—can lead to knowledge that is fragmented. It is like what you learn by dissecting a frog: you know the parts, but you cannot put them together to understand the animal. And, in cutting the frog apart, you have killed it.

Native American education, in contrast, has always been experiential and holistic. If you wish to know how to make baskets, you go to a basket maker and watch that person at work. If you are patient and watch long enough, eventually the basket maker may ask you to do something—to hold onto this coil of sweetgrass here, to help shave down that strip of ash. If you return the next day, and the next and the next, then one day you discover that you, too, know how to make a basket.

But making a basket is not all you will have learned. A basket maker knows which trees and other plants can be used and at which times of the year they can be prepared. Thus, you will have gained a knowledge of botany and of the rhythms of the seasons. When cutting a tree or uprooting a clump of sweetgrass, a basket maker gives thanks to that plant for sacrificing its life to help human beings. Tobacco is left in exchange, as a sacrifice.

Thus, basketmaking has a religious dimension. Stories also will have been learned—about the materials used in crafting the basket, about the significance of patterns and designs. Among the Pima people, the figures of the whirlwind or the man in the maze appear on baskets, and the stories connected to these figures are part of the basket maker's lore.

There may even be songs. A Pomo basket maker once sang her basket song for me as she worked, explaining that it had to be sung a certain number of times in just such a way. When the song had ended, the basket was finished. Making a basket is not something easily learned out of a book. For American Indian basket makers (and, I am sure, basket makers in other traditional cultures), it involves much more than a simple handicraft.

Children, as any sensible teacher knows, respond to *doing* things. Activities are almost always the favorite part of a day for a child. Children also respond to stories. A good story, in fact, is very much like "doing something," for the events of the story come alive and the trials and accomplishments of the central character become the listener's own. The listener is more of a participant than a passive observer, as is the case with a television viewer.

Ray Fadden, an Elder whose Mohawk name is Tehanetorens, knows the power of traditional Indian stories and has shown how they can be used in contemporary Western education. When Ray began teaching in the public schools in New York State four decades ago, many Native American people were turning away from their heritage. The old stories that taught people respect for nature were disappearing. Ray learned and retold those stories in his classes, and Indian and non-Indian children responded with enthusiasm. He became known as one of the foremost experts on the history of the Iroquois people, and recorded legends and traditions in beaded belts he made himself, drawing on the forms of the wampum record belts of past centuries. Eventually, without the help of any government or foundation funding, he built the Six Nations Indian Museum in Onchiota, New York, at the northern edge of Adirondack Park.

The museum is built in the shape of a longhouse, its walls lined with display cases, its rafters hung with artifacts from the rich cultural heritage of the Iroquois. Many of the items in the museum, like the stories Ray tells, were given him by Iroquois people. Though he has retired from the public schools now, he keeps the museum open to the public through the warm months of the year, with the help of his artist son, Kahionhes. He charges a modest admission fee, except for American Indian people, who are admitted free. It is his way of repaying them for the knowledge they have shared with him over the years.

On any given day during what he calls "the tourist season," he may be found at the museum reading one of his belts. It may be one that tells an old story, such as that of the brave hunters who followed the Great Bear up into the Skyland; or it may be a more recent tale of the damaging of the chain of life, which began with the destruction of the natural habitat and the extermination of natural species.

Ray Fadden explains conservation as the Indian saw it, an ecologically sophisticated view of the interrelatedness of all things; a relationship that, as his stories indicate, was part of the Iroquois way for countless generations.

His stories are first and foremost for children. "You youngsters get in here and sit right down. I have a story that you need to

hear." But anyone who sits down and listens quickly realizes that his stories are for young and old alike. "These stories are so strong that they were only to be told in the winter time when Mother Earth is asleep. If the stories are told during the summer, then the other creatures might hear you and neglect their work. That's how strong these stories are."

Ray lives what he teaches about responsibility for preserving the great chain of life. He has posted the land around the museum and maintains hundreds of feeding stations for the birds and other animals (feeding stations made necessary because acid rain and spraying for black flies have damaged the food chain in many parts of the Adirondacks so that it is hard for animals to find their natural food). The area serves as a sanctuary for many Adirondack animals, among them the huge black bears, which have a special relationship to Ray. In some of his stories, he tells how to show respect for bears. When the bears meet him in the woods, they lower their heads in greeting, and he does the same. (Though this may be hard to believe, I have seen it happen more than once.)

When Tehanetorens first taught in Indian schools in New York State, the idea of imbuing children with traditional Iroquois values or telling Indian stories was unthought-of or forbidden. Today, thanks to work like his, something closer to the old patterns of Indian teaching may be found within the walls of such institutions as the Onondaga Indian School in Nedrow, New York, in the heart of the Onondaga reservation.

A school run by the Onondaga community with the approval of the State Education Department, OISA uses Iroquois traditions in the school curriculum. The children's Indian heritage is even honored by the school calendar, which provides a vacation for students and staff during the time of the midwinter ceremonials, when the Dancing Stars (the Pleiades) are at the height of the winter sky.

At the traditional thanksgiving to the maple trees, when the sap is gathered in March, the school holds a maple festival. The students tap the trees and gather the sap, and a sugarhouse is kept running out back, close to the school kitchen, to boil down the syrup. When it is time to dig wild onions, a group of students and teachers goes out into the fields around the school to harvest it.

In the bilingual classroom supervised by Audrey Shenandoah, Onondaga students introduce themselves to a visitor by speaking their clan names and their own Indian names in Onondaga. Storytelling is one of the favorite activities here, for students from preschoolers to the upper grades. The walls and pillars of the basement room are decorated with paintings of clan animals—Wolf, Eel, Snipe, Bear, and Deer—and the figures of Iroquois mythology.

Looking at those pictures, one sees that Native American traditions create from birth a sense of closeness to nature that most young people of European ancestry have never experienced. Among the Iroquois and most other Native American people throughout the continent, children are born into a clan. In the case of the Iroquois, you inherit your clan from your mother. Each clan is represented by an animal (among some other Native people, natural forces such as Sky or Wind may take the place of a clan animal) and you identify with it. Just as in the majority culture, astrology suggests that you are affected by your star sign (an enormously popular idea, no matter how often it is debunked or scoffed at), so too for Native Americans your clan seems to have some effect on your personality.

I have often heard it said that members of the Bear Clan tend to be big and strong, that those who are "Wolves" are quick-moving and volatile, that "Turtles" are slow-moving and careful. Certain traditional stories are associated with different clans. A Mohawk story, for example, tells how the Bear Clan was given the secrets of medicine plants by the Creator, and throughout the continent there are "bear doctors." It is believed that bears suffer from many of the same sicknesses people do and that by watching what herbs a bear eats when it is sick you may learn to cure certain human illnesses.

Having a clan animal with which one is intimately connected is only one instance of how American Indian culture and stories create a sense of closeness to nature for Native children. The forces of nature are personified in ways that I feel to be essentially non-romantic and usefully realistic. The four winds, for example, are associated with certain animals. The north wind is called the White Bear by some Indian Nations. It is strong and cold and brings the snow. The east wind is called the Moose by the People of the northern maritimes. They see it walking out of the water with its great strength and shaking the moisture from its wide antlers. The south wind is the Gentle Fawn. It arrives bringing warmth, new flowers, green grass. The west wind is the Panther, striking with sudden force. Those names accurately describe the characteristics of those winds, are easy to remember, and make those forces, because they are better understood in the shapes of animals, less threatening.

Even the calendar is seen differently through the eyes of American Indian culture and stories. Instead of learning the names of the months of the year through the old rhyme, "Thirty days hath September..." American Indian children are still, through their Elders and in schools such as the Onondaga Indian School, taught the 13 moons. The time around November is for the Abenaki *Mzatonos Kisos*, "The Moon of Freezing," the time around October *Pebonkas*

Kisos, "The Moon of Leaves Falling," around May, *Kikas Kisos*, "Planting Moon." Each Native People has its own names for the moon cycles, names that similarly reflect the condition of the natural world and also remind human beings of the activities they should be undertaking.

I can never think of the year without seeing in my mind the Turtle's back. In the stories of a good many Native American people, from California to Maine, the earth was built on the back of the Great Turtle, who agreed to support the world. A St. Francis Abenaki Elder and teacher of mine, Mdawilasis, once told me the stories connected with the Turtle's back.

"Count the number of squares on the Turtle's back," he said. "You'll see there are always 13. That is how many nations there were of our Abenaki people. Turtle remembers when others forget."

Then he went on to show me how the Turtle's back is also a calendar. There are 13 squares for the 13 moons. Around those large plates on the back of Turtle are always 28 smaller plates, for the number of days in every moon. "There are stories in everything around us," he said. "You just have to know how to look in order to see them."

The teachings that have been given to generations of Native American children in stories are ones that need to be understood by all of us. One of my favorite Abenaki stories is that of Gluskabi's game bag. It is a tale I have frequently told to students and used in workshops on storytelling and the Indian view of ecology.

Gluskabi is the transformer hero of stories told by the different Abenaki Nations, from the Passamaquoddy of Maine to the St. Francis Abenaki of Vermont. In the story, Gluskabi goes hunting but is not successful. Angered, he seeks out his Grandmother and convinces her to make him a magical game bag, which will stretch to fit anything placed within it. He then goes into the woods and puts the bag in the middle of a clearing. Then he begins to weep and moan. The animals come out and ask him what is wrong. "It is too awful," he says. "I cannot tell you." Finally, though, he does. "The world is going to be destroyed," he says.

Now the animals become afraid. "What can we do?" they ask. "Ah," says Gluskabi, "You can hide in my game bag." Then all the animals in the world, even the great bears and the moose, climb into the game bag and Gluskabi ties it shut. When he takes them home, his Grandmother sees the game bag is very full and asks, "What do you have there, Gluskabi?" "Nothing," he says. But she persists and he opens the game bag so she can see in. There are all the animals in the world looking up at her. "Now," says Gluskabi, "We no longer have to work to hunt. We can just reach into the game bag for food."

But his Grandmother shakes her head. "Animals cannot live in a game bag," she says. "And what about our children and our children's children? If we have all the animals now, what will they have to eat?" Then Gluskabi sees he was wrong. He goes back to the clearing, opens the game bag, and says, "All you animals, come out. The world was destroyed but I put it back together again." Then the animals come out and return into the forest.

Today, when the secrets of Gluskabi's magical bag, which can catch and destroy all of the animals of the world, are known all too well, it is important for such stories to be told. For ourselves and for our children's children.

Taking Another Look

Mary Gloyne Byler

American Indians have had to struggle for more than their physical survival. It is not only land that has been appropriated; it has also been a fight to keep mind and soul together, for along with the United States Cavalry, missionaries, educators and the "Americanizers," have come the writers of books about Indians.

Down through the years the publishing industry has produced thousands of books about American Indians—a subject that fascinates many. Fact and fiction—it is not always possible to tell which is which—have rolled off the presses since "frontier" days. But American Indians in literature, today as in the past, are merely images projected by non-Indian writers.

Most minority groups in this country have been, and are still, largely ignored by the nation's major publishing houses—particularly in the field of children's books. American Indians, on the other hand, contend with a mass of material about themselves. If anything, there are too many children's books about American Indians.

There are too many books featuring painted, whooping, befeathered Indians closing in on too many forts, maliciously attacking "peaceful" settlers or simply leering menacingly from the background; too many books in which white benevolence is the only thing that saves the day for the incompetent, childlike Indian; too many stories setting forth what is "best" for American Indians.

There are too many stories for very young children about little boys running around in feathers and headbands, wearing fringed buckskin clothing, moccasins and (especially) carrying little bows and arrows. The majority of these books deal with the unidentified past. The characters are from unidentified tribes and they are often not even afforded the courtesy of personal names. In fact, the only thing identifiable is the stereotyped image of the befeathered Indian.

This depersonalization is common in books for children. In *Good Hunting, Little Indian* (Young Scott Books) the characters are referred to as Little Indian, Mama Indian and Papa Indian, calling to mind Mama Bear, Papa Bear and Baby Bear. But, in *Granny and the Indians* (Macmillan) the same author personalizes the "Granny" by giving her a name (Granny Guntry) while the other characters are simply "the Indians"—who are made to look silly and ridiculous both in the story and in the illustrations. The pictures in both of the books contain a baffling hodge-podge of Indian dress.

The device of repeatedly referring to people in this impersonal and anonymous way, and then reinforcing the anonymity with illustrations that are nondescript, creates the impression that one is not dealing with full-fledged human beings.

Many books parody Indian life and customs, holding them up to ridicule and derision. *Indian Two Feet and His Eagle Feather* (Children's Press) is about a little boy (Indian Two Feet) and how he earns the right to wear an eagle feather. This makes a mockery of those tribes that consider eagle feathers symbolic of courage and honor, and it equates the process of earning them with child's play.

A much-used theme is that of a child in search of his "real" name. According to the jacket copy on *Little Indian* (Simon & Schuster), readers will "gleefully" discover that there is more than one way to acquire a name. This story distorts and makes fun of the name-giving practices of some tribes and makes of them whimsical, meaningless exercises to be viewed with humor.

The degree to which non-Indian authors' concept of things "Indian" is distorted and an example of how distortions are kept alive are demonstrated in a book called *Buffalo Man and Golden Eagle* (McCall Publishing Co.).

The book begins with that quaint old "Indian" expression, "Many moons ago." Why not simply say "a long time ago"? According to the story, Golden Eagle (also referred to as "the Indian") hunted six days a week, but on the seventh day he would don "his most beautiful headdress, put his peace pipe in his mouth, and stroll off into the hills."

The six-day work week is misplaced in the context of time; it did not exist for American Indians. The tribes that wore headdresses wore them only on special occasions, not to "stroll" around in. Peace pipes were smoked ritually and in the proper ceremonial setting. So while Golden Eagle, or "the Indian," adheres to the biblical injunction against working on the Sabbath, he is disrespectful towards ceremonial and religious articles that are particularly American Indian—all in five lines of text with a total of 75 words.

It is one thing to write about imaginary beings from an imaginary time and place, but American Indians are real people and deserve the dignity of being presented as such. These little books with their "charming" stories, fanciful illustrations and cute little characters put Indians in the same category with ogres, giants, fairies, and baby animals.

Some authors indulge in what amounts to acts of cultural vandalism. An example of this is in *Pink Puppy* (Putnam's). The setting is among the Cherokees in North Carolina.

The book opens with a wake for Cindy Standingdeer's mother. The author's understanding of a Cherokee wake and of the dynamics involved is highly superficial. Cindy, an eight-year-old, feels that because people are singing they are happy. Since most Cherokee children are taken to wakes from the time they are infants, it is unlikely that an eight-year-old would so grossly misunderstand the hymn singing in this way.

The old "stoic Indian" cliché is thrown in when the author has Grandmother Standingdeer say to Cindy, "Cherokees don't cry. You'll have to learn the old Indian way—it's a good way." The school teacher (white) arrives and urges Cindy to cry, saying, "That's all right, Cindy. Go ahead. You'll feel better." And later she adds, "I'll cry with you, Cindy."

The author cannot have attended many Cherokee wakes or funerals or it would be obvious that Cherokees do indeed cry. However, if it were true that Cherokees do not cry, and if it is really the "old Indian way," then the teacher, in encouraging the child to cry, is interfering with behavioral and cultural patterns in a very direct way. She is undermining the grandmother's position and is saying, in effect, that the "old Indian way" is not a good way, after all.

Cindy is "glad her grandmother didn't come up close and put her arm around her the way the white people do." But, she accepts the embrace of the teacher, "a young white woman," without qualm.

Cindy becomes abstracted and it is alleged that "somebody had a medicine man conjure her." It is irresponsible of the author to introduce the subject of witchcraft and medicine men. Responsible scholars hesitate to make judgments about the extent to which present-day Cherokees in western North Carolina believe in or practice conjuration.

Whatever the Cherokees think or feel about conjuration, a medicine man is a figure to be respected and should not be equated with a capricious "wicked witch" who casts spells on innocent children.

Cindy's father keeps her home from school "day after day" because he is lonely. He agrees to take his family (three children and himself) to live with his mother because her house is "bigger and is better built."

A book of this sort is all the more insidious because it is well meant and is not obviously bad. The language itself is not derogatory. It is the impressions the words convey that are objectionable: the grandmother is a cold person untouched by the death of her daughter; the father is an industrious but incompetent and selfish man who cannot provide his family with adequate shelter.

The teacher is the only person who comforts or sympathizes with Cindy. She is warm, understanding and concerned.

The book is supposedly about a young Cherokee girl, but it is really about the pretty young white teacher who copes with the problems created by the death of the girl's mother. The implication is that it is the non-Indian only who can solve problems and make decisions for American Indians because Indians are not capable of doing so.

This patronizing attitude is indicative of an arrogance that sometimes borders on the grotesque. In *Trading Post Girl* (Frederick Fell, Inc.), the following passage occurs:

> Libby gave Barney a teasing glance. 'Red earth, white clouds and blue water—Daddy, are you patriotic!'
>
> 'Well, now, Punkin, I guess you're right. This really is a piece of our American life, right among the Indians. You wait and see, some day they'll be real fine American citizens.'
>
> 'Oh, Daddy, not those savages.'
>
> 'They've got a lot of things to learn, too, honey. Give them time. They've got lots of good in them.'

The author, under the guise of fairness, is telling us that American Indians are not "patriotic," are not "real fine" citizens, and that they have "lots of good in them" in spite of the fact that they are "savages."

A number of authors have taken it upon themselves to establish the humanity of American Indians by presenting arguments for and against the idea. Humanness is not an arguable point.

One of the factors that significantly contributes to and nourishes this kind of arrogance is the way American Indians are portrayed in history books. This description of "the Indian" appears in *The French and Indian Wars* (American Heritage Junior Library):

> To the Indians pity was a form of cowardice. Their captives were no longer persons but things to be exchanged for ransom or tortured for amusement according to their shifting savage moods. The custom of scalping was symbolic of the Indian mind, a mind so apart from that of the whites as to remain incomprehensible. So heedless were the red men of human suffering that the word cruelty seems inadequate to

describe their ingenious tortures. Even the gentle Roger Williams called them 'wolves with the brains of men.'

This description is in sharp contrast to the following statements from Hodge's scholarly *Handbook of American Indians North of Mexico*:

From the days of Columbus to the present travelers have given testimony of customs and manners of Indians...which displayed a regard for the happiness and well being of others....Abundant evidence might be adduced to show that Indians are often actuated by motives of pure benevolence and do good merely from a generous delight in the act....Truth, honesty, and the safeguarding of human life were everywhere recognized as essential to the peace and prosperity of a tribe, and social customs enforced their observance....The care of one's family was regarded as a social duty and was generally observed....Honesty was inculcated in the young and exacted in the tribe.

Non-Indian writers have created an image of American Indians that is almost sheer fantasy. It is an image that is not authentic and one that has little value except that of sustaining the illusion that the original inhabitants deserved to lose their land because they were so barbaric and uncivilized.

This fantasy does not take into account the rich diversity of cultures that did, and does, exist. Violence is glorified over gentleness and love of peace. The humanistic aspects of American Indian societies are ignored in the standard book.

A book of "Indian stories" for young readers published in the 1930s proclaimed itself a "fine collection of exciting stories in which Indian war whoops fairly echo through the pages and painted savages peek out behind each word."

The world has changed a lot since then, but the publishing industry has not. In 1968, Harper & Row published *Indian Summer*, an "I CAN READ History Book" for children ages four through eight. According to the jacket copy it is "wonderful—geared to that important group, late first through third grade...It is a perfect book."

The setting for the story is a log cabin in a Kentucky forest during the time when the American colonies were fighting to gain independence from Britain. While the man of the house is away fighting with the American forces, men of some unidentified tribe skulk around the cabin. The "pioneer" woman outwits them and they retreat hastily into the forest. The author, in a fit of incredible cuteness, has contrived to work the sound "ugh" into the story.

The message a child gets from this "history" book is that the settlers are good, peaceful people who love their homes and families, and that American Indians are menacing but stupid creatures called "redskins" who can be made fools of by a lone woman. The "pioneer" woman is bravely and courageously defending her home and children. The father is patriotic and dutiful. There is nothing in *Indian Summer* indicating that American Indians are also fathers and mothers with families and homes.

Undoubtedly, it is accurate that settlers were threatened by, and afraid of, Indians, but Indians were equally, if not more, threatened by the settlers and they had much more to lose. The history books and story books seldom make it clear that Native Americans, in fighting back, were defending their homes and families and were not just being malicious.

It is rarely, if ever, mentioned that non-Indians scalped people, but scalping as an Indian practice is emphasized in most of the books about American Indians, including the textbooks used in schools throughout the country.

For example, in *Indian Summer* these statements occur: "Those Indians are after your scalps." "Then they could have scalped you a long way from the cabin. That's an old Indian trick." A book called *Tough Enough's Indians* (Walck, Inc.) has this to say:

'Injuns didn't go fussin' up their critters that-a-way,' Beanie said. 'They didn't have time. They were too busy huntin' and fishin' and beatin' drums and scalpin' other Injuns and white folks, cuttin' their skin and hair right off, somethin' terrible, and burnin' 'em up at stakes.'

Pontiac, King of the Great Lakes (Hastings House) contains this sentence:

A warrior had only to drop his canoe into the water and he was on his way to a council, a feast, or some scalp-taking expedition of his own.

The frequency with which non-Indian authors mention scalping, and the relish with which they indulge in bloody descriptions, would indicate that it is they, rather than Indians, who are preoccupied with scalps.

Contrary to what people have been led to believe, scalping was not a widespread custom among American Indian tribes. Rather, as the *Handbook of American Indians North of Mexico*, compiled in the 1800s, states,

The spread of the scalping practice over a great part of central and western United States was a direct result of the encouragement in the shape of scalp bounties offered by the colonial and more recent governments...

The Puritans offered rewards for Indian heads. As early as 1641, New Amsterdam (New York City) paid bounties for Indian scalps, as did other colonies.

In 1755, Massachusetts paid £40 (about $200) for the scalp of an adult male Indian and £20 (about $100) for the scalps of women and children. The French and English, in addition to paying for Indian scalps, offered rewards for the scalps of white people. Many non-Indians took advantage of the opportunity to supplement the family income by collecting scalp bounties.

There were many tribes who never took scalps. In all fairness, a more balanced approach is needed. In 1972, in an obvious attempt to counteract such books as *Indian Summer, Tough Enough's Indians*, and *Pontiac*, Harper & Row brought out a book entitled *Small Wolf*, in which Small Wolf, a young boy from an unidentified tribe, goes hunting on what is now Manhattan Island. He sees many strange sights, including a man whose face is "all WHITE." He brings his father to the island and they are run off at gunpoint by an irate Dutchman. The settlers grow in numbers, occupying more and more land, repeatedly forcing Small Wolf and his family to pack their belongings and move.

While it is admirable that Harper & Row is willing to attempt to present an Indian point of view, the book is not without flaws. The man whose face is "all WHITE" is described as having "a fat jaw and cracks between his teeth," so that Small Wolf thinks he is wearing a "devil mask." The illustration shows a fat, leering Dutch man. The implication is that "bad" people are physically unattractive—not to be confused with good, clean-cut Americans.

Historically, the "devil mask" is misplaced; the devil is a Judeo-Christian concept, not an American Indian one.

This book fosters a common misunderstanding about American Indians and the concept of land ownership. "They (other Indians) had no right to sell the land. The land and the sky and the sea are all Mother Earth for everyone to use," says Small Wolf's father.

This bit of dialogue presents a simplistic and highly romanticized version of what were various practical concepts of land ownership. It leaves the impression that American Indians had no concept of land ownership at all.

The Native peoples of this country were not rootless wanderers drifting about the country helter-skelter. Certainly, when the colonists landed, the people who owned the land did not have deeds and fee-simple titles to whip out and exhibit as proof of ownership; however, the various tribes and bands did claim sovereignty over specific areas of land, dwelling, hunting, and farming within well-established boundaries.

The people who came here to establish colonies were, after all, in search of a piece of land to own. Historically and philosophically, one rationalization for the seizure of Indian-owned lands is that nobody owned the land anyhow. Much book space has been, and is being, devoted to maintaining that myth. Apparently the producers of books feel that the American public and system of government cannot stand the truth.

The ending of *Small Wolf* gives the impression that American Indians eventually just faded into the sunset. This denies the fact that there are American Indians around today.

While non-Indians are portrayed negatively, they ultimately come across as being strong and aggressive. Small Wolf and his family evoke a feeling of pity. American Indians want respect, not pity—it is demeaning and denies human dignity.

This book is a sincere effort to offset the negative images portrayed in books like *Indian Summer*. But both of these books exemplify a flaw common to most books about Indians: they are portrayed either as noble superhumans, or as depraved, barbarous subhumans. There is no opportunity for them to behave like mere human beings.

A more direct assault is made upon the humanity of American Indians by the use of key words and phrases which trigger negative and derogatory images. Words such as savage, buck, squaw, and papoose do not bring to mind the same images as do the words man, boy, woman, and baby.

Descriptions of half-naked, hideously-painted creatures brandishing tomahawks or scalping knives, yelping, howling, grunting, jabbering, or snarling are hardly conducive to a sympathetic reaction to the people so described. Ethnocentric bias is translated into absurdities, i.e., making a point of the fact that American Indians could not read or write English when the Pilgrims arrived; they did not have clocks; they had no schools.

Broad generalizations are made, obliterating individuality. Such generalizations, while convenient, serve to foster and sustain stereotypic misconceptions. For example, in *The Indians of the Plains* (American Heritage Junior Library), this pronouncement occurs: "War was the Indian's career and hobby, his work and his play."

The author does not mention that some tribes considered warfare to be an aberration. Others strove to maintain peace and harmony in all phases of their existence. Besides, it is doubtful that there was actually much inter-tribal "war" before the coming of the white men.

Extensive cultural bias is evidenced by the comparisons invited by authors in their descriptions of people. In *Something for the Medicine Man* (Melmont), the "Granny," a Cherokee woman, is described as having a face that is "dried up like a persimmon." The teacher (non-Indian) is "tall as the trees," not "old like Granny," and has eyes "like blue flags"—the baby (Cherokee) has eyes "like a baby fox." The Cherokee family eats "like hungry dogs."

The non-Indian teacher in *My Name is Lion* (Holiday House) is young, and smells "like too many flowers." A Navajo lady is described as "an old woman" who is sitting "huddled in a blanket." Lion, a Navajo boy who finds he does not "mind" the way the teacher smells, discovers that the Navajo woman "sure" does not smell "like that flower teacher." Lion's grandfather is drunk, dirty, and "whining in Navajo about money." The positive intent of both of these books is cancelled by the negative aspects of the implied comparisons.

The repeated juxtaposition of person and animal serves to instill and reinforce the image of American Indians as being not only subhuman but also inhuman beings. In *Captives of the Senecas* (Hale & Co.), Senecas are described: "A ring of painted Indians was closing in on them, darting like huge weasels through the grass of the intervale." A later sentence reads, "Indians were coursing the ground like hunting dogs." *The American Indian* (Random House) has this to say:

> The Indians hung around New Amsterdam, as the colony on Manhattan Island was called, and made themselves a nuisance. They were lazy, insolent, and thievish as monkeys.

The French and Indian Wars (American Heritage Junior Library) puts forth this thought: "The Indian might turn gentle, but as with a tame wolf, it was a gentleness never to be trusted." *The Secret Name* (Harcourt Brace) has this statement: "Dad thinks Indians are like wild animals...You can tame them a little bit, but not all the way."

It has been well established by sociologists and psychologists that the effect on children of negative stereotypes and derogatory images is to engender and perpetuate undemocratic and unhealthy attitudes that will plague our society for years to come.

It is time for American publishing houses, schools, and libraries to take another look at the books they are offering children and seriously set out to offset some of the damage they have done. Only American Indians can tell non-Indians what it is to be Indian. There is no longer any need for non-Indian writers to "interpret" American Indians for the American public.

Storytelling and the Sacred
On the Uses of Native American Stories

Joseph Bruchac

Storytelling is a serious business. It should not be undertaken thoughtlessly, for if stories should be retold during the growing season life must come to a halt as the friendly spirits of nature become enthralled by their magic spell and neglect their appointed function of providing sustenance for the coming winter. So then also that part of the spirit which remains and wanders aimlessly when people die might be enticed into the community when stories are told, making them long again for the fellowship of the living and perhaps stealing the spirit of some newborn to keep them company. People must prepare for stories, and youngsters be protected by a buckskin thong on the wrist to tie them to the world so they might not be "spirited" away by the dead. Just as many ceremonies must be postponed until the cold- time, so also stories should be reserved until then.

—William Guy Spittal, from his introduction to
Myths of the Iroquois by E.A. Smith.[1]

Native American Stories and Non-Indian Tellers: Some Problems

There is a great deal of interest throughout storytelling circles in American Indian stories, and almost all storytellers seem to know and tell at least one such story. These tales are often among their favorites. They also find that their audiences ask for and respond to them with enthusiasm.

It is understandable that there should be this interest in Native American stories; after all, this country was founded on "Indian Land." (And on more than that, if we are to take the word of Mohawk storyteller and historian Tehanetorens. He concludes that the American people of today live more like the Indians their ancestors first encountered—in terms of dress, food, and material culture—than they do like their European ancestors. Even the form of our government seems to owe a greater debt to the Constitution of the Six Nations of the Iroquois than to any European document.)

The stories of the many Native Nations of what is now the United States speak to both the Indian and the non-Indian in ways unlike any other tales. Moreover, the many Native American tales already collected and in print constitute one of the richest bodies of myth and legend found anywhere in the world. There are currently to be found in books tens of thousands of Native American tales from the more than 400 oral traditions of North America—tales filled with those memorable and exciting details which attract both storytellers and audiences. Iroquois stories, for example, abound in such wonderful creatures as stone giants, monster bears, flying heads, magical dwarves, vampire skeletons, and more than a dozen different trickster figures.

For many storytellers, American Indian tales are untapped and fertile ground. A storyteller first "finding" an American Indian story which speaks in that special voice to him or her must feel as Balboa (not Cortez) felt on that peak in Darien when he first saw the Pacific Ocean.

There are, however, a number of problems related to the current uses—and misuses—of American Indian stories by non-Indian storytellers. These problems stem in part from that very newness, that undiscovered quality, which makes the stories so attractive and exciting to a storyteller seeking new ground. In addition, not only are the stories new to the potential teller, so too are all of the real (rather than stereotyped) aspects of Native American culture, past or present.

Difficulties also arise due to the sources from which the majority of non-Indian storytellers appear to draw the stories they are telling. Although American Indian tales come from oral traditions, the storyteller usually encounters them first in a book rather than from the lips of an American Indian. Unfortunately, many of the written versions of Native American stories which are still alive in the oral tradition of a particular people are either incompletely or inaccurately recorded.

It is a sad truth that the average non-Indian American today knows less about the American Indian than the first European settlers on the continent—who survived because of the help and friendship of Native Americans. Even people who live within a few miles of large and active American Indian communities either know little about their Native American neighbors or express disbelief that they even exist. Again and again I have gone into a town and on asking if there were any local Indians been told there are none, only to meet numerous local Indian people shortly thereafter.

The myth of the "Vanishing Red Man" is more alive in the minds of most Americans than the vital, continent-wide, growing population of Native Americans which prompted Simon Ortiz, Acoma storyteller and poet, to say in one of his poems: "Indians are everywhere."

Along with the lack of knowledge about the existence of the present-day Native American goes an ignorance of the place and proper use of American Indian stories. No story—in any culture—exists in isolation from the life of its people. The problems of the rationale, effectiveness, and validity of transplanting stories from one culture to another do not just relate to American Indian tales. The best storytellers are usually aware of those problems and may even engage in heroic efforts to understand the origins and cultural contexts of the tales they use.

Yet many storytellers—including some of the best—know only that the American Indian stories they tell came from this or that book or were told by this or that other non-Indian teller. Ironically, they may know less of the origin of an American Indian tale—which grew from this soil—than they do of one from ancient Babylon or the Fiji Islands.

Almost universally, the non-Indian tellers using an American Indian tale have never heard a word spoken in the particular American Indian language from which that tale comes, have no knowledge of the intellectual or material culture of that particular Indian nation, and have never met a living American Indian from that tribal

Nation. In many cases, they don't even know where the story comes from—other than that it is "Indian." And they almost certainly do not know the strong relationship between storytelling and the sacred which exists throughout the many Native American Nations.

Before going further, let me make it clear that my aim is not to discourage non-Indians from telling American Indian stories. The stories of Native American people are, to a degree, now part of the heritage of all Americans. The lessons they teach—and I will speak more about the lesson-bearing qualities of Native American tales—are probably more needed today by all of us than they were hundreds of years ago by those who first told them.

These are powerful stories, powerful as medicine or tobacco. But, like medicine or the tobacco whose smoke is used to carry prayers up to Creator, stories must be used wisely and well or they may be harmful to both tellers and hearers alike. Every Native American storyteller I have spoken with about this—Vi Hilbert in Washington, Ed Edmo in Oregon, Kevin Locke in North Dakota, Simon Ortiz and Harold Littlebird in New Mexico, Keewaydinoquay in Michigan, Tehanetorens in New York, and many others—agrees that there is no reason why non-Indian storytellers who understand and respect should not tell American Indian tales.

But there is a great deal to understand, and respect implies responsibility. It is my hope that this article may lead non-Indian tellers to a better understanding of American Indian storytelling and suggest some directions they may then follow to develop the proper relationship with the stories they wish to tell.

Native American Uses of Stories

Hey-ho-wey—I tell a story,
A story from the Ancient Ones,
Hey-ho-wey—I place asseyma
For their spirits...
Hey-ho-wey—I tell a story,
Listen—and learn.
     Hey-ho-wey—Hey-ho-wey...

—Keewaydinoquay, from her
Origin Tale *Mukwah Miskomin,
Gift of Bear* [2]

How are Native American stories used by Indian people? Native American stories have been used traditionally to teach the people those lessons they need to know to cooperate and survive. American Indian cultures, throughout the continent, place high premiums on both the independence of the individual and the importance of working for the good of all.

Coercion was seldom used to force an individual to conform and the lack of police, strict laws and jails was often remarked upon by European travelers who noticed that the American Indians they visited also seemed to have no crime. This lack of coercion was particularly evident in the child-rearing practices of Native American peoples. Universally, it was regarded as deeply wrong for any adult to strike a child. The European rule of "spare the rod and spoil the child" seemed perverse to the Native Americans, who believed that beating children would produce only negative results. Striking a child could serve only to break the child's spirit or stir resentment. Such a cowardly act was a terrible example. One who beat children could expect one day to be beaten by those children when they became stronger than their parents.

Instead, when children did wrong, the first thing to be done was to use the power of storytelling to show the right way. If children were disobedient, rude to an Elder, or doing things which might be dangerous to themselves, then they would be told one or more lesson stories designed to show what happens to those who misbehave.

The power of the stories—which are told to this day—was usually enough. If stories and other measures—such as throwing water on them—did not work, then various shunning practices, such as pretending they did not exist or (in the case of the Abenaki) blackening their faces and sending them out of the lodge to be ignored by all in the community, were used. As soon as the children indicated willingness to behave properly, the shunning ended.

(In the case of adults who consistently acted against the welfare of their people, the most drastic—though seldom used—measure was banishment from the lands of that tribal Nation. Adults, too, were told stories to help them see the right paths to follow.)

Because such lesson stories were of great importance to the welfare of the individual and the Nation, they had to be charged with great power. A good story, one which is entertaining, creatively effective, is more likely to affect its hearer. The role of the story as a social guide makes it all the more important that the story be memorable. Because of this, it is important that non-Indian tellers understand clearly the message which a particular story is meant to convey. If you are unaware of the way in which the story is used, then *you* may be more likely to misunderstand or misuse it. Stories are like food. We eat food because we like it, but we also eat food because it keeps us alive.

I think it is no exaggeration to say that all American Indian stories, when used in the right context, can serve as lesson stories and as important tools of communication. That is still true to this day among Native

American people. In fact, even jokes may be used in that fashion in Native American communities.

If an American Indian tells you a joke, listen closely to it. Invariably that joke will apply to something which you have done or said. The joke may be intended as a lesson for you or even as a reprimand if you have overstepped your bounds in some way. But because Native American people still believe in non-interference in the actions of others—except in indirect ways—a joke may be the chosen way to point something out.

It is important to remember, too, that Native American culture is holistic. By this I mean that there is no separation between church and state, none of the convenient pigeon-holing we find in western culture which makes it easy to separate the "sacred" from the "everyday." In the American Indian universe, everything is sacred.

A book I strongly recommend to anyone interested in the role of stories in contemporary Native American life is *Wolf That I Am* by Fred McTaggert. It chronicles the efforts of McTaggert, then a graduate student at the University of Iowa, to collect and write about the stories of the Mesquakie People, whose settlement was not far from Iowa City.

Although he thought he would be collecting quaint folktales from the remnants of a dying culture, he soon found himself confronted by people who believed strongly in themselves, their language, and their religious rituals. Far from dying, the Mesquakie way was very much alive. Far from being ready to share their stories with the tape-recorder-bearing graduate student, the Mesquakie people were protective of their traditions.

At the advice of a Mesquakie friend, also a student at the University, McTaggert once trudged through a snowstorm to reach the house of a man who was said to know many stories. But when McTaggert knocked on the door and Tom Youngman stepped out, closing the door behind him, this is what happened:

> "I was told you might be able to help me out with some information about stories."
>
> The man's deep brown eyes looked into mine for several minutes. I sensed in his eyes a power and a calmness that I was not at all familiar with. He was wearing only a flannel shirt, but he did not even shiver in the cold, piercing wind. As he stood in front of the closed door, looking deeply into my eyes, he somehow put me at ease, and I felt neither the fear nor the guilt that I usually felt when first meeting people on the Mesquakie settlement. His silence was an adequate communication and when he finally spoke, I knew what he was about to say.
>
> "I can't tell you stories," he said softly. I had no trouble hearing him over the whistling wind. "I use my stories to pray. To me, they are sacred."
>
> I thanked him, and he opened the door again and retreated into his small lodge...[3]

Later, McTaggert realized that he had been tricked by his Mesquakie student friend. At first he was angry and confused, then he realized that by being tricked—as in the Mesquakie story of Raccoon and Wolf which he read in an old collection (*Fox Texts* by William Jones)—he had learned a lesson.

There are also stories, and this varies from one Native American Nation to the next, which are part of healing rituals. The most obvious example may be the Navajo stories which are part of the various healing way ceremonies. Figures from those stories are made in colored sand on the earth, and the person to be cured is placed on top of that sand painting—made a part of the story—in a ritual which may go on for days.

In other Native American Nations some stories are only to be told to certain initiated

people and even then only at certain times. What responsibility does the storyteller have when discovering one of these stories and wishing to tell it outside of the original context? I am not sure that I know the right answer, but I do know that taking sacred things lightly is not a good idea and that caution is more advisable than foolhardiness. There are stories told about characters, Coyote, for example, who take the sacred too lightly and do things the wrong way. Within the stories, they always pay for their mistakes.

It appears to be a continent-wide tradition that all Native American legends are only to be told at certain times and in certain ways. Keewaydinoquay, an Anishinabe medicine woman and storyteller, has a song which begins each storytelling. She always offers *asseyma*, or tobacco, for the ancestors during its singing. Those who have studied with Keeywaydinoquay do the same.

In most parts of North America, stories are to be told only during the winter seasons. In some cases a story may be told only at night. Further, to mention the names of certain characters in stories—Coyote, for example—outside of the stories is an invitation to bad luck. Coyote, say some of the California Indian people, might hear you mention his name and then come to visit you and do mischief.

One can, I suppose, find logical reasons for these prohibitions. To engage in storytelling during the growing season when one should be working in the fields or gathering food might be seen as counter-productive. People have greater need for the stories in the winter when food may be scarce and nights are long and cold; then a good story helps keep up one's spirits. But the prohibitions against storytelling out of context are, I have been told, not enforced by human beings. Instead, the powers of nature step in.

Tell stories in the summertime, the Iroquois say, and a bee will fly into your lodge and sting you. That bee is actually one of the Little People, the *Jo-ge-oh*, taking the shape of a bee to warn you that you are doing wrong. The Abenaki people say that if you tell stories during the growing season snakes will come into your house.

For whatever reasons, I only tell certain stories in the months between first and last frost. A non-Indian friend of mine who wanted to tell Indian tales, however, neither knew nor cared about such prohibitions. He looked up some stories from a 19th century text and began to memorize them. Finally, he had learned them well enough to tell them in public. But the first time he told one of those stories, he became ill. I advised him to learn more about the tales. Instead, he told another one in public and had a serious accident immediately thereafter. Once again, I suggested he might look into the history of these stories and learn more about the Native people who tell them. His response, however, was that he now had to find out if this was just a coincidence.

Quite deliberately, he told another of the tales in public. This time he became so ill that he almost died. He concluded that he *did* need to know more about the stories, made a trip to Oklahoma to visit with some old people from that Native American Nation, and discovered the stories he'd been telling were night-time stories, only to be told at a certain time of the year and never (as he had done) in the light of day.

Native American Stories and Non-Indian Tellers: Some Possible Directions

What I want to share here is not a set of hard and fast rules, but some possible directions for a non-Indian storyteller to follow when wishing to use Native American tales. They come from my own approach to the stories that I tell, ones which come from the traditions of my own Abenaki ancestors and the other Native American people from whom I have learned:

1. Instead of learning Native American tales solely from books, learn them from the life of the people. Visit with living American Indian people, try to find out more about their ways of life and their languages. When using written texts, fully research the versions of the story if more than one version exists. A knowledge of the language and people from which the story comes should help you develop a version truer to the original.

2. When visiting with Native American people, remember that listening and patience are cardinal virtues. The old stereotype of the stoic Indian comes in part from the fact that all too often non-Indians monopolize the conversation. It is common practice in western culture to interrupt others when engaged in conversation. Such interruptions effectively terminate conversation with Indian people. When asking questions, avoid leading questions or ones with a simple "yes" or "no" answer. Native people place great value on politeness and will often say "yes" just to avoid disagreeing with you.

3. Know what type of story you are learning. Find out if there were certain times when it was to be told and be aware of the way the story's construction fits into the culture and worldview of that particular Native Nation. If you are not certain of a story's use or origin, *don't tell it*. Further, if you wish to use a story which you have heard from a Native American teller, always get that person's explicit permission to tell it.

4. When telling a Native American story, try to avoid subtly racist language or language that stereotypes. Many non-

Indians, for example, do not realize that it is deeply insulting to refer to a woman as a "squaw," a child as a "papoose," or a man as a "brave." Remember that Native American cultures, rather than being "primitive" or "ignorant," were often politically and culturally more sophisticated than most European nations at the time of Columbus. As Alvin M. Josephy says, "Belief in the freedom and dignity of the individual was deeply ingrained in many Indian societies." (Josephy's *The Indian Heritage of America* should be read by any teller using Native American tales.[4]) Moreover, Native American women in many tribal Nations—such as the Iroquois, where they owned the houses, controlled the agriculture and both chose and deposed chiefs—played central roles.

One of my favorite Iroquois stories is of the Storytelling Stone. It tells of how the first legends were taught to a boy by an ancient rock. In exchange for each story, the boy gave the stone game that he had shot. It is an important story for anyone who wishes to tell Native American tales to remember, for it reminds us of the principles of reciprocity and the right relation to the earth which are at the root of Indian stories and Indian culture. A storyteller, whether Indian or non-Indian, who keeps those principles in mind, will be well on the way to making use of Indian stories as they were meant to be used—for the people, for the earth.

Footnotes

1. Smith, E.A., *Myths of the Iroquois.* Ohsweken, Ontario, Canada: Iroqrafts, 1983.
2. Keewaydinoquay, *Mukwah Miskomin or Kinnickinnick, Gift of Bear.* Minis Kitigan Drum, 1977.
3. McTaggert, Fred, *Wolf That I Am.* Boston: Houghton Mifflin, 1976.
4. Josephy, Alvin M., *The Indian Heritage of America.* New York: Alfred A. Knopf, 1968.

Not Just Entertainment

Lenore Keeshig-Tobias

("Not Just Entertainment" cuts straight to the heart of what this book is about. Indians are public property, the other half of "cowboys and..." Teachers speak to their students of "our" Indian heritage; writers think nothing of "adapting" any story—excuse me, myth or legend—and always for children. Anthropologists tell us that they know more about our history than we do; they speak of us as having lost our cultures. Well, these "myths and legends" are the stories we live by. Have, and will. You might not have noticed, but the People are dancing again, the People are growing out their hair. Mourning is over. Now we fight back.)

The issue is not about *Where the Spirit Lives*, an award-winning and subtly racist TV-movie about the Native experience in residential schools, written and produced by white people from their own perspective. The issue is not about Darlene Barry Quaife's *Bone Bird*, a "celebration of Native spirituality" written by a white woman who says "writing from imagination is an incredibly free process." The issue is not about W.P. Kinsella's *Miss Hobbema Pageant*, a collection of malicious and sadistic renderings of stories about Native people, written by a white man who maintains, "When I need facts I invent them." The issue is not just a white perspective of history, an oversimplification of Native spirituality and lifeways, or mean-spirited and racist renderings of our stories. The issue is not censorship or the shackling of imagination, both naive and thoughtless responses voiced by many non-Native writers and storytellers, and even a few Native writers who want to keep up their good relations with the fort.

The issue is culture theft, the theft of voice. It's about power.

The issue is not unlike the struggle women waged, not so very long ago, to get their voices heard, their stories published. The issue is not unlike the French Canadian struggle for their language and their culture. The Quebecois have a unique voice in North America because they have fought to ensure that their language remains intact. Language is a conveyor of culture. Language carries the ideas by which a nation defines itself as a people. Language gives voice to a nation's stories, it's *mythos*.

The question I ask Canadians is: Would you accept an American definition of Canada and Canadians? How would it be if Germans were to write Jewish history? And white Americans writing Black history?

Stories are not just entertainment. Stories are power. They reflect the deepest, the most intimate perceptions, relationships and attitudes of a people. Stories show how a people, a culture thinks. Such wonderful offerings are seldom reproduced by outsiders.

Picture this—the outsider (oppressor) crawling into the skin of the oppressed without asking and before the skin is even vacated. Now, suppose the skin is already empty. What happens if it is too big or too small for the outsider? And then once inside, whose eyes are looking out?

Cultural insight, cultural nuance, cultural metaphor, cultural symbols, hidden subtext—give a book or film the ring of truth. Images coded with our meanings are the very things missing in most "native" writing by non-Native authors. These are the very things that give stories their universal appeal, that allow true empathy and shared emotion.

Yet, Native images, stories, symbols, and history are all too often used by Canadians and Americans to sell things—cars, tobacco, movies, books. But why hasn't Basil Johnston's *Indian School Days* become a best-seller? Why hasn't *HalfBreed* by Maria Campbell been reprinted? Why, for that matter, has Maria Campbell, as one of Canada's "celebrated" authors, never received a writer's grant?

With First Nations people struggling for justice in Canada's legal system, in land claims, in education, what makes Canadians or anyone else think Native peoples have equality in the film industry? In publishing? With granting agencies? Or in the arts?

Unconsciously perhaps, but with the same devastating results, the Canadian cultural industry is stealing Native stories as surely as the missionaries stole our religion and the politicians stole our land and the residential schools stole our language. As Leslie Marmon Silko writes in *Ceremony*, stories "are all we have, you see—all we have to fight off illness and death."

As a storyteller, I was advised by an Elder that there is a season for storytelling—winter. "Blackflies, mosquitoes and other creatures like those stories," she cautioned. How quaint, I thought at the time.

Nonetheless, I respected her advice, and as time went on, I began to understand. If storytellers sit around all summer telling stories, then quite naturally they'll become the feast of blackflies and mosquitoes. But my Elder was telling me more. She was telling me these stories are meant for certain ears only—and I don't mean non-Native ears.

She was also telling me that storytellers have a responsibility for the stories they tell. So powerful are stories that, in Native cultures, one storyteller cannot tell another's story without permission. Alexander Wolfe, a Salteaux storyteller, in his introduction to *Earth Elder Stories*, sets this down: "Each family handed down its own stories. Other stories, belonging to other families, could not be told, because to do so would be to steal." This aspect of Native lifeways and values, the copyright, existed long before the Europeans arrived in North America, and it still applies to the written word, in fact any story, fiction or non-fiction, that is put out to the public.

But rather than confront and deal with issues of appropriation, rather than recognize the fact that we can tell our own stories and that there is protocol for the acquisition of stories, and rather than accept responsibility to and for the stories they tell, many non-Native writers and "storytellers" cry censorship and decry self-censorship.

Some traditional stories tell how Trickster attempts to recreate the actions, the magic of another. Motivated more by laziness, incompetence in providing for his own family and his great need to impress these same friends with his handling of their magic, Trickster fails. Not only are the friends not impressed, but the magic always backfires.

Our Elders and traditional teachers want to share the beauty of Native culture, the Native way. But appropriation is not sharing, and those who fool themselves also fool the public by drawing away from the real issues and struggles facing Native peoples. Appropriation exploits and commercializes Native cultures, and is harmful to innocent people.

Consider also that when Native and traditional people go out to gather medicine (roots and herbs), they do not go out and just pick and take. They ask, talking to the plants and rocks, telling of their needs and what is in their hearts. They leave a tobacco offering in place of what they take.

Native stories deal with the experiences of our humanity, experiences we laugh and cry and sweat for, experiences we learn from. Stories are not just for entertainment. We know that. The storyteller and writer has a responsibility—a responsibility to the people, a responsibility for the story and a responsibility to the art. The art in turn then reflects a significant and profound self-understanding.

Now tell me, why are Canadians and their American cousins so obsessed with Native stories anyway? Why the urge to "write Indian"? Have they run out of stories of their own? Or are their renderings nostalgia for a simpler more "at one with nature" stage of human development? Now there's a cliché for you.

Maybe, Canadian and American stories about Native people are some form of exorcism. Are they trying to atone for the horrible reality of Native-white relations? Or maybe, they just know a good story when they hear one and are willing to take it, without permission, just like archeologists used to rob our graves for their museums.

What about the quest for Native spirituality? It is mostly escapist, and people, like Darlene Barry Quaife, Lynne Andrews, and other would-be shamans, would rather look to an ideal, romanticized "Native" living in never-never land than confront the reality of what being Native means in this dominant society.

What makes white Canadians and Americans think they are privy to the stories of First Nations people, anyway? And why is speaking for ourselves and telling our own stories so threatening to them? Because stories are power? They have the land now, or so they think, do they now want our stories, our voices, and our spirit, too?

Residential school survivors tell of children being forced to eat their own vomit when their stomach could no longer hold down the sour porridge. They tell of broken knuckles from fingers being rapped. Some even tell of having pins stuck through their tongues as punishment for speaking their Native language. (Now, *that's* censorship.) And what about the teacher who was removed from one residential school for abusing children? He was simply sent to another, more remote, school.

It's not as if these stories have never been told. It doesn't mean the stories have never existed. Nor does it mean Native writers and storytellers are incompetent and inexperienced as W.P. Kinsella would like us to believe: "If minorities were doing an adequate job, they wouldn't need to complain," he has said. "They don't have the skill or experience to tell their stories well."

It means our voices have been marginalized. Imagine—white Canadians and Americans telling Native stories because their governments outlawed Native languages and Native lifeways, and punished those of us who resisted.

However, as Métis author Maria Campbell (to whom we Native writers affectionately refer as the Mother of us all) said on public radio last fall, "If you want to write our stories then be prepared to live with us." To this I have to add—not just for three months either, and 18 months is little better.

Heed the voices of the wilderness. Be there at Big Mountain and Akwesasne. Be there with the Lubicon, the Innu. Be there with the Teme-Augama Anishnabai on the Red Squirrel Road. The Saugeen Ojibway. I dare you.

Well I say, a mouse dances on my head, and if you want these Native stories, then fight for them. I dare you.

AAA-IIII-EEE Y-AAH!
Clear the way.
In a sacred manner I come.
The stories are mine!

—an Ojibway War Song

Grandmothers of a New World
Beth Brant

(The truth is, a lot of writing for children is done for purposes of indoctrination. Deliberately or not, writers put into children's books the things they think kids need to know in order to survive and become full human beings, or the things they want them to believe. Of all the distortions, misrepresentations and outright lies which have been used to justify the treatment of the original inhabitants of these continents, none have been more extreme than those applied to the women. At the heart of every Native Nation are its women. The Cheyenne people acknowledge this when they say, a Nation is not conquered until the hearts of its women are on the ground.

Because the white men who came here so little valued their own women, one of their first missions was to reduce ours to the same status—beast of burden, important for the production of sons, but little else: squaws. You will not learn from the history books about the Cherokee Beloved Women or the Iroquois Clan Mothers. You will certainly not learn of the continued influence of women in Native life. Since it began with Pocahontas, it seems appropriate that telling the truth should begin there, too.)

Pocahontas and Nancy Ward hold a special fascination for me because of the legends that have risen around their names and lives. At the same time, some Indians have attached the word "traitor" to describe them. Deified and vilified. What were the lives of Pocahontas and Nancy Ward really like?

Somewhere outside their legends the real truth lies. And as a poet, rather than a historian, I feel I have a freedom of sorts to explore and imagine what those truths are.

According to "history," Pocahontas was a favored daughter of Wahunsonacock ("Powhatan"), chief of the Algonquian Confederacy in what is now called Virginia. In 1607 or 1608 she saw her first white man, John Smith, as a ship from England sailed into the harbor. She immediately became enamored of his color and promptly fell in love with him. Wahunsonacock, being the savage he was, hated John Smith and for no apparent reason gave the order to have him

executed. Right before he was to be tomahawked, Pocahontas threw herself on Smith, telling her father that he'd have to kill her too. Since Pocahontas was willing to die for this particular white man, then there must be something wonderful about all white men, so Wahunsonacock spared not only John Smith's life but the lives of the rest of his crew.

Smith eventually returned to England, leaving Pocahontas to pine away until she met John Rolfe. Pocahontas must have thought that all white men looked alike because she enthusiastically fell in love with him and became a good christian. She also became a good capitalist because she helped her husband grow rich in the tobacco trade, took up wearing white women's clothing, had a son, went to England where she was a celebrity, and finally died happily in England—her soul eternally saved.

Quite a story. Even Hollywood couldn't improve this tale.

But I can.

Wahunsonacock had 20 children, ten of them daughters. Pocahontas was a favored daughter, but more than that, was a child of her father's confidence. She understood only too well what the invasion of Europeans meant for her people. I also must tell you that at the time Pocahontas met John Smith, she was 12 or 13—a woman by Indian standards of the day. Pocahontas was not just a good listener, she had ideas that were listened to. When she spoke, the Pamunkey people heard her and respected her voice. While not a true matriarchy like the Mohawks or the Cherokee of Nancy Ward, Pamunkey women held sway in the disposition of enemy warriors and matters pertaining to war. John Smith's so-called rescue was, in fact, a mock execution—a traditional ritual often held after capture of enemies. This ritual, in the eyes of John Smith, held all the dramatic trappings of a play. Smith saw himself cast in a starring role and played it to the hilt. Pocahontas also played her part. She chose to adopt Smith as her brother since this was her right as an Indian woman. Smith began writing letters back home of how his life was saved by a genuine Indian princess, and how he held the Algonquian Confederacy in the palm of his hand. Of course, this was and is nonsense.

Wahunsonacock and his daughter/ confidante were not fools. They had a sophisticated view of the English and the other European nations who were clamoring to capture the "new" continent and claim it for their own. The English seemed mighty, so why not choose them to

make alliances with? The continuation of the Indian people was uppermost in the daughter's and father's minds. Then, as now, survival was the most important thought on North American Indians' agendas. Also, the art and practice of diplomacy was not a new concept to Indian people. If Indians were as savage and warlike as the history books would like us to believe, there would not have been any of us left when the first white man set his feet on this continent. So Pocahontas was probably the first ambassador to the English, just as La Malinche was to the Spanish in Mexico. Not an easy task for anyone, let alone a 12-year-old woman who could not read, write, or speak the language of the intruders, and who most likely figured out early on that the English held little esteem for women—especially if they weren't white. Pocahontas saw the alternative to genocide as adopting John Smith as her brother.

The history books speculate on whether Smith and Pocahontas were lovers. It may seem an insignificant thing to wonder about, but I wonder too, because the failure of John Smith to sire a child by Pocahontas must have been a tear in the delicate fabric of the tie that had sprung up between the British and the Algonquian Confederacy. A child born of an Indian ambassador and a British father stood a chance of truly being the child of a new world; a child would contain the elements necessary for the continued existence of the Indian people. But it is probably just as well that Pocahontas did not bear a child by John Smith. Boastful and self-involved, he eventually left the Jamestown Colony and went home to England. He hadn't made his fortune, but he was to make a mark on history through his lies and distortions of the Indian people. There are reports that Pocahontas and her father were greatly angered at Smith's leavetaking. Why? Did they see it as a withdrawal of protection by the British?

Through Smith's adoption, they had woven a tenuous connection between the two nations that had so far been mutually rewarding. The Algonquian Confederacy had lost few people to these British invaders. Their confederacy was still strong in the eyes of other Indian Nations they traded with, and they were not weakened by the relationship with the British, due to the diplomatic skills of Wahunsonacock and his daughter.

The British had done fairly well in the new colony too. Indians had taught them what to eat, how to eat it, how to plant what they ate. It often amazes me how Thanksgiving is portrayed as whites and Indians sharing their food with each other in a loving gesture of friendship. The pilgrims had nothing to share. What they ate on that mythical day was entirely due to the generosity and loving spirit of the Indian people. And it was this kind of generosity that frequently became the beginning of the end for all Indian Nations. Indian people have many languages, but there is not a single word, except in English, that describes the word "stingy" or "selfish." But that winter when John Smith left for England, Wahunsonacock and Pocahontas left the Jamestown settlement and went home. They enjoined other Indians to do the same. And Jamestown suffered heavy losses of life. They literally starved. Was this a punishment on the part of Wahunsonacock? Did he see his daughter as a woman scorned? Most likely not. Did he see his daughter as a humiliated woman? There we can come closer to the truth.

Indian women chose whom they wished to love or not love, whom they wished to have children by, whose families they wished to unite. By adopting Smith as lover/brother, Pocahontas was, in effect, opening her home and family to him. Smith violated this most basic precept of Indian values by leaving Jamestown without even

a goodbye or thank you. To be impolite to an Indian is humiliation to the whole family, clan, and Nation. Smith and the other settlers might not have been aware of this humiliation, simply because they chose not to be aware of the system of values that governed Indian thinking. Literally turning their backs on the Jamestown settler (another subtlety that the British chose to ignore), Pocahontas was sent on varying missions to other Nations by her father. Serving as a spokeswoman for the Algonquian Confederacy, she arranged new trade agreements, cemented old friendships, built new ones. Of this there can be no doubt—Pocahontas was a skilled orator and a politician. It fills me with rage that the only stories we have of her are the sickly sweet, romantic variety, so racist and untrue.

During this time, Pocahontas took an Indian husband. Of him, we can find no trace. I wonder if she had children by him. What happened to them and him? Was Pocahontas happy? When Wahunsonacock and Pocahontas were ready to visit Jamestown again, they were taken prisoner. I suppose the settlers wanted to vent their anger on them for being deserted. It would never have occurred to the pilgrims that their own stupidity and racism had led to the death of so many British. Pocahontas and Wahunsonacock were not free to leave the settlement, but could wander among the people and houses. They found a man who must have intrigued them no end. He was a missionary, and he was teaching people to read. Reading was something the white men did, and because of it, they held a certain power over the Pamunkey people. Bargaining with the British, Pocahontas arranged for her father to be sent home and she would stay to learn more about the christian way. The accounts given at the time show Pocahontas to be an eager convert.

I submit that her conversion to christianity was only half-hearted, but her conversion to literacy was carried out with powerful zeal. And besides, the Church of England was not without some appeal. The rituals of prayer and communion must have been appealing to a Pamunkey woman who had grown up in prayer and communion with the spirits. The message was different, yet the idea of life after death was one that Pocahontas could identify with. In Indian life, everything had its own spirit, not just human beings. When things die, they go to the spirit world and become influences on the living. And while some aspects of christianity must have seemed harsh to someone of Pocahontas' sensibilities, it served a nobler purpose in her mind. Please don't think of this as hypocritical or calculating. Pocahontas was using the tools that the spirits and Creator were giving to her.

And that brings me to something that I feel in my heart is true—Pocahontas was guided by divine power. Not a god in christian terms, but a communion with Creator. Indians of pre-christian times spent their lives in this kind of communion. "Living with the spirits," my father would say. Pocahontas lived with and listened to these spirits. There is a term that has been used for centuries—"Manifest Destiny." It is a white man's term and logic, meant to imply that whites are superior to Native peoples and, therefore, it is nature's law that the white race hold dominion over all natural things. In other words, the white man is king and emperor over all—people, animals, plants, the very air.

But I propose that Pocahontas had her own manifest destiny to fulfill. That of keeping her people alive. Would Wahunsonacock and his people have listened and learned from Pocahontas so readily if she had not already proven to be the kind of person who did "live with the spirits"? Was Pocahontas a shaman? Don't forget, her name means "playing with the spirits," or better, "getting joy from the spirits." Name-giving in Indian culture is serious business. Many signs and omens are consulted before giving a person a name. In many tribes, it was the role for the berdache, or homosexual, to bestow this honor. History will not tell us that Pocahontas was a shaman, but there is a feeling inside me that tells me this is so. A very unscholarly and unacademic feeling on my part. But I am not a scholar or an academic. I am an Indian woman poet and storyteller who believes there were and are prophets of the future among my people. Pocahontas was such a prophet.

Linda Hogan, a Chicasaw poet, has written to me in letters about the "new people." These are people like her and myself—the half-breeds, the mixed-bloods. Did Pocahontas envision nations of new people? Did she envision a new world? A world where people would say "I am a human being of many races."? Is this the real manifest destiny? I may be stepping on many toes, for there is always debate on who constitutes a real Indian, depending on the blood quantum. But I remember what Vine Deloria once said. He said, "Blood quantums are not important; what really matters is who your grandparents were." These women I am talking about were our grandparents. They were our grandmothers in spirit, if not actual blood ties. This does not mean that I think every person is a spiritual Indian. That would be dishonorable to my ancestors. And I emphatically do not believe that our culture and rituals are up for grabs. A person does not become an Indian by participating in a sweat, or observing a Sun Dance, or even working on political issues that affect Indians, such as Big Mountain. One does not become an Indian like one chooses new clothes, or chooses religion. And one is not like an Indian simply by believing in our value system.

While learning to read and write, Pocahontas had as one of her teachers, John Rolfe. The accounts come down to us through history that he admired Pocahontas. He may indeed have admired her. She was a powerful voice in Jamestown, her father held great wealth of land, she knew the many secrets of growing tobacco which Rolfe had come to realize could make him a rich and respected man. Rolfe came from gentry stock, but was a fairly poor man compared to others of his station. Why else go to the "New World," except in search of untold wealth, ready for the taking? But the history books tell us that Rolfe was taken with Pocahontas because of her "regal bearing, her christian demeanor, her wisdom." All this may be true and perhaps love even entered into it.

But I tread carefully when I speak of love, because it means so many different things. Did Pocahontas love John Rolfe? Perhaps. Did her spirits tell her that Rolfe was the right choice? More than likely. There were other white men waiting in the wings to have the favor of Pocahontas and her father. For one was not possible without the other. But Rolfe was a man easily handled by those who held more power and charisma than he. And he was not ugly or diseased. The courtship began, but not without obstacles. The court of King James was very adamant in discouraging contact between the races. The issue of class was an equal barrier to the marriage. This is why we end up with the ridiculous legends of Pocahontas being a true, imperial princess. John Smith had started the flame of this particular bonfire when he wrote home about having his life saved by a princess of the realm. And John Rolfe added more fuel to the story in his desire to be married. Thus Wahunsonacock is made a king and Pocahontas his favorite princess. In reality, of course, kings and princesses—royalty—did not exist among Indians.

Of a dowry, there is no mention, but it would be fair to say that Rolfe acquired quite a parcel of land to experiment with tobacco. The smoking of tobacco was a great hit in England among the royal court. King James was said to disapprove of it, but it doesn't look like too many paid attention to what he had to say. His own wife, Queen Anne, was addicted to the stuff and her court of ladies spent hours smoking and gossiping in the palace. The legend of Pocahontas makes us believe that after marrying Rolfe, she quickly became a lady of leisure, even acquiring the title of Lady Rebecca. I find this choice of names especially intriguing. Did she choose it for herself? In her quest for literacy, the Bible was the only tool she had at that time. Did she read the story of another ancient legend, Rebecca, when she was told "Be thou the mother of thousands of millions, and let thy seed possess the gate of those which hate them?"

When Pocahontas found herself pregnant, what must she have felt? The joy any new mother feels? A special joy because she was going to have a child of her new world? A child of differing races, who would learn to read and write as a matter of course and would take a place in this new world with Pocahontas' wisdom and cunning and political skills?

To insure this child of her new world would come into the best of all possible worlds, Pocahontas surrounded herself with female relatives and her father. John Rolfe may have been alarmed that Lady Rebecca was choosing to have her child in this most primitive and heathen of manners, but maybe he wasn't. We only know that in 1615 Pocahontas gave birth to a son, Thomas, amidst the chanting and singing of her people. So much for Pocahontas' christian submissiveness. After the birth, the relatives stayed on.

One has to wonder at John Rolfe's attitude toward this. But unlike John Smith,

Rolfe recognized the honor of being part of an Indian family. When a non-Indian becomes part of an Indian household, whether through marriage or friendship, the Indian family takes over. This is assimilation of a kind that is never written about or discussed. The non-Indian is swallowed up and loved and may have to put up small battles to hang onto a distinct personality as opposed to the personality of the Indian group.

I have seen this happen to my non-Indian uncles, my non-Indian mother, my non-Indian lover. Soon they are talking like Indians, joking like Indians, using the term "we" instead of "you" and "I." The prevailing Indian culture and world-view becomes the non-Indian's view as well. But, again, this is not becoming an Indian. It is a process of assimilation that is whole. Many parts make up the integration of a community. This is a difficult concept to explain to people who are not part of an Indian community. Each part is distinct, yet each part acts in accordance with the whole.

One way I might explain this integrity is through the example of the Sun Dance of the Plains Indians. Each person entering the circle to dance has a definite objective in mind. Whether he or she is dancing for one purpose, for example strength, or the curing of a sickness of the body or mind, that purpose must reflect on the community and be for the good of the community. In Oklahoma a few years ago, a Vietnam veteran asked to participate in the Sun Dance in his wheelchair. This had never been done, but a way was worked out that a guide would maneuver him through the rigorous ceremony. This was not an easy task the veteran and his guide had taken upon themselves. The dance can last for hours; it has been known to last for days until the communion with Creator has taken place. Later, when the dance was over, the vet told a friend of mine that he was dancing to be absolved of the "sins" (his word) he had committed in Vietnam.

But all the while he was dancing, he was reliving his experience in Vietnam, and he began dancing for his buddies, he began dancing for the Vietnamese people, he began dancing for peace and the end to racism in the world. What has this story to do with Pocahontas? Everything, I think. While not belonging to the Indian world-view that produces the Sun Dance, Pocahontas was doing her own dance for the good of the community. And her community, because of the child she bore, was an enlarged one. And so I believe was John Rolfe's idea of community. At least I am hoping so, for the sake of Pocahontas and that little boy child Thomas.

Pocahontas and John Rolfe were invited to England to be presented to King James and Queen Anne. The tobacco industry was a profitable one to the British monarch. He wished to thank the Rolfes in person, but more than that, he wished to meet Pocahontas, the "princess" of the Indians. North American Indians were becoming the rage in England at that time. The novelties of Black Africans were wearing thin and British royalty wanted a new toy to play with. Indians were the "in thing," and I daresay, Europeans haven't changed all that much. To this day, North American Indians are an object of fascination to European peoples. I honestly think they believe we still live as we did 400 years ago. And they think we are all alike. But Americans are not much better. I'm afraid they tend to think that Indians are pretty much extinct, except for the Southwest, and that we all hold the same world-view and tell the same stories.

The England of the 1600s was a primitive, filthy place and must have been a terrifying sight to Pocahontas and her relatives. For she did not travel to London with just her husband and son. She took many female relatives and her uncle, who was a medicine man. I often wonder, since Pocahontas knew how to write, if she kept any kind of account of her journey. It has been recorded that while in London, Pocahontas and her Indian family swam daily in the waters. This was seen as a primitive aberration by the British, who took baths maybe once a year. But some of the Indians became ill from the polluted waters and had to stop their cleansing routine.

Pocahontas met the king and queen. It was reported that they were impressed. Was Pocahontas? We have no account that she was. Illness began making inroads on the Indian family. John Rolfe got permission to take them to the country where the air and water were cleaner. Thomas could play, and Pocahontas could relax from the stares and pointing fingers and rude comments. It has also been recorded that Pocahontas visited schools. The sight of pale little boys being disciplined by the cane and given no physical endearments of any kind, must have made her fear for her own child, and more determined that although a child of both cultures, her son would receive the proper kind of childhood—an Indian one.

Pocahontas also met up with her old friend, John Smith. Smith wrote that she seemed angered with him. He was probably quite angered himself. This grand reception that was accorded Pocahontas and Rolfe could have been his if he had been more far-thinking. It must have rankled him that the "princess" of his making was truly being treated as royalty.

Pocahontas fell ill. She had already lost some of her people to England's diseased air and had spent her time in the country in mourning. The Rolfes prepared to take their leave and go back home to Virginia. Thomas was ill also, which must have sent his mother into a frenzy of trying to get him away from a country that did nothing but kill her people. They set sail, but in Gravesend, in the county of Kent, the ship had to stop and

Pocahontas was removed to receive medical care. The consensus is that she had tuberculosis. Her uncle, Uttamatamakin, performed healing rituals over her.

This may have been enough to ease her mind and spirit, but British doctors came and purged her and applied leeches. This treatment weakened her further. Pocahontas died and her last reported words were "it is enough the child liveth." John Rolfe failed Pocahontas in death, since he had her buried christian-style. Uttamatamakin was infuriated and the anti-white feelings that had always been present, but were held at bay during Wahunsonacock's rule, began stirring and set the scene for hard times to come in Virginia.

Why did John Rolfe fail Pocahontas? It may be the fact that his son was still very sick and he wanted to leave for Virginia as soon as possible. Rolfe was not a strong personality and may have chosen the most politically expedient way to placate his English hosts, and Pocahontas was no longer there to strengthen him. This final act on Rolfe's part was that of a fool. Pocahontas' relatives were token christians as she was, and they would have gone along with the christian burial, *if* they also knew that Pocahontas would be sent on her proper way to the Spirit World through their Pamunkey ministrations. But it did not happen this way, and Pocahontas was interred at Gravesend in full English dress and tradition.

Wahunsonacock died within a short time after receiving the news of his daughter's death. He longed to stay alive to take his grandson to live with him, but that was not to be. And the precious child Thomas, so important to Pocahontas' vision of a new world? He stayed in England and was reared by his father's uncle. John Rolfe went back to Virginia and died shortly after the Indian uprising that took place. With

Pocahontas and Wahunsonacock dead, the so-called Peace of Pocahontas was at an end. As a teen, Thomas Rolfe did return to Virginia and experienced the great urge to see his mother's people and the place where he first drew breath. He journeyed to the Pamunkey, which was considered enemy territory by the British.

What happened to Thomas as he visited the land and language of his birth? For a few years later he was commissioned a lieutenant in the colonial militia and took up duty as a colonist against the Indians. Had his mother lived, would the outcome have been different? It is hard to say. La Malinche lived to see her son by Cortez take up arms against her people, and his. The Pamunkey people and those of other southeastern Nations were on the path to extinction. Some by war, but most through the greatest weapon the Europeans had—disease. It is estimated that two-thirds of Indian people in North America were wiped out because of measles, chicken pox, tuberculosis, smallpox, and the common cold. Did Pocahontas see this also in her vision? It's ironic that Pocahontas became grandmother to an estimated two million people who lay claim to being her descendants. It is ironic to me because a Virginian who would recoil in horror at having a Black ancestor, points with pride at the Indian blood in his body.

The British did their job well, annointing Pocahontas a princess while excising her Indianness. We are left with a story of a woman who was made into an "incidental" Indian. And this is the biggest and most hideous of lies surrounding Pocahontas. There was nothing incidental about her. She fought for her people and for the future of her people. She spoke in her own language even at the last. She brought her son into the world through Indian womb and hands. And even her final words, "it is enough the child liveth," speaks volumes of her plans, much more eloquently than I ever could.

Nancy Ward was also a woman committed to a vision. When she was born in 1738, she was given the name Nanye'hi, which means "Spirit People" or "Spirit Path." This name, like Pocahontas— "getting joy from spirits"—describes Nancy's communion with a dream that gave direction to her life.

Nanye'hi became the wife of Kingfisher in 1750 and the legends about her began at that time. While a mother of two young children, she went into battle with her husband to fight the Creeks, traditional enemies of the Cherokee. The Cherokee Nation was a true matriarchy, meaning that blood lines flowed through the mother. Clans of the woman became the clans of her children. Women influenced all political and family matters. Accompanying her husband into battle was not a new phenomenon to the Cherokee people.

For a reason known only to Nanye'hi and her spirits, she went to Georgia with Kingfisher and when her husband was killed, she took up his arms and continued the fight. This inspiration led her people into ultimate victory over the Creeks. Stories began to circulate among the Cherokee about Nanye'hi's heroism. She soon was chosen to become a Beloved Woman of the Cherokee. Beloved Woman means exactly what it implies. She was beloved by the people, but even more, she had a direct link with Creator who spoke through the Beloved Woman's voice.

It seems to me that only Indians could come up with this particular model of behavior. Most of us knew stories about christian saints who supposedly were in communion with god or christ, but the Indian people so cherished and personalized Creator and all the spirits that made up the mysteries of the universe, that this mystery chose to speak through women's voices. This is not unique to just the Cherokee. In many Nations across North America, you will hear Creator's voices coming from the women. In fact, Creator is usually a female/male deity or one who has no sex, who just is. Again I think of christian women saints who had to die before achieving that state of grace they so desired. How much more human, and yes Indian, to be in a state of grace constantly. And I must quote my father again when he says there are "people who live with the spirits."

This particular state of grace called being human was and is a source of amusement and wonder to Indian people. We have thousands of stories that tell the tale of being human. It is not an exalted position. In many instances, humanity is a result of Creator or our tricksters playing a joke. How's that for making us humble? And if the state of being human is a joke, how much more important it is for us to have our spirits to guide us.

I once wrote a short story about a young man who had conversations with his dog. The young man despaired about the human species, wondering if they could ever be smart. His dog told him that was an impossibility. Dogs buried bones and occasionally dug them up and chewed them, but pretty much left them alone. Humans left bones lying all around their lives and tripped over them and piled them up so high that eventually people couldn't move and had to stay in one place forever. And that is because human beings are stupid and young and don't know any better. The young man had to agree, for after all, it is the truth. And the young man came to the conclusion that if humans were as smart as dogs, the human would be the pet and get to sleep all day and eat food already prepared for him and be welcomed into bed on a cold night.

I give you this story because I want you to know what it is to grow up an Indian and know your place in the scheme of things. Women like Nanye'hi and Pocahontas knew what their places were. Perhaps we can

imagine a little of how they felt when we put it into modern terminology. Non-Indian and Indian women of today live with fear as a constant. Yet, at the same time, some of us try to set things right. So it was with Pocahontas and Nanye'hi.

When Nanye'hi became the Beloved Woman, the Cherokee were literally caught in the middle between France and England. Each European nation was panting for the Cherokee lands and it became Nanye'hi's job to placate each nation while retaining and preserving the strength and power of her own Cherokee Nation. Again, like Pocahontas, she had to be a diplomat of skillful integrity. Nanye'hi's uncle Attakullakulla worked hand-in-hand with Nanye'hi at maintaining this precarious balance of power. Imagine it, if you can. These two people, young woman/mother and aging man, holding war at bay for years, while gathering strength to withstand the onslaught they knew would eventually come. And because of maintaining this balance, Nanye'hi was seen by many of her descendants as being a traitor and lackey to the British. The same has been said of Pocahontas, La Malinche, and Molly Brant (my own ancestor—I am not going to write about her here because there simply isn't room).

These women called traitors, what was their treachery? Neither handed over their people or lands to the white man. For one thing, it would not have been in their consciousness as Indian people to do so. Land was given by Creator. They were simply human; who were they to give land to someone else? These women called traitors, did they fraternize with the enemy? What does fraternization mean? Sleeping with the enemy while giving away secrets? Neither woman did so. They married white men, but again I must remind you, these women lived with the spirits. They knew what was in their vision. Some may say things did not work out the way they were supposed to. Or did they?

Gloria Anzaldua, Chicana poet and editor of *This Bridge Called My Back,* has told me that she sees La Malinche as a hero of heroes—because of her there is a new race of people, the Chicano. There are ways and then there are ways of looking at history.

In 1757, Nanye'hi married a white trader by the name of Bryant Ward. She had a daughter, Elizabeth. The unusual thing about Bryant Ward is that he did not live with Nanye'hi and the Cherokee. Why is this? My own guess is that Nanye'hi didn't want him to. She sent him away after her child was born. The words of Pocahontas come back to me: "It is enough the child liveth." Was this Nanye'hi's thought also? To carry on the vision of a new people?

In 1775, the Watauga Purchase took place. Twenty million acres of Cherokee land was sold to the British for 2,000 pounds. There is no record of Nanye'hi's voice at this time. But a woman who always counseled "never sell the land" must have been appalled at what she saw as a break with Indian tradition and spirit. But already, whether because of her marriage to Bryant Ward or her repeated negotiations with the British, Nanye'hi, Beloved Woman, was losing her influence.

In 1776, a Cherokee faction, led by Dragging Canoe and Old Abram, set siege to the Watauga fort. They captured a white woman, Lydia Bean, and were going to burn her alive. It is reported that Nanye'hi stepped to the fire and shouted, "No woman shall be burned at the stake while I am Beloved Woman." This whole episode has a familiar ring to it. But it probably happened as it was recorded. The Cherokee, tired of years of staving off the white man, was nonetheless learning from him.

The very notion of murdering a woman, regardless of her being non-Indian, is a telling story of how the Indian system of values was deteriorating. In all the horror stories of actions between whites and Indians, I find this one the most horrific—how Indian attitudes toward women had changed. Not everywhere, and not everyone, but enough of it to freeze my blood and anger me almost beyond reason. Nancy Ward must have been feeling the same kind of rage and fear. For if attitudes against women could go against Creator's wishes, what other horrors must follow? And this is not to say that we Indian people brought destruction upon ourselves. Such a statement would even be beyond the stupidity allowed for merely being a human. We are all familiar with the "blaming the victim" syndrome. Yet at the same time, I do not see my people or myself as victims, since that word implies a giving-up, a loss of self. And certainly it's evident we are still here, as bothersome as we have always been.

After saving Lydia's life, Nanye'hi took her to live at Chote, Nanye'hi's ancestral home. History does not say how long they resided together, or what they talked about. How I wish I could hear them! Did they talk of politics and raising children? Did they learn about each other's peoples and ways? Did they become lovers? One thing is known: Nanye'hi learned to make butter and cheese from the milk of the "white man's buffalo," the cow. She later used this knowledge to introduce dairying into the Cherokee Nation. But what of Lydia Bean? Did she learn of the spirits? Did she learn of the woman's voice being the conduit of Creator? Did she learn a lesson in being a woman? Did she become assimilated into the Indian way of thinking like so many do who live with Indians?

I want to know the answers to these questions because it is essential to understanding between Indian and non-Indian women of today. But once again, the answers and questions are meant for us to decipher and translate. Are we doing it? If there truly is a new world as I believe, and as Nanye'hi and Pocahontas believed, we must get down to this basic at once.

I am reminded of a time when my non-Indian lover and I went to my reservation for a visit. We stayed with one of my many great-aunts and cousins. One night we sat at the kitchen table and shelled beans. We all sat for hours, about five of us, just doing women's work—preparing food for our family. There was a magic to that evening. Probably because it was the most simple and primal act of love—feeding those we love. And my lover, Denise, always aware of the fact that she is a white woman among the Mohawks, felt loved and filled and thankful to be a part of this act. And we Mohawk women felt the same. I have thought of that evening many times, especially when I am asked to speak or read in unfamiliar places. Nancy and Lydia made food together—of the physical and spiritual kind. It must be possible for us to do it too.

War intensified between the Cherokee and the emerging American nation. The Cherokee found themselves defeated at every turn, while Nanye'hi stood her ground and shouted for peace. In 1781, trying to negotiate a peace treaty, Nancy Ward cried, "Peace,...let it continue. This peace must last forever. Let your women's sons be ours. Our sons will be yours. Let your women hear our words." This speech is the most stirring of all speeches to me. The idea that differing races could belong to each other in love and peace was and is the most radical of ideas. Did the women hear Nancy's words? It is doubtful. How could they have heard them unless their men chose to tell them?

The year 1785 found Nanye'hi still living at Chote with her children and grandchildren. Her daughter by Bryant Ward had married an Indian agent. Her two children by Kingfisher had married and produced children. All lived with Nanye'hi. She had also opened her home to orphans, of which there were many. Things had changed. Life was changing for the Cherokee people. They were becoming farmers and, as I mentioned earlier, Indian culture was giving way to some of the values of the white man.

But in 1817 the last Cherokee Council meeting was held, and Nanye'hi was expected to speak and give counsel. Being old and ill, she sent her son Fivekiller to represent her and to read her written message. And here we have another conundrum. Nancy Ward was a literate woman. Where are her words? It frustrates me no end as an Indian woman, that history has not deemed it worthwhile to remark on the fact that Nanye'hi and Pocahontas could write and therefore must have put ideas and thoughts on paper. Nancy and Lydia Bean must have corresponded. Where are these documents I long to see? Does someone have them? Were they burned or thrown out with the trash? Were they deliberately lost? After all, it must not be known that the savage, the barbaric, the primitive could read and write. It would completely change history and the attempts by white North Americans to make us invisible—a silent genocide. (As an aside to all this, I must tell you of Sequoyah, who devised a spoken and written alphabet of the Cherokee language—and he never knew how to read or write. Imagine the genius and spirit of such a man.) Fivekiller read his mother's message to the people and I'd like to quote some of it here.

> Your mothers, your sisters, ask you not to part with any more of our lands. We say you are our descendants and must listen to our request. Keep the land for our growing children for it was the good will of our Creator to place us here. Keep your hands off of paper for it is our own country. If it was not, they (the white man) would not ask you to put your hands on paper. It would be impossible to remove us all for as soon as one child

is raised, we have others in our arms. Therefore children, don't part with any more of our land but continue on it and enlarge your farms and cultivate and raise corn so we may never go hungry. Listen to the talks of your sisters. I have a great many grandchildren and I wish them to do well on our land.

Nanye'hi's words were a prophecy, especially about the impossibility of removing all the people from the land. Even during the forced removal of southeastern Nations to Oklahoma, known popularly as the Trail of Tears, many Cherokee escaped and blended into other families and races.

Nancy Ward died in 1818. She had lived a long life compared to Pocahontas. When she died, there were no last words recorded, but her great-grandson reported that a light rose from her body and fluttered like a bird around her body and her family in attendance; then it flew in the direction of Chote, Nanye'hi's ancestral homeland. If Nanye'hi had spoken last words, I imagine they would have been words she had spoken all her life: Don't sell our land. Let the women hear my words. Our cry is for peace.

My friend Awiakta, a Cherokee writer and champion of Nancy Ward, has told me of the historic reunion of the Cherokee Eastern and Western Councils in 1984, at the Red Clay Historical Area in East Tennessee. "These are the same council grounds," Awiakta said, "where the last council met before the Removal and also where Nancy Ward came during her lifetime. (Her homesite and grave are in the vicinity.) The Cherokee had carried the Sacred Fire with them on the Trail of Tears. At the Reunion they brought brands of it back. On a hill, in a receptacle made of native stone, they relit the Sacred Fire, which will burn eternally."

Awiakta tells me that 20,000 people were there. Descendants of Nanye'hi's dream of a new world. Red and white, red and black, red, white and black. All these glorious mixtures come together as family. "Let your sons be ours; our sons be yours." How prophetic those words! If I leave you with any thoughts, let them be that Pocahontas and Nanye'hi were not what history has made them. They also were not goddesses or superhuman. They were human women who communed with the spirits.

History has given us some truths and many untruths about these women. What is women's history? Is it the history of all women, not just those who were white and privileged? Does it mean the changes that women have wrought in history, not just the history of the European nations, but of all nations? I hope it means that. As an Indian, I am forever on my guard about what I read or hear about my people. So much is distorted through ignorance or misunderstanding.

I recently became a grandmother. When I held my newborn grandson in my arms for the first time, I was so awestruck that I think I stopped breathing. For I realized that this truly is a new child of a new world, or as Linda Hogan said to me, "New atoms and their beginning in the human form." This child, Nathanael Brant, is a child of many people—Mohawk, Polish, French, Cree, Irish. And he will grow up knowing all of them.

A Pamunkey shaman and a Cherokee Beloved Woman—they did not fail their communities. Their dream should be ours, together. What we can do in their memory and honor is to continue the search for truth in all things.

WE ARE SOVEREIGN PEOPLES.

OUR FAMILIES ARE FOUNDATIONS OF OUR NATIONS.

WE MOVE FORWARD WITH OUR GRANDPARENTS AS OUR GUIDES, AND OUR CHILDREN IN OUR ARMS.

STOP THE INDIAN LAND GRAB

Book Reviews

Ashabranner, Brent

Children of the Maya: A Guatemalan Indian Odyssey

> Dodd
> *1986; grades 6-up*
> *Maya*

Morning Star, Black Sun

> Dodd
> *1982; grades 6-up*
> *Cheyenne*

To Live in Two Worlds: American Indian Youth Today

> Dodd
> *1984; grades 6-up*
> *all Nations*

These three titles prove that it is possible for a non-Native person to write about aspects of Native life, in a way that is not racist or insensitive. In *Morning Star*, Ashabranner discusses the confrontation between the Northern Cheyenne and the energy companies. He lets the people speak for themselves, too, and gives the last word to Joe Little Coyote:

> Every generation of Northern Cheyenne must have strength to fight for survival or we will disappear. Sweet Medicine told us we must not forget who we are. Well, we do not intend to forget.

Two Worlds tells, through the words of young people, what it is like to be young and Indian in America, right now. Maybe the overall picture drawn here is a little too optimistic, but it makes a nice change from the "vanishing Indian" stories.

In *Children of the Maya*, Ashabranner tells of the refugees who have found their way to Indiantown, Florida, and how the people there have welcomed them and are trying to help them make a new life. This is not an everyday story. First, the author tells about the town, then about Guatemala and the 150,000 Mayan people who have been forced to flee their villages. After that, in a method more effective than any other he could have chosen, he just lets the people talk. The only word for this book is gut-wrenching:

> One of the boys had seen soldiers decapitate a guerrilla. When he told the psychologist about it, he spoke in a whisper and his face was sweaty. "I saw it all," he said, "but they didn't see me."

Ashabranner's calm tone makes the facts all the more damning.

These are fine books. Paul Conklin's photographs give each an added dimension.

Awiakta, Marilou

Rising Fawn and the Fire Mystery

St. Luke's Press
1983; grades 4-up
Choctaw

"It was the fourth night of the Cold Moon, the winter of Rising Fawn's seventh year." She and her family were waiting for her father to come back from the Council, at which it would be decided whether the Choctaw people would stay in Mississippi, or make the journey to Indian Territory. The decision is made to go—"any of us who stay...are a marked people"—but Rising Fawn and her family never get the chance. In the middle of the night, the soldiers come. "A shout brought her awake, a white man's shout...'Burn it down. Gimme that torch. I'll throw it!'" Rising Fawn is saved by one soldier less brutal than the rest, and taken to a childless white couple. She is sustained by the last words of her Grandmother: "A voice like the embrace of wind in the pines: 'Be like the seed...live deep in your spirit.'"

Rising Fawn is cared for, physically, but she never speaks. "From then on, only the fire was real to her. She thought of the white couple as simply 'The Man' and 'The Woman.'"

Eventually, at Christmas time, Rising Fawn is won, by the kindness of James and Amanda, and the story of the Christ child.

> She felt the wisdom in the story...she thought of the Christ child...of her own wandering...of her own hearth where the fire was kindled every year from the source of all life...From the heart of the candle flame Rising Fawn saw the Grandmother's gnarled hands slowly unfold and spread like a wide cup to hold the sacred flame...She understood that her spirit was safe...Rising Fawn folded one small hand around the Man's rough knuckles, and the other she placed within the upturned palm of the Woman. With a soft voice, she said, "My name is Rising Fawn."

Because the Woman uses words like "pagan" and "heathen," because of the way the story ends, the unperceptive reader might conclude that Awiakta intends to show that Rising Fawn has gone through a perhaps painful, but necessary, transition on the way from savagery to civilization. Nothing could be farther from the truth. *Rising Fawn and the Fire Mystery* is the profoundly affecting story of a child, secure in the peace of a loving family, and lifeways of a very ancient society, whose whole world, in an instant, is destroyed by barbarians. In the light of her own Fire, Rising Fawn sees and understands a way to live in this new world. Her story—with variations—was repeated thousands of times. Awiakta has set it down with honesty and beauty.

Baker, Betty

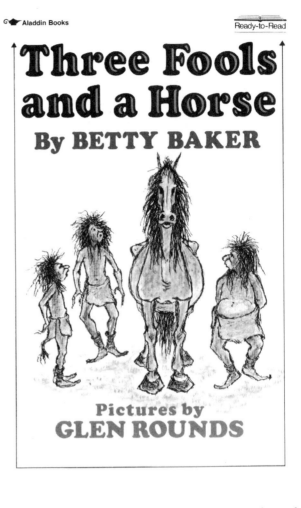

Three Fools and a Horse

Macmillan
1975; grades 1-2
Apache

"A long time back, the Foolish People lived on Two Dog Mountain. Most of the people knew nothing. Some knew a little more. But all were foolish." Their names are Little Fool, Fat Fool, and Fool About. A more spavined, knock-kneed, straggle-headed bunch would be hard to find. In the first story, Little Fool wins a horse from the flatlanders—the owner is called Big Nose—by out-running it. In the second, they try to ride it. In the third, Fool About stays on the horse by gluing himself to it with pine sap. "But he could not sit down for many days." The end.

Not funny, you say? Not so you'd notice. According to the author's notes, the Foolish People were a "tribe" invented by "the Apaches...so they could make jokes about themselves...Many stories have been printed in folklore and anthropology magazines ...Several have been combined, slightly changed and much elaborated in the writing of this book." I guess. Lord only knows what they were *really* like. They were probably learning stories and they probably were funny. In translation, however, they are a miserable production that holds Native peoples up to ridicule, and could only be painfully embarrassing for any Native child unfortunate enough to stumble across the book. The author's treatment is particularly unforgivable, because she has written for beginning readers who will have little or no frame of reference in which to place the stories. They will have no way, given the level on which history is taught, to know that these are not representative Native Americans. The illustrations, in Glen Rounds' usual scurfy style, add immeasurably to the effect.

This is a very bad book.

Baker, Olaf

Where the Buffaloes Begin

Warne
1981; grades 3-5
Siksika/Blackfeet

Around the campfires, it was said that, if you arrived at a certain strange lake in the South, at the right time, you might see the buffaloes rising from the water. You might see that, because this was the sacred place where the buffaloes begin. One early morning, Little Wolf sets out to find that place, and he does see them. "They were there, hundreds and hundreds of them, rising out of the water...a lake of swaying bodies...his nose inhaled the sharp moist smell of the great beasts." But that is not all of the story. It is the buffaloes, running with Little Wolf, who destroy the Assiniboines, "deadly enemies of the tribe," who are sneaking up to attack Little Wolf's people. And now, "they always add the name of Little Wolf to the legend, for he is the boy who led the buffaloes and saved his people."

The book is beautifully written, obviously by one familiar at first hand with Plains life. The pictures, by Stephen Gammell, have power. There is no attribution for the story. More seriously, this lovely book is marred by the many references to "his people's enemies, the Assiniboines," who, given half the chance, would kill you and scalp you, "as neatly as could be," who "could come creeping along the hollow...like wolves...on moccasins noiseless as the padded feet of the wolves, as intent, and almost as cruel."

Wolves are not "cruel"; that is a whitepeople concept. And—one more time—Indians are not animals. But given the time in which it was written—1915—it could probably have been worse. The book is authentic in so many other ways that I might use this with children, but change a few words.

Banks, Lynne Reid

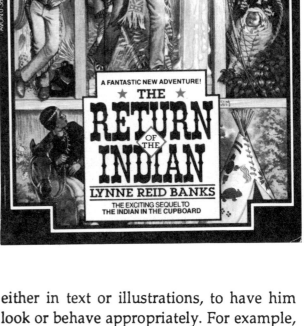

The Indian in the Cupboard

Avon
1980; grades 4- 6
Haudenosaunee/Iroquois

Return of the Indian

Doubleday
1986; grades 4-6
Haudenosaunee/Iroquois

Lynne Reid Banks has written two books which, while not intended to have a specifically Native American theme, do depend, for major plot turns, on an Indian character. Both books have won critical acclaim for fine writing, and were praised for having a "wonderful collection of characters."

The setting is England. On his birthday, Omri is given a small, white cupboard. When, for lack of a better idea, he puts a plastic "Indian" in it, the little figurine comes to life, still tiny, but very much a human being. Omri's life becomes centered around the needs and wants of "Little Bear." The object here was not to draw an authentic Native person, but to create an arresting literary device. Although the little "Indian" is called Iroquois, no attempt has been made,

either in text or illustrations, to have him look or behave appropriately. For example, he is dressed as a Plains Indian, and is given a tipi and a horse.

This is how he talks: "I help...I go...Big hole. I go through...Want fire. Want make dance. Call spirits." Et cetera. There are characteristic speech patterns for those who are also Native speakers, but nobody in the history of the world ever spoke this way.

As with *The Indian in the Cupboard*, the writing in *The Return of the Indian* is vivid, and the dangers faced by Omri and his friend Patrick are compelling and real. However, one of the talking points for those who loved the first book was that it showed clearly the boys' growing realization that the manipulation of these very real little people was wrong. Why, then, bring Little Bear back?

What one reviewer describes as "some lively battle scenes," are among the most graphic war scenes in modern children's literature. As a whole, the book is brutal, and the Indians are horrifying:

> He saw an Indian making straight for him. His face, in the torchlight, was twisted with fury. For a second, Omri saw, under the shaven scalplock, the mindless destructive face of a skinhead just before he lashed out...The Algonquin licked his lips, snarling like a dog...Their headdresses...even their movements... were alien. Their faces, too—their faces! They were wild, distorted, terrifying masks of hatred and rage.

My heart aches for the Native child unfortunate enough to stumble across, and read, these books. How could she, reading this, fail to be damaged? How could a white child fail to believe that he is far superior to the bloodthirsty, sub-human monsters portrayed here?

Not any amount of fine writing excuses such abuse of the child audience.

Baylor, Byrd

Before You Came This Way

Dutton
1969; grades 2-up
Nation unspecified

The Desert is Theirs

Scribner's
grades 2-up
Tohono O'odham/Papago

A God on Every Mountain Top

Scribner's
1981; grades 2-up
Nation unspecified

Hawk, I'm Your Brother

Macmillan
1976; grades 2-up
Nation unspecified

They Put On Masks

Scribner's
1974; grades 2-up
various Nations

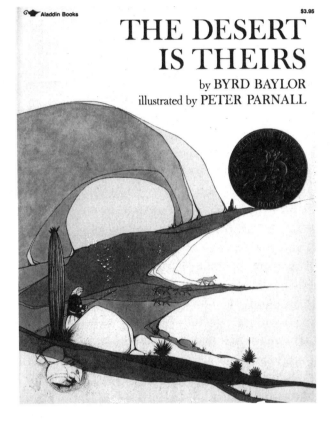

Over the years, Byrd Baylor has produced a number of visually appealing and poetic books. Most of them, in one way or another, depend on a Native frame of reference. In *Before You Came This Way*, "you" are asked to suppose that you are walking down a canyon where there are rock paintings and petroglyphs, and to speculate upon the people who came before. The illustrations are done on amatl paper, "a rough, handmade bark paper made by the Otomi Indians of Puebla, Mexico." Some of the figures look a little weird, but some give that chill up the spine produced by the originals. For the most part, Baylor eschews interpretation, being content to raise questions about what might have been the meaning of the work. Occasionally, her statements make assumptions: "Their artists drew those great fierce faces..." Whether or not the artists, or the people who looked at them, thought of them as fierce, or in an entirely different way, I don't think the author can have any way of knowing.

The drawings in *The Desert is Theirs* are spectacular. Earth, sky, and space are stretched, flattened, turned, and folded in upon themselves in ways that explode conventional notions of picture-book art and to speculate upon the people who came before. I would guess that Baylor's intent was to show the ways in which Native people live *with* the Earth, and not against Her. What comes across, unfortunately, throughout the book, is an equivalence between Indians and animals.

> This is no place for anyone who wants soft hills and meadows and everything green...This is for Hawks...and lizards that run in the hottest sand and coyotes...And it's for strong brown desert People...Papago Indians. They're Desert People...You'll see doves dipping down for the juicy red fruit that grows high on a cactus...and you'll see Indian children hold out their hands for the same summer treat. You'll see pack rats.

And further on, when talking about medicinal plants: "No one has to tell Coyote or Deer and no one has to tell the Papagos." On another page, "Hawks call across canyons. Children laugh for nothing. Coyotes dance in the moonlight."

I wish I hadn't noticed this imagery. It's like seeing a distortion in a beautiful painting, and never being able *not* to see it again. *Why did she do that?*

A God on Every Mountain Top is a little different. It is a collection of "Stories of Southwest Indian sacred mountains." They are told in Baylor's words, but the material is, for the most part, handled respectfully, and, for me, it lives. The author says: "There are dozens of versions of each story included here, and there are other stories not included because they were too private to tell outside." The illustrations are beguiling little figures, that non-Native readers are probably going to find "cute."

Rudy Soto would like to be a hawk. "There, playing alone on the mountainside, a dark skinny boy calling out to a hawk...That's Rudy Soto." "He thinks people can learn to fly (he was too young then to know he'd never get his wish.)" "And when he met new people he would look at them carefully. 'Can you fly?'" So he steals a hawk "out of its nest before it could fly," and puts it in a cage. Eventually, when the bird is grown, the boy comes to terms with what he has known all along: the hawk is miserable. So he takes it back and releases it.

It is hard to believe that a boy old enough to go get the hawk is young enough to really think that people can fly. What seems completely implausible is that he would be allowed to keep the bird. Perhaps for something he needed to learn? If so, that has not been made clear. Despite the talk about people "wise enough to understand such things," and "There is a hawk that is my brother, so I have special power," I feel that this book belittles the concept embodied in that statement. As well, *Hawk, I'm Your Brother* is not satisfactory as a piece of writing—almost as though the author was not convinced, either.

The problem with *They Put On Masks* is easily stated. Masks are a very sacred part of all Native religions. Many of them can be seen only by initiates, even within Nations. To reproduce them casually in a book would be the equivalent, to a Christian, of blasphemy. Many of these masks should never have been written about, much less illustrated. I don't even like to look at the book, or talk about the masks. The author even says that some of them "are being worn in ceremonies today." Some things are not appropriate subjects for books; some things should just be left alone. If the People have told Baylor some things, that doesn't necessarily mean they wanted her to go and tell everyone else. After discussing masks from many Nations, the author says,

> Now think what kind of mask your mask would be. And think what kind of songs that mask would bring out of you...and what strange unknown dances your bones would remember.

It makes the hair stand up on the back of my neck.

Benton-Banai, Edward

The Mishomis Book: The Voice of the Ojibway

Red School House
643 Virginia Street
St. Paul, MN 55103

1979; grades 8-up
Anishinabe/Ojibway/Chippewa

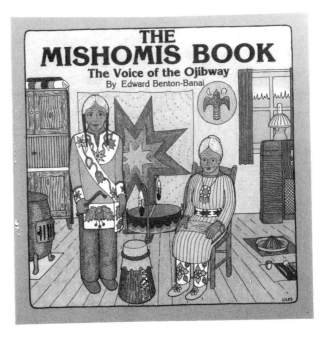

Edward Benton-Banai, Executive Director of The Red School House, and a member of the Fish Clan of the Ojibway Nation, has, out of a concern for the negative and inaccurate ways in which Native life is portrayed in this country, given us these teachings of his people. *Mishomis* is Ojibway for Grandfather, and this is truly Grandfather's book. In the first chapter Mishomis invites us to begin a journey with him, "to find what many of our people left by the trail...a journey to rediscover a way of life that is centered on the respect for all living things."

Mishomis begins with the Creation Story, and tells how Original Man came to be on the Earth, how he learned his name, how he found his Grandmother, how he searched the Earth for his Mother and Father, and how, as Waynaboozhoo, he became a hero and a teacher for the Ojibway People. As a child must be guided to grow in understanding, so does Mishomis take the reader from the simplest beginnings to the complexity of meaning of the Midewiwin and Sweat Lodge Ceremonies.

The Mishomis Book is a spiritual odyssey as well as an historical one, and as such, it is deeply moving. There is so much here that it is impossible to touch on half of it. Although the form is that of a children's book—and I have seldom seen one that I would rather give to a child—Benton-Banai's book is far from being "just" for children. People familiar only with the Judeo-Christian tradition will undoubtedly be surprised at the "sophistication" and the richness of the beliefs embodied in it, and the beauty of the language in which they are expressed.

The book so totally confounds the usual Indian stereotypes that I would recommend it highly to anyone who wishes to introduce children of the dominant culture in a more realistic and truthful manner to the lives and cultures of the tribal peoples of America. It is hard to imagine that anyone could read this and not come away from it at least a little more open to the beauty and strangeness of life.

Bierhorst, John

Doctor Coyote

Macmillan
1987; grades 2-4
Nation unspecified

According to the author, "Less than a hundred years after Columbus discovered the New World, a ship from Spain crossed the Atlantic carrying a book of Aesop's fables...Once in America, they fell into the hands of the Aztec Indians, who saw them as trickster tales and in retelling them made the Native American coyote the chief character." With regard to Columbus and the "new world," I must say that Bierhorst should have known better. As Wilma Mankiller, Chief of the Cherokee Nation, has said, "You can't discover a place where there are people living already, and you can't claim to have done so unless you don't value those people as human beings."

With regard to Aesop, well, maybe. Bierhorst cites a manuscript in the National Library of Mexico. While I have no way of knowing how closely the author has adhered to the originals, these sound neither very much like Aesop, nor particularly "Indian." The morals frequently seem to be beside the point. Here is one example:

One day a dog came into the kitchen while Coyote was busy cooking and ran off with a sheep's heart in its teeth. When Coyote saw what had happened, he said "All right, take it! That's what you were born to do. You know that when I hear your voice again, I'll take care of you and protect you. Did you steal my heart? You have given it back to me many times over." Moral: When we lose something it sometimes makes us see that we are luckier than we thought.

My quarrel, however, is not even so much with the words, as with the illustrations. All of the characters are animals dressed up like Indians; not from back then, but right now. Coyote wears blue jeans, a squash blossom necklace, and a windband; and drives a pickup. The female coyotes wear shawls and big silver-and-turquoise bracelets. Coyote lives in a stereotypical reservation shack—you know, yard full of junk, outhouse in the back.

All Native peoples have stories of the times when animals could talk, and of beings who transform themselves, now one thing, and then another, sometimes both at once. And trickster tales serve an important purpose in all Native societies. We do not, however, think of ourselves as animals. Watch them, yes—learn from them too, and see that there are more similarities between animal and *all* human behavior than you might suppose. Given the historical tendency of white people to think of the Native population as being somewhere between animals and real human beings, these pictures are, to say the very least, unfortunate. They make what might have been a passable book, completely unacceptable.

Big Crow, Moses Nelson (Eyo Hiktepi)

A Legend from Crazy Horse Clan

Tipi Press
P.O. Box 89,
Chamberlain, SD 57325
1987; grades 4-up (younger for read-aloud)
Lakota

Tashia Gnupa (Meadowlark) and Mesu (Little Brother), her baby raccoon, are inadvertently left behind when her camp is scattered by a stampeding herd of buffalo.

> She went to sleep in the middle of a noisy village with children, horses and barking dogs. Now, there was nothing at all but an awful smell in the air and a cloud of dust.

Tashia and Mesu wait many days, but no one finds them.

Comes a morning, when a buffalo calf, checking out the world, stumbles across the two, and, in the manner of young things sometimes, refuses to take no for an answer. Tashia and Mesu are scared to death of him.

> Tashia tore away and ran as fast as her feet ever moved...The baby buffalo stood there puzzled. Then, he realized he had made a friend who wanted to play. With a loud bleat he jumped up, spun around, and ran after.

And so Tashia joins the Buffalo Nation.

Many years later, Tashia is found by warriors, one of whom unknowingly kills her beloved Wechokcha. For three days, the young woman mourns him, and then the hunters return with her to their camp. Each person knows of her. She has become legend.

> In the years that passed, Tashia married an Oshkay'ki warrior...By the time they grew old one of their sons was the pride of all Lakota. He led his Oshkay'ki brothers into battle against the United States Army and was known as Tashunke Witko (Crazy Horse).

Moses Nelson Big Crow is telling a story that comes from his people, from his own family, out of a language that is his own. It makes a world of difference. He knows exactly what he is doing, what each thing means, just how to set it down. The explanatory introduction seems almost superfluous, so strongly does the story live.

It would have this life, were there not a picture in it, but the illustrations, by Daniel Long Soldier, give visual expression to the power of the words. The cover illustration is a strong and beautiful painting. This is no doe-eyed "Indian maiden"—this is indeed the mother of warriors.

A Legend from Crazy Horse Clan is a remarkable book. The events it describes seem only a breath away—as though, if you know the right way to do it, you could step sideways, and be there.

Blood, Charles, and Martin Link

The Goat in the Rug

Four Winds
1976; grades ps-up
Diné/Navajo

This is the story of how the goat, Geraldine, gets involved—literally—in the making of a rug. While her friend, Glee 'Nasbah, makes the rug, Geraldine describes each step, from the hair clipping and carding to the dyeing and weaving. This is one of the very few titles on a pre-school level that is both a good story *and* treats Native life as though it were simply a normal part of human existence. The writing has warmth and humor, and without any particular attempt to "sound" Indian, seems very real.

Brescia, Bill, editor

Our Mother Corn

United Indians of
All Tribes Foundation
Daybreak Star Press
P.O. Box 99100
Seattle, WA 98199
1981; grades 5-up
Hopi, Pawnee, Seneca

Our Mother Corn discusses the origin of corn, and its place in the lives and cultures of the Hopi, Pawnee and Seneca peoples. Companion planting and crop rotation, songs, games and stories, as well as a list of where to get corn products, are included. One good thing is that questions are sometimes raised, without the exact answers being given. If you want to know, you have to think about them. There is a lot more here than the history of corn. Any teacher who would like to instill in students some understanding of, and respect for, Native history and cultures, will find the book extremely useful. The design of the book, with illustrations by Roger Fernandes, is quite appealing. A good first purchase.

Brewer, Linda Skinner

O Wakaga: Activities for Learning About the Plains Indians

Daybreak Star Press
1984; grades 4-6
Lakota

O Wakaga (I Made It) is a serious attempt to deal with Native subjects in an entertaining yet meaningful way. This is an informative book with emphasis on the Lakota people; there is a remarkable amount of information on lifeways and language, with accurate phonetic spellings, which is unusual for a children's book.

Broker, Ignatia

Night Flying Woman

Minnesota Historical Society Press
1983; grades 7-up
Anishinabe/Ojibway/Chippewa

This is a true story. It was written because Ignatia Broker's children were

> of that generation of Ojibway who do not know what the reservation means, or the Bureau of Indian Affairs, or the tangled treaties and federal—so-called—Indian laws which have spun their webs for a full century around the Native People, the First People of this land. Now my children are urging me to recall...It is important, they say, because now their children are asking them...It is well that they are asking, for the Ojibway young must learn their cycle.

"As it is told, many of the events and circumstances pertaining to Ni-bo-wi-se-gwe were unusual, even from the time before birth." *Night Flying Woman* is her story.

Oona, as she came to be called, had a traditional and very happy childhood.

> The fire...made patterns that made Oona laugh and coo...Mother would go about her work, and often she would stop and whisper softly to Oona...Father would come in blowing cold air and smiling, his strength and presence making everyone feel that all was well.

She lived through some of the worst times in Anishinabe history, a time of harrowing changes, and great loss. Through it all, she was a source of caring and strength for her people. She helped them to adapt, she helped them to survive. "The children of Oona, E-quay, and Mary were Sa-gwa-de Anishinabe, mixed-bloods, but they were true in the spirit of the Ojibway."

And so it has been. Oona had grandchildren, great-grandchildren, and great-great-grandchildren. And when she was old, she thought about Ojibway children, and wondered if they no longer cared about the legends and stories from the "old life." She thought, "if this is so, then our history will be lost." "There was a knock, and Oona turned and saw a small girl in the doorway...'I should like,' said the child, 'to hear the stories of our people.'"

This beautiful book is a blessing, a gift, an antidote for all the poisonous lies about our past that we have had to endure. It is full of courage, and love. This is how it *really* was.

Brown, Dee

*Teepee Tales of the
American Indian: Retold for
Our Times*

Holt, Rinehart
*1979; grades 5-up
all Nations*

Because Dee Brown is the author of *Bury My Heart at Wounded Knee*, I would not have expected this book to be done with so little sensitivity. Brown has chosen 36 stories from collections made in the late 19th and early 20th centuries by such ethnologists and folklorists as Frank Cushing, Henry Schoolcraft and George Bird Grinnel. They are arranged in categories: Before the White Man Came, Allegories, Tricksters and Magicians, Heroes and Heroines, etc. In the introduction, Brown cites the "archaic" language, disconnected incidents, and obscure plots and meanings of the first English versions, as a reason for retelling them. I disagree. Many early collectors cared deeply about the people whose tales they recorded; they shared their lives, learned their languages and they were zealous about getting it down and getting it down straight. George Grinnel, for instance, spent some 40 years visiting the Cheyenne people every summer, and his material is about as authentic as a person from another culture can get.

I am disturbed that in the introduction and the brief lead-ins for each category, Brown refers to the People primarily in the past tense, and that he finds it necessary to say things like, "Had it not been for a few far-sighted anthropologists, ethnologists, folklorists...we would now have almost no legends of these people," and "Many of the stories were chosen because they are sprinkled with the delightful touches of fun and humor that are characteristic of American Indians." Thanks a lot.

There is no evidence that Brown spoke with the People about these tales. He seems to have gone through the literature, lifted out whatever appealed to him, and set it down in a fashion that seemed to him to be OK. (If some old Indian on a reservation can tell a good story, surely a person of Dee Brown's background and intellectual attainments shouldn't have any trouble with it.)

Bruchac, Joseph

Iroquois Stories

Tape.
Good Mind Records
2 Middle Grove Road
Greenfield Center, NY 12883
1988; all grades
Haudenosaunee/Iroquois

It's the time of deep snow...people of all ages gather now, around the old man or woman who knows how things came to be, why things are the way they are...and now that old person raises a hand...'I will now tell a story.'

So begins Joseph Bruchac's tape of stories from the Haudenosaunee, the People of the Longhouse. They are from *Iroquois Stories: Heroes and Heroines, Monsters and Magic,* and include: "The Creation," "How Buzzard Got His Feathers," "Turtle's Race with Bear," and "The Crayfish," on side one. Side two has women's stories: "The Wife of the Thunderer," and "The Brave Woman and the Flying Head."

Reading a story, no matter how beautifully set down, is nothing like hearing it told. It also helps if the teller is good, and Joseph Bruchac is—very. He has a wonderful voice for stories, and knows exactly how to use it—just the right pacing, this perfectly timed pause, that lowering of pitch. And incidentally, he makes a great bear...

A word of caution: If you do not believe in the value of being frightened in a safe place, then "The Brave Woman and the Flying Head" is not a story for very young children.

This is an excellent recording, and I recommend it highly.

Bruchac, Joseph

Iroquois Stories: Heroes and Heroines, Monsters and Magic

Crossing Press
Trumansburg, New York 14886
1985; grades 5-up
Haudenosaunee/Iroquois

Iroquois Stories is among the best of the collections. It has a deliberate structure and background, beginning with the introductory material. "Telling the Stories" gives background, both about the ways in which Native American stories have been set down, and how the author himself came to tell them. "The People of the Longhouse" gives history. "The Storytellers" discusses the place of stories among Native Peoples, and how the stories still live.

The first story is called "The Coming of Legends." Then comes "The Creation," which tells how Sky-Woman came to earth. "The Two Brothers" tells how her grandsons became the Good Mind and the Bad Mind; and how corn, beans, potatoes, tobacco and squash grew from the body of their mother, who died giving them birth. And so on, through "how"

stories—which tell how things came to be—stories of heroes, stories that teach us how to be in right relation to all that is around us.

There may be other collections that have such wholeness; if so, I do not know of them. A People's stories say who they are. So it is with *Iroquois Stories*. Joseph Bruchac has shared the spirit and the heart of the People with us. Because this is so much a part of him, he has also given us something of himself. For this gift, we should be grateful.

A wise leader of the Seneca said, "Our religion is not a thing of paint and feathers, but of the heart." So it is true of the stories of the Hotinosonni, the longhouse people. The stories do not need longhouses, or central fires, or fur robes or ceremonial garments to come alive.

Bruchac, Joseph, editor

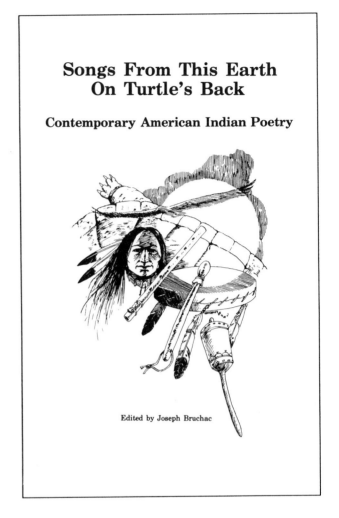

Songs From This Earth On Turtle's Back

Contemporary American Indian Poetry

Edited by Joseph Bruchac

Songs From This Earth on Turtle's Back: Contemporary American Indian Poetry

Greenfield Review Press
1983; grades 6-up
various Nations

Among the best of the anthologies, *Songs From This Earth on Turtle's Back* contains selections from the work of 52 Native American poets. Although definitely intended for an adult audience, this collection could easily be used with students of high school age, and some of it, even with older children. The quality of the writing—all of it—is outstanding. From N. Scott Momaday, who, perhaps more than anyone else, has mastered the forms of English literature and made them speak with a purely Indian voice; to the scathing fire of Diane Burns or Janet Campbell Hale; from Paula Gunn Allen to Ray Young Bear, this is real poetry.

Deprived of their languages, many of them, these poets have taken the one forced on them and made it sing for them in ways never thought of. They also show that real poetry is about real things, no matter where they may exist on the continuum from physical to spiritual.

There is a brief autobiographical introduction by each of the contributors to her or his work, and generally a photograph. As Joseph Bruchac says in his introduction,

> It is a collection of contemporary writers, not a compilation of chants or songs put together in the 19th century by a non-Indian ethnologist...the heritage of American Indian oral literature...is still very much alive today...if anything, its real range, meaning and contemporary relevance have yet to be explored.

Do not be put off by the small print. You don't just sit the kids down and make them read it; you read these poems to them.

Bruchac, Joseph

The Wind Eagle and Other Abenaki Stories

Bowman Books
1985; grades 4-6
Abenaki

Joseph Bruchac is a writer and storyteller, who has retold a number of Iroquois and Abenaki stories. His preface gives a short history of the Abenaki People, and says what we always have to keep saying: "Listen well, an ancient voice is speaking. The People have not disappeared, it is only that other eyes and ears are just beginning to open!" This collection will help them to see and hear. They are all Gluskabi stories, and it is easy to tell that the author is a true storyteller, because the words go easily from the page to being said. This is one you need.

Cameron, Anne

Raven Returns the Water

Harbour Publishing Co., Ltd.
Box 219, Madeira Park,
British Columbia V0N 2H0
grades ps-up
Northwest Coast Nations

"There came a time when the water began to disappear," and the people, the animals, the huge trees, all suffered greatly. "Raven was so thirsty she thought she would die...She knew she had to do something." In "the last green valley on earth," Raven finds a frog, gigantic with all the water of the world. Raven tricks frog into giving up what she has swallowed—although it is a very gentle trick.

> Raven knew force was not the answer. Raven knew fighting would not solve the problem. Even if Raven managed to best Frog...there would come another day and Frog would again steal the water...unless Frog learned to respect the water, and share it, and live in harmony again, there would be no peace...or safety.

So Frog is taught a lesson, and is forgiven.

It is hard to say how much this story may have been changed. The "moral" is drawn a little more obviously than is usual for Native tales. One odd thing is that Raven is referred to as "she." In traditional telling, trickster figures—Coyote, Iktomi, Raven—are male. Speculation as to whether they might ever have been—or could *sometimes* be—female, is beyond the scope of this review. Stories may be changed, for a purpose, but you have to know what you're doing. "Adapting" them, in order to make them more accessible—or acceptable—to a non-Native audience, is almost always a disaster. This does not appear to have been Cameron's intent. She tells us: "When I was growing up on Vancouver Island, I met a woman who was a storyteller. She shared many stories with me, and later, gave me permission to share them with others."

As it stands, *Raven Returns the Water* seems to work, particularly as an introduction to Indian storytelling for non-Native children. Anne Cameron is a wonderful writer, and there is nothing here that offends me. Whether or not there would be, if I came from the Northwest Coast, might be another story.

Charging Eagle, Tom, and Ron Zeilinger

Black Hills: Sacred Hills

Tipi Press
Box 89
Chamberlain, SD 57325
1987; grades 4-up
Dakota

The Black Hills of South Dakota is one of the most sacred places on earth. They remain so, despite the abomination of Mount Rushmore and the tourist traps, despite the gold mines. The Black Hills are holy.

> They are...called 'O'onakezin' which means they are a place of shelter...They are sometimes called 'Wamakaognaka E'cante' which means that they are 'the heart of everything that is.'

They have also been the source of controversy for more than 100 years. This situation has been referred to as "complicated." It isn't. The appropriation of the Black Hills by the United States government was one of the clearest and most flagrant examples of out-and-out theft and treaty violation in the annals of Native-white relations. The introduction, by Frank Fools Crow, gives a brief summary of that event.

The book itself tells clearly, and in terms easily understood, what the Black Hills mean to the Dakota Peoples. The authors have chosen to explain this in terms of Christian symbolism, which, of course, has nothing to do with it. Nevertheless, it probably helps the non-Native reader to understand, when comparison is made to Mt. Sinai: "It reminds us of the times that Jesus and Moses went to the mountain top to be alone and pray to God."

> Today the largest gold mine in this part of the world, making 85% of all the gold in the United States, is located in the Black Hills. The 'heart of everything that is' lies open and bleeding, scarred by men and their machines, seeking profits for their own generation while forgetting the generations to come.

Black Hills: Sacred Hills is a good introduction to a matter that, for Native people, is as vital as anything that confronts us. There is not anything else at all on the subject for children.

Collura, Mary-Ellen Lang

Winners

Dial
1984, grades 6-10
Siksika/Blackfeet

At 15, Jordy Three Bears is a veteran of foster homes—11 in eight years. Now, he is on his way back to the Ash Creek Reserve and the Grandfather he hardly remembers. It's an uneasy arrangement. Joe is no all-wise, all-seeing, all-forgiving, super-Indian Grandfather. He doesn't know what to do with this kid, either. So he does the best possible thing: leaves him alone.

Joe's gift of a horse, and a new friendship, begin to make Jordy's life seem "agreeably simple," and he nearly loses it all, because of the inexplicable, but implacable, hatred of one whiteman.

Parts of *Winners* seem contrived; not that the events described could not have happened, but that they would not have happened in just this way. Then, too, it is not hard to tell that Collura is not a Native writer, when she refers to Jordy's "swift, bronze ancestors," and Joe's long hair as "the one mark of Indianness available to

him." Even so, Mary-Ellen Collura is so interested in her characters, as people, that her story transcends its flaws. I would guess that she has known, and liked, some Indians, maybe even called them friends. She pays Native people the compliment of allowing them to be human beings, full of complexities and surprises. She is a writer with the gift to make you see what she is describing:

The stallion had been trying to get up but he lay still now, his head raised and turned toward Jordy, a desperate plea in his eyes. Jordy...could see the broken skin on the knees and the thick blood...he knew the horse was finished and he couldn't do a thing for him—not make it easier for him, not even put him out of his misery. He sat down and cradled the horse's head and cried.

Presently he became aware of another sound...He supposed it must be Brady. At that moment Jordy hated Brady with a pure and terrible hatred. The fate of his mother and the fate of the stallion came together...both helpless victims of the same viciousness. He wanted to kill the man.

When Jordy wins, both the race and a matter of far greater endurance, it seems both believable and right.

I like this book, a whole lot.

Cooper, Amy Jo

Dreamquest

Kleitsch, Christel and Paul Stephens

Dancing Feathers

A Time to Be Brave

Annick Press, Ltd.
Distributed by Firefly Books
3520 Pharmacy Ave., Unit 1-C,
Scarborough, Ontario M1W 2T8
1987; grades 5-up
Anishinabe/Ojibway/Chippewa

These three books come from the Spirit Bay series, and are based on films of the same titles. *Dreamquest* contains two stories. The first, "The Big Save," is told twice.

Rabbit is a macho little dude, fresh from Thunder Bay, and he cannot stand the idea of having a girl on his hockey team. He makes her life a living hell. But when the school bus is caught by a blizzard on the way home from a game, it is the timid Rose, and not Rabbit, who knows what to do until help comes. Rabbit and Rose take turns telling the story. "So you listen to both stories, listen carefully. Then maybe you can figure out what the real story is."

"Hack's Choice" tells what happens when Hack's uncle, Coleman Blackbird, comes back to Spirit Bay. Hack idolizes Coleman, once a professional hockey player.

Only gradually, does Hack realize that his mother's distrust of her brother is justified. Uncle Cole's reason for returning to Spirit Bay forces Hack to make some decisions about what is worth keeping and what, no matter how much you may want it, is better to give up. The story is complex in the way that Native stories frequently are, with layers of meaning that we think about long after the telling is done. Bernard Mide, an Elder, tells Hack about the crow: "In all our legends we are taught to be aware of him. His coat is shiny, and attracts our eye, but he is a trickster and a thief." But he also says, "I knew Coleman Blackbird when he was little. He was a good boy." What does it mean? "Be careful. Every storyteller has his tricks."

A Time to Be Brave tells how Tafia Shebagabow goes for help, even though she is terribly afraid, when her father is injured at their winter camp. In *Dancing Feathers*, Tafia tells about "one time last summer," when "I sure got myself in a lot of trouble..." The "trouble" concerns a pow-wow in Toronto; a jingle dress, left behind accidentally-on-purpose; a stolen painting; and two kids, lost in the big city.

These are very good books. First of all, they are just plain good stories that would hold the interest of a young reader. Then, they deal with people who are real—not just somebody's idea of "Indians"—living meaningful lives, rooted in place. Relationships are warm and caring. Elders are not just treated with respect, but valued.

There is humor. The white man who comes to see Tafia's father talks non-stop and can't get "Shebagabow" right on a bet. His best shot: "Sherhoogahooboos."

This is not to say that there are no false notes. At one point in *Dancing Feathers*, a white friend says, "You know, Frank, I never think of you as being Indian." Did the authors but know it, this is a "compliment" we get a lot from white acquaintances. Frank's response? "Yeah, I know...I forget it myself sometimes." Being Indian isn't something you forget—ever. And please. When we dance, we do *not* "hop, hop, hop." In view of the overall excellence of the series, however, these are pretty small flaws.

D'Aulaire, Ingri and Edgar Parin

George Washington

Doubleday
1936; grades 3-5
Nation unspecified

Pocahontas

Doubleday
1949; grades 3-5
Pamunkey

Ingri and Edgar D'Aulaire have produced a number of books that are part of the canon of beautifully illustrated and classic writing for children. Although quite old, most of them are still in print, and show up regularly on recommended lists. And they contain some of the most blatantly racist writing to be found in modern children's literature.

In *George Washington*:

Virginia was once a wilderness. Wild beasts lived there, and swift Indians ran through grass and swamps...Then across the sea came the men from England and chased the Indians away.

Along with all the other wild animals, presumably. As a young man, on a surveying trip, George

met a tribe [really? A whole tribe?] coming from war with scalps at their belts. George Washington and his friends gave them presents, and the Indians danced their war dance for them...he

[George] thought their war dance was very funny.

Back at the plantation, the "slaves and servants" welcomed their master home "with beaming faces." "Now Washington was happy. He walked peacefully over his fields, where the slaves were singing and working."

The illustrations suit the text. The Indians leap around on one foot, waving their arms in the air. This, I guess, is their "war dance." The Black people are lined up by the front steps to greet the Great General. They are beautifully dressed, plump and immaculate, fuzzy-headed, smiling, "darkies." I always like a book that has something to offend nearly everyone.

Then, there is *Pocahontas*:

In the dark woods of Virginia, where dusky owls hooted over the treetops and prowling beasts howled at the moon, there lived a stern old Indian chief...He had a little daughter who was the very apple of his eye. She was as sweet and pretty as he was ugly and cruel.

In this version of the story, Pocahontas is an "Indian princess." Thoroughly spoiled by her father, she gets to run and play with the boys, while the "squaws and their girls" must work "from morning till night." When the white men come, the people react with childlike awe and fear, immediately recognizing the superiority of the newcomers, who "were not afraid of offending Powhatan even though he was so mighty that everyone trembled when he frowned. They must be dangerous sorcerers, Powhatan's people thought." But Pocahontas is fascinated. "She was certain their magic could not be evil." So she saves John Smith.

Later, while the guest of a "village chief and his wife," who are "ugly and cruel people," she is sold by them to an English sea captain. "Thus was the Princess Pocahontas sold for a copper kettle." While in Jamestown, she meets John Rolfe, and the rest, as they say, is history.

This book must surely contain every verbal and visual Indian stereotype known to humankind. The Native people are both naive and cruel, the women are squaws, the men are braves. The women do all the work, while the men and boys get to hunt, fool around, and capture white colonists. All the Indians are fascinated by white culture, which is clearly of a much higher order than their own. Of a compass: "There was a little spirit that lived in the box. The spirit always pointed straight to the North." The King of England's house was "of snow-white stone," and "as large as a whole Indian village. There, little princesses ran about clad in silk and silver and gold and played with pearls and diamonds."

The Indians behave in the fashion one would usually expect from savages: "The medicine men were scowling as they danced and shouted and worked their magic."

Out from the trees whirled Pocahontas, leading a band of young girls. The girls were painted in gleaming colors and each had a pair of antlers tied to her head. Leaping and yelling, they stormed up to the fire, and danced an Indian dance around it.

The illustrations are, well, astonishing. "Powhatan" wears a robe composed entirely of what appear to be raccoon tails, everybody wears feathers sticking straight up, and most of the time, Pocahontas wears something that looks as though it was left over from "Sheena, Queen of the Jungle." The people (mostly men) look just alike. They sit just alike—arms folded across chests, and they stand just alike—arms folded across chests. The boys all wear whole raccoon hides—heads, tails, paws and all—folded over the backs of their belts.

The facts of the matter are these: Powhatan was the name of a town on the "James" river. "Powhatan's" name was Wahunsonacock, and he did not "rule over 30 tribes." He was the founder of the Algonquian Confederacy of Nations that the invaders, not knowing any better, also called Powhatan, after what they thought was the name of its "chief."

The story about John Smith is not true. Historians believe Smith was the one who made it up; he was known to be a great liar. The book does not say that Pocahontas "never returned to her home across the great water" because she contracted what was probably smallpox—one of the great blessings bestowed on us by the whiteman—and died.

One. More. Time. Native women were not drudges and beasts of burden. Medicine men were not evil sorcerers. The colonists did not buy corn from the People—they stole it. Native people were neither more naive nor more cruel than the white invaders. John

Smith was no man of honor, and the bunch he brought with him were adventurers, criminals, and the sweepings of the English gutters. Et cetera, et cetera, et cetera. And this is the book, whose jacket gushes unashamedly,

> With real humor and many wonderful details the characters come alive...In the story of Pocahontas [the D'Aulaire's] have recreated another important historical period...in lovely color lithographs and storytelling that combine[s] charm and authenticity.

DePaola, Tomie

The Legend of the Bluebonnet

Putnam
1983; grades ps-3
Commanche

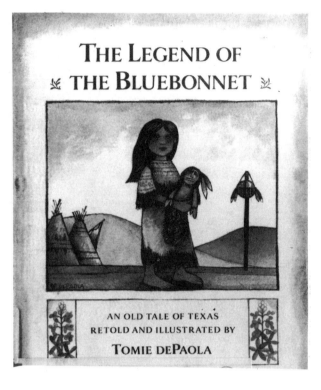

There is a great drought, and "The People called Commanche" are seeking to discover how they have offended their "Great Spirits." The shaman tells them that "The People have become selfish...the People must sacrifice. We must make a burnt offering of the most valued possession among us." Of course, nobody believes that it is his/her dearest treasure that will be required, with the exception of one little girl, called She-Who-Is-Alone because her whole family was lost to the famine. What she has left is a doll dressed like a warrior. She-Who-Is-Alone dearly loves her doll, and she knows what she has to do. That night, she takes the doll and one firestick and goes to the hill to do what is necessary. In the morning, the hills and fields are covered with flowers, "beautiful flowers, as blue as the feathers in the hair of the doll"; the rain comes, and She-Who-Is-Alone is given a new name: One-Who-Dearly-Loved-Her-People.

And every spring, the Great Spirits remember the sacrifice of a little girl and fill the hills and valleys of the land, now called Texas, with the beautiful blue flowers. Even to this day.

The courage of children is always very moving, and the emotional impact of the book is strong. The illustrations are among the loveliest DePaola has ever done. The sequence of evening sky, shading from lavender to blue to star-flecked night, has a luminosity rarely seen.

Some of the book's flaws are trivial; others, more serious. For one thing, the Christian sweetness of this story seems far enough from the spirit of the people from whom it supposedly came to cause one to speculate upon its original form. Secondly, in the context of tribal life, the little girl's complete isolation seems a bit unconvincing. Clearly, someone takes care of her. When night came, she "returned to the tipi, where she slept, to wait...Soon everyone in the tipi was asleep." Who are they?

A further word about the illustrations. DePaola's people are not, with the exception of She-Who-Is-Alone, drawn as individuals.

They have a homogeneous set of features; they are "Indians."

While it is disappointing that DePaola did not manage to avoid some of the more common pitfalls, I would not hesitate to use this book with small children. I do not think that white children can pick up any unfortunate attitudes from it; there is nothing here to shame or hurt an Indian child. Whatever else, the author does not condescend to his material, and his portrayal of She-Who-Is-Alone is not demeaning.

The story is animated by the same love and respect for children that lie behind all his other work.

Durham, Jimmie

Columbus Day

> West End Press
> P.O. Box 27334
> Albuquerque, NM 87125
> *1983; grades 7-up*
> *all Nations*

Anger is counter-productive, they say, and "provocative." They talk about "building bridges to understanding." I can think of no better bridge to understanding than *Columbus Day*. Of course, it isn't the kind of understanding *they* mean. They mean that we should be patient for another 500 years. They mean we should gladly share our cultures, now that they are interested. They mean that we should stop being "exclusionist" about "Native spirituality."

Well, Jimmie Durham isn't having any of that. The subtitle of his book is "Poems, Drawings and Stories About American Indian Life and Death in the Nineteen-Seventies." He says,

> The decade from 1970 to 1980 was a very important time for American Indians. It

sounds silly...since the 1490s the decades have all been extremely difficult.

In those years, the People have died—sometimes quietly, often brutally and horribly. The Death in that subtitle is not a "metaphor." It stands for the names of people we all know: Pedro Bissonette, Buddy Lamont, Wesley Bad Heart Bull, Anna Mae Aquash, Jimmy Little, Frank Clearwater, Raymond Yellow Thunder, Byron deSersa, Hobart Horse, Jo Ann Yellow Bird. And others. Not to mention the maimed and the disappeared. These names remind us that the possibility of violent death is a constant for Native people in 20th century America, in "heroic times, for people who of course feel unequal to that for which their ancestors and children call them."

Columbus Day is almost a mini-history of Indian America, and there is not a word of it that is not true. Do not, therefore, assume that it is also polemic. Jimmie Durham is a very accomplished writer:

> I want my words to be as eloquent
> As the sound of a rattlesnake
>
> I want my actions to be as direct
> As the strike of a rattlesnake
>
> I want results as conclusive
> As the bite of a beautiful red and black
> coral snake.

White society has great investment in the idea that to show feeling is to "lose it"—"it" being cool, control, dominance. That rigorous and disciplined poetry can also be written with passion, about real things, will, no doubt, be surprising to some readers. As well, the truths in this book may be hard ones to accept. Nevertheless, if you can read it with an open heart, you may truly begin to understand the reality of our lives. There is humor in the writing, and great beauty, as well as a clarity that makes the use of *Columbus Day* with older children perfectly possible. The drawings extend and embellish the text, occasionally telling a story of their own—although it is all one story, really...

Before you teach "Indians" again, next year, think about this book. Think about it a lot. Then see if you can still have your class make paper-plate Indian faces, with yarn braids, and take "Indian" names for the day. See if you can tell those children, with the same nonchalance, about "contributions" the Indians have made for the well-being of white society. See if you have the heart to ask the one Native child in your class to bring some rugs or pots, or tell an "Indian" story, for the Thanksgiving assembly.

"What last words can I give us?" asks Durham.

> We will not vanish; we will stand in some manner...The world and its own history is catching up with the U.S. At some point the people of the U.S. will be forced to face themselves and their inane reality. They will someday be forced to admit that they are neither the center nor the answer but only some people among other peoples, but living an inch above the earth in some strange fantasy land. Someday they must turn and face their terrible history, and ask the world if they can make a deal. Then we will have our chance, that so many Indians have sacrificed so much to insure.

**Franklin Northwest
    Supervisory Union Title IV
    Indian Education Program**

*Finding One's Way: The
Story of an Abenaki Child*

Abenaki Self-Help Association, Inc.
P.O. Box 276
Swanton, VT 05488
1987; grades 4-6
Abenaki

Growing up in that state, I often heard from white people that there had never been any Indians in Vermont. Oh, the Mohawks used to come over on a "raiding party" now and then, but none of them *lived* here...

The Abenaki People of Vermont, the "Saint Francis Indians," are not alone in being presumed not to exist. They share that with the Wampanoags of Massachusetts, and many another Nation. *Finding One's Way* deals with that state of non-being, in a way that may be used to good advantage with either Native or non-Native children. It has a teacher's guide with which to "help all children increase their awareness of Vermont Native Americans."

It's the day before Thanksgiving. Louis's teacher is talking about Indians. A child asks whether there were Indians in Vermont, too. The teacher says that there were Abenaki Indians, but that they had not been "friendly." Louis, with more courage

than discretion, perhaps, says, "I'm an Abenaki Indian." "Really, Louis," says the teacher, "whatever makes you say that?" After class, the children taunt him:

"You're not a real Indian...you don't even look like one."

"Where's your wigwam, Louis?"

"If you're an Indian, why don't you wear feathers and walk around naked?"

"How come you and Mom and Granpa all tell me I'm Indian?" he asks his father. The rest of the book tells how Louis's family introduces him to his heritage. "Why (his father) wondered, had he not said anything about this to Louis before?"

Although written for instructional purposes, the story is neither didactic nor textbookish; the people seem very real. The places described are there; some are illustrated with photographs. The events described are true to the lifeways of the Abenaki People. Some of the topics covered in the teacher's manual are: Stereotypes and Prejudices, Discovering Your Heritage, Cooking With Native American Foodstuffs/ Recipes, Life Cycles, Dance and Music, and Study of Vermont Pre-History. Activities are, for the most part, excellent; very little of it involves encouraging non-Native children to "act like Indians."

A few caveats: "Squaw" is not a good word to use. And I would be happier if the children were encouraged to write their own legends, out of their own lives, rather than to write "their own Indian myth or folktale."

One activity I reproduce practically in full, because I think it is so good:

> When Louis wanted to discover more about his background, he went to a primary source—his grandparents. Primary sources are those which are first-hand knowledge, i.e., someone who was actually there or can tell you what they experienced...If you are fortunate enough to have grandparents who are alive, they could be the beginning of a whole new discovery for you; a journey into the past...An excellent way to begin is just by talking with your parents or grandparents. Ask them questions about what life was like when they were little, favorite memories they have, and changes they have seen over the years. If they feel comfortable, you may wish to bring a tape recorder. In this way you can actually preserve a part of your heritage for years to come.

In the introduction, the writers say, "It is hoped that the sensitivity of the subject will allow room for individual growth and self-acceptance, as well as an appreciation and better understanding of others." *Finding One's Way* will do those things, yes, and perhaps help teachers find the gentleness to value all their children, and an interest in teaching this material, not just as a lesson plan they have to do for Thanksgiving, but as an important reality.

Friskey, Margaret

Indian Two Feet and His Horse

*Children's Press
1959; grades 1-3
Nation unspecified*

There's this little Indian, see—no Nation, just Indian. His name is Little Two Feet (as opposed to the rest of the Indians, who have only one foot?) And, he doesn't have a horse. "He had to walk, walk, walk. He could sing. He could dance. He could skin a deer for hide. But he could not ride a horse. He had to walk."

"'Little Two Feet,' said his father, 'you must think like a horse to find one [old Indian lore, right?]. Go find one.'" After running into a buffalo in a clump of grass ("If I were a horse, I would put my nose into this grass"), and a moose in the river (now *there's* an interesting denizen of the High Plains), Two Feet takes a nap. And a horse finds him. Turns out to have a sore foot. Horse and boy walk home together. "Little Two Feet has a horse!" said his father. "And they all danced and sang." The boy "worked with that horse's foot until the foot was well. And then he rode to the woods. He rode to the river...he had a horse!"

The illustrations show High Plains grass, mountains, mesas, and cactus. All the tipis have three poles (wish *we'd* thought of that—would have made the load a lot lighter). Two Feet wears an eagle feather (an honor, to be earned). His father wears ceremonial headdress, and holds a pipe shaped like a tomahawk. The "dance" consists of four men hunched over, patting their mouths with their hands—you know, *woo woo woo?* There are four women in the book: three "maidens" who sit in doe-eyed admiration of the dancers, "Indian style" (and, by the way, Indian women did not sit cross-legged—it was considered extremely immodest); an old woman with a load of wood on her back, and a mother with a baby on her back, and a pueblo-style pot on her head. There's a lot of tearing around on horseback, to no discernible purpose, by the warriors.

There are several more of these "Indian Two Feet" books, which, unbelievably, are still in print. Don't buy them.

Fritz, Jean

The Double Life of Pocahontas

Putnam
1983; grades 4-7
Pamunkey

Pocahontas is one of the handful of Indian names immediately recognizable to most white Americans. The little that is actually known about this young woman can be covered in a few short paragraphs, yet she has been the subject of countless articles, stories and works of non-fiction. (At least a half-dozen children's titles based, in one way or another, on her life, are currently available.) More than any other individual, with the possible exception of Sacagawea, Pocahontas is the embodiment of whites' romantic mythology of the American Indian.

Although most historians now acknowledge that John Smith lied when he told of having been saved by Pocahontas, the popular conception remains unaffected. Jean Fritz's "biography" will do nothing to change this. She reproduces the standard version, intact, with enough chunks of history of the Jamestown colony thrown in to make it book-length. There is plenty of speculative padding: "she would have" and "she must have" are common phrases. John Smith is portrayed as a hero, and there is more about him in this book than there is about Pocahontas. The Library of Congress CIP data notes: "A biography of the famous American Indian princess, emphasizing her life-long adulation of John Smith and the roles she played in two very different cultures," and that about says it.

There is considerable emphasis on the trickery, savagery and childish naiveté of the Native people:

> Yet other Indians were not one bit friendly. Once they killed an English boy and shot an arrow right through President Wingfield's beard. Often they

lay in the tall grass...waiting for someone to come through the gate...Not even a dog could run out safely. Once one did and had forty arrows shot into his body.

And here's another quote: "Perhaps the strangers would leave soon, Powhatan thought...In the meantime, he might get guns from the strangers. How he marveled at the power of guns!" The suggestion here is of a simple-minded person naively awed by the "power of guns" rather than of someone encountering a new technological achievement. And this is the same man who led a confederacy of 30 Nations, comprised of more than 9,000 people, in 200 villages. And it must be noted that the man referred to as "Powhatan" by the English

colonists—and everybody else since—was actually named Wahunsonacock. He was the founder of an Algonquian Confederacy that also came to be called Powhatan by whites. Powhatan was the name of the town where Wahunsonacock lived.

And surely it should not *still* be necessary to point out that there has never been such a thing as an Indian king, queen or princess?

It would serve no useful purpose to go through this book page by page, separating fact from fantasy. Suffice it to say that Fritz has added nothing to the little already "known" about Pocahontas, and that this little is treated with neither sensitivity nor insight.

Fritz, Jean

The Good Giants and the Bad Puckwudgies

Putnam
1982; grades ps-3
Wampanoag

Fritz has combined "fragments of old legends collected by Elizabeth Reynard in a fine book called *The Narrow Land*," to tell how Cape Cod and the Islands came to be. The story is that the good giants, Maushop, Quant, his wife, and their five sons are in conflict with some nasty little guys called puckwudgies. Maushop becomes enamored with the sea woman, Squant, and the five sons are killed by the puckwudgies' poisoned arrows. Their parents bury them at sea: "Laid out in the water, the five sons became five islands, long whalelike islands, their backs humped."

There are a few other complications, but they don't matter a lot. Wampanoag friends to whom I showed the book were deeply offended by this distortion of their stories.

Fritz has felt no more need for authenticity with Maushop than she did with the more recent *Double Life of Pocahontas*. In a note at the end she says,

> I have adapted and added dialogue and scenes, telling the story as Maushop might tell it today. And if he's picked up some yankee speech in all these years, what else would you expect?

Now, "new people" are in the land, ones who don't "understand magic." In fact, Native peoples live there still, and they do not talk a sort of fake "New England hillbilly." They live their lives in as traditional a manner as possible, and do what they can to protect their heritage.

This book is an insult to them.

García, Maria

The Adventures of Connie and Diego/Las Aventuras de Connie y Diego

Children's Book Press
1339 61st Street
Emeryville, CA 94608
1986; all grades
Chicano

Connie and Diego are twins, born "with many colors all over their little bodies. They looked so funny that their sisters and brothers started to laugh." And that's the way it is until the twins are old enough to run away, in search of a place where "no one will make fun of us." However, the animals they meet make them realize that they are human, and cannot live in the forest. Connie and Diego decide to go home, "where nothing had changed. But *they* had..."

Some may be disappointed that the story does not have a more fairy-tale ending. But for those of us born "different" in the "melting pot" of America, there seldom is a fairy-tale ending. The best we can hope for is to be allowed to grow in ways that will enable us to do the best we can with what we have been given. Sometimes, of course, that best is quite a lot. This book is for us.

Goble, Paul

Buffalo Woman

Bradbury
1984; grades 3-4
Plains Nations

The story is of a kind common to many cultures: The hero is given a supernatural wife but loses her through some fault of his own or through the maliciousness of others. Sometimes he gets a second chance, sometimes he doesn't. In this case, a "great hunter" who has always been respectful of the buffalo is rewarded by the Buffalo Nation with a beautiful wife. They have a son, Buffalo Calf, but the hunter's relatives are unkind, and on a day when the hunter is away, the Buffalo Woman takes the boy and leaves the camp. The hunter follows, but he must face danger and pick his wife and son out from the herd. This he does, with the help of his supernatural son, and he is then transformed by the Buffalo Nation into "a young buffalo bull."

As usual, Goble treats the material with great respect, and, as usual, his illustrations are lovely.

Goble, Paul

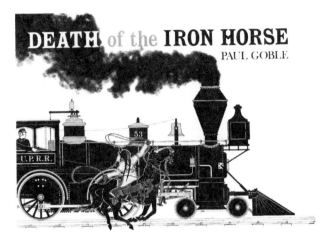

Death of the Iron Horse

Bradbury
1987; all grades
Cheyenne

"There have been many trains wrecked by Indian people in the pages of fiction, but it really happened only once." *Death of the Iron Horse* is Goble's telling of that event.

On August 7, 1867, a Union Pacific freight train was derailed by Cheyennes...The derailment was only a minor incident, but one that the Cheyenne people have remembered with pride and amusement.

As always, Goble has honored the history of the People. He begins with Sweet Medicine's vision of the coming of the white men, and the destruction that was to follow. Those things did happen, and the railroad was built all across the land. The iron horse caused great fear. So some young men went out to protect the People.

"Let us see the trail it leaves," they said to each other. But nobody had ever seen anything like its tracks.

"These must surely be the iron bands binding our Mother Earth...We must cut them apart and set her free."

The train is derailed, the trainman killed and all the marvelous objects the train contained are examined with wonder. The young warriors gallop across the plain, trailing bolts of cloth that fly behind them in the wind of their going. "When they came to be old men, they loved to laugh about that day."

In many beautiful and subtle ways, the illustrations compliment the text. The title page illustration shows the new iron horse and the fresh, clean land it runs upon. The last is of the same land, plus Amtrack train, power lines, jet planes, and a litter of cans and bottles.

Those who object to the trainman full of arrows should also note the preceding page on which he is shooting at the riders beside the train. Or the illustration on the second page of the story: A small encampment nestles in the bend of a blue-green river. The silvery, smoke-darkened lodges stand out against the white of new snow. Look closely. The vivid splashes of color are burning tipis, and the woefully broken bodies of the dead, most of whom are women. One little figure lies with her feet just in the river. Another, fleeing with a cradle board, starts to fall, just as we look at her. The encampment is under attack from the bluecoats.

As Goble says in his introduction,

Like everything to do with war, the derailment had sad and unpleasant aspects. But from this distance in time, we can see that the Cheyennes were simply fighting for their lives, liberty, and their own pursuit of happiness.

One hopes that might sound a certain note of irony in this "constitutional year." A brilliant and powerful book.

Goble, Paul

Star Boy

Bradbury
1983; grades k-up
Siksika/Blackfeet

Star Boy is Goble's retelling of the Blackfeet story whose purpose is to tell how the Sun Dance was given to the Blackfeet people. The illustrations are lovely as usual, although I am always a little bothered that Goble's people never have real faces.

As with his other books, Goble closes with a poem, in this case a Sun Song by Black Elk. Maybe it would have made his book stronger if he had said that Black Elk was not Blackfeet but Oglala, and that the Sun Dance is a sacred time shared by many of the Plains Nations.

It is hard to resist the beauty of the book, and the story. If taken just for what it is, it is coherent and does no violence to the spirit of the original. I would not object to using this with very young Native children, particularly those growing up away from their homelands. *Star Boy* would also, if used by a knowledgeable adult, be a good way to introduce non-Native children to a spiritual concept that is central to the lives of a large number of Native peoples.

Green, Richard

Wundoa; I'm Number One

Ricara Features
P.O. Box 664
via Sanborn, NY 14132
1983; all grades
Mohawk

I have been told that anyone who is not Indian is not going to *understand* this book, let alone find it funny. Maybe so. Green, who is Mohawk, has written a comic-strip story of a blind horse, who used to be a polo pony before getting hit on the head with a polo mallet. Now the horse communicates telepathically. This would be interesting to try with kids who like such racist monstrosities as *Tin Tin.*

Haseley, Dennis

The Scared One

Warne
1983; grades 1-5
Lakota

An especially timid child, called "The Scared One," finds an injured bird and in the process of trying to care for the bird, overcomes his own terror. Later, after an encounter with Old Wolf, an ambiguously drawn Elder to whom his mother has sent him for help, some boys try to take the bird away from The Scared One. At this point, he seems to undergo some sort of visionary experience, and the bird, described previously as having a broken wing, stretches out its "flashing wings, his wings of flame," and flies. The boy is transformed and cries, "I will never fear! I will never die!" Then the bird "rose into the flame of the sky into the blood of my life!" The end.

The author demonstrates neither insight into the mind and being of a Northern Plains child, nor sensitivity to, or understanding of, Native life. The people in this story don't *have* a culture; the boy has no family or tribal ties. He has not a friend in the world, and no relatives, other than a mother, who, for no apparent reason, is incapable of helping her child. States the protagonist,

in school, they told us that my tribe [unnamed—although the few non-English words used in the text are identifiable as Lakota] was once proud although today only a few old people know the language.

If Haseley knew what he was writing about, he could not have made such a ridiculous statement. Old Wolf is a version of that very necessary creature in fiction about Indians, the evil medicine man, and the supernatural elements in this story—if that is what they are supposed to be—are not successfully dealt with at all.

I have to say that neither the author's degree in Clinical Social Work nor his residence in South Carolina, Vermont, and Brooklyn seem to have qualified him to write an authentic book about the Lakota people and their beliefs. I feel sorry for the illustrator, Deborah Howland, whose drawings are beautiful, but if she is as familiar with the people as her art work seems to indicate, she should have known better than to get involved with this.

Henry, Edna, Wechappituwen (Blue Star Woman)

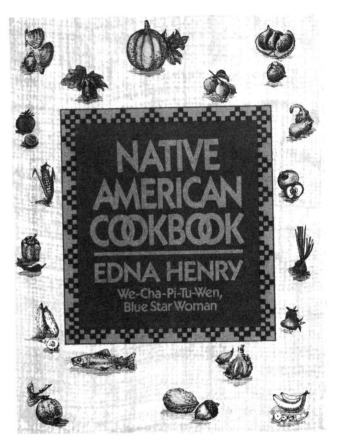

Native American Cookbook

Messner
1983; grades 5-up
various Nations

This is a collection of authentic recipes from Nipmuk, Iswa, Shinnecock, Narragansett, Miccosukee (Seminole), Cuna, Lakota, Inupiat, as well as a few that are called just "Southwest." Each section incorporates historical and cultural information, and entertaining snippets: "The turkey is not quite so dumb as some people think, but he is a curious bird...Sometimes turkeys will stare at their reflection in the water, fall in, and drown. 'Hey, turkey'!" The recipes are not always strictly traditional, but maybe more healthful. For example, the fry bread recipe calls for whole wheat flour. Henry, who is Nipmuc and Cherokee, gives substitutes for Native foods that may not be obtainable in a given area. Some of these work better than others. Having tried most of the recipes at one time or another, I can say that this book is interesting, informative, and full of good eating.

Henry, Jeannette, and Rupert Costo

A Thousand Years of American Indian Storytelling

Indian Historian Press
1981; all grades
All Nations

This is a treasure trove, more than 40 stories, from a vast spectrum of Native time and culture, down to the present day—literally a thousand years, at least. They "do not pretend to be scholarly works or treatises delving into the why and wherefore of the spirit that belonged to the ancient Natives of this continent." Perhaps this is the reason that they retain some of that spirit.

The excellent introduction by the editors discusses the place of storytelling in Native American life, and points out that "Indian storytelling has never ended. It continues and lives, especially when Indian people gather together in celebrations, festivals, pow-wows, or tribal affairs." One of the best things about the book is that it presents some of the modern stories, as well as a few by children. Another good thing is that there is some humor. Indians are always fooling around, and I seriously doubt whether any of us would have survived, if we hadn't been able to laugh. This is not readily apparent from collections gathered by non-Native writers.

It would be difficult to select a favorite story, but I particularly like "Mario and the Mountain Lion," and the eerie beauty of "The Dancing Arrows." And I love "Miracle in Woody End," in which Lance Michael, "a man to stay away from," gets his heart's desire, by "accident," by being a good person.

The illustrations are in a variety of styles, and suit the stories. Some are funny, some are frightening, and some are very beautiful.

Get this book, and *read* it.

Highwater, Jamake

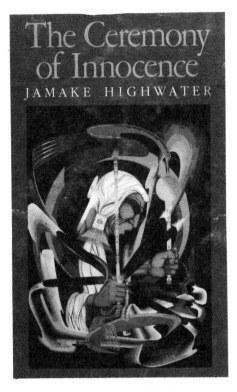

Ceremony of Innocence

Harper
1985; grades 7-up
Siksika/Blackfeet

The second book of Highwater's Ghost Horse Cycle finds Amana, of *Legend Days*, a mother, and struggling to survive in the post-Wounded Knee world. Having loved a white man, been abandoned by him and borne a child, she has now become helpless, vulnerable to each twist of fortune, a leaf in the white wind that has overwhelmed the Native world. Rescued from being sent to a reservation by her friend Amalia, Amana and her daughter, in a section very reminiscent of part of Maria Campbell's *Halfbreed*, are given a home in Amalia's "whorehouse."

One might be tempted to cite the author for his helpless and ineffectual women, were it not for the fact that none of his characters seem competent to cope with life on any level. The reader unfamiliar with true Native history will be at a loss to understand from this book how the People managed to survive at all.

Recently, Jamake Highwater's identity as a Native person has been called into question by a noted political columnist, and by *Akwesasne Notes*, a highly regarded and widely distributed Native newspaper. On the basis of this book, it seems likely that they may be right.

Hirschfelder, Arlene

American Indian Stereotypes in the World of Children: A Reader and Bibliography

Scarecrow Press
*1982; grades 10-up
all Nations*

AMERICAN INDIAN STEREOTYPES IN THE WORLD OF CHILDREN: A Reader and Bibliography

ARLENE B. HIRSCHFELDER

If the majority of non-Native people in the U.S. think about Indians at all, it is certainly not as people, on the same level of humanity as themselves. The enormous labor of putting together *American Indian Stereotypes* has been done in the hope that this might be changed—to show how children absorb the little they do "know" about Native Americans and to demonstrate ways in which the racist attitudes they learn can be counteracted.

While this book was not intended for children, chapters of it will surely be useful in teaching older students to "unlearn" racism.

The reader part of the book contains articles on children's misconceptions about Indians, on the portrayal of Native peoples in textbooks and children's literature, and on the inauthentic and insulting use of "Indian" imagery by the toy industry. Native American religious ritual by Boy Scout/Girl Scout/Campfire Girls- type organizations is also examined in an article that asks,

> Can you imagine a group of non-Christian children pretending they are Catholic for an evening once every two weeks; the group of non-Christian children and their fathers taking holy names such as Jesus Christ, Saint Paul, or the Pope...taking communion, making a crucifix, or saying Hail Mary?

Good question.

The bibliography is divided into two parts. The first lists articles and books that describe and analyze the treatment of Native people in a wide variety of printed materials, as well as movies, TV, the arts, etc. The issue of stereotyping in general is also covered. The second section—of necessity much shorter—lists "corrective" materials.

No brief summary can do justice to this book, and it is hard to believe that any but the most determined bigot could come away from a reading of this book unchanged. I cannot recommend it highly enough. It is an invaluable resource and should be required reading for anyone who bears any responsibility for what gets into little kids' heads.

Hirschfelder, Arlene

*Happily May I Walk:
American Indian and
Alaska Natives Today*

Scribners
*1986; grades 5-up
all Nations*

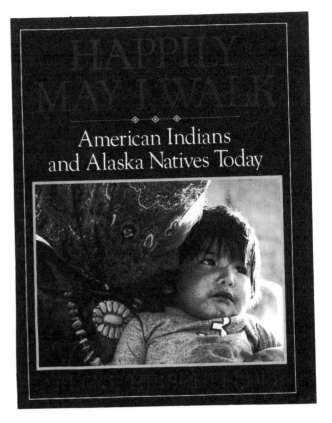

The stated purpose of this book, "containing new information about the ways Native Americans live in the United States today," is to "help you 'unlearn' Indian stereotypes." The range of material is so enormous that the text becomes almost a listing, rather than a narrative. It is to Hirschfelder's credit that she has accomplished so much of her purpose in 143 pages. Included: tribal governments, reservations, Alaska Natives, language, daily lives, religious ways, dance and music, sacred healers, Elders, children and education, Native Americans in cities, reservations, resources, economic life, treaty rights, Native American-U.S. government relations, termination and self-determination, performing artists, sports and pow-wows, Native American organizations, and writers and journalists.

While Hirschfelder writes with objectivity, she does not negate the ways in which Native peoples have suffered from the stupidity, insensitivity, greed, and outright malice of some whites: "Many sacred grounds have been destroyed...In Arizona, authorities flooded a sacred site of the Navajos to create Lake Powell...ignoring Indian protests." And, "Government education meant getting Indians to think, live and look like non-Indians, to stop being Indians." Children were forcibly removed from their families and homelands: "Some children...did not see their families for months and sometimes years." Native religious beliefs are dealt with honorably. "Superstition" is not a word you will find in this book. Compared to most other titles on Native subjects written for young people, this is a marvel of unbiased, fair reporting.

Having said that, I must also say that there are certain points in the text with which I must take issue.

- To say that "before 1960, very few Indians completed high school," is fairly misleading. Comparatively few, maybe. There are many Native people in the 30-50 age range who have at least a high school diploma; not a few of these also have been graduated from college. Some hold PhDs. You still have to be twice as good at everything to make it through the white educational system, which is one thing Hirschfelder does not say.

- The Council of Energy Resources Tribes (CERT) is not universally regarded by Native people as an unmixed blessing.

- Hirschfelder asserts that "Indians do not want the Bureau of Indian Affairs destroyed." There is a difference of opinion about the BIA. While many Native people feel the need for some such organization to stand between them and the rest of non-Native America, others feel that the BIA has been the biggest stumbling block in the way of Native self-determination.

- "States provide many services to Indians, as they do to all people living within their borders...schools, mental hospitals, nursing homes, prisons..." I'm sorry, the law may say so, but any Native person could tell you that these things—with the possible exception of prisons—are simply not available to Native people on the same basis as for whites. Native health care in this country is a national scandal.

The chapter on arts is one of the least satisfactory. Because Native cultures have not made a distinction between life and art, Indians tend to be multi-talented. This is an area in which their contributions have been of a very high quality, and yet remain, for young people, completely unknown. Moccasins, beads and buckskins is the level at which children are familiar with Native arts. In an area where many Native peoples do excel, it is a shame that Hirschfelder neglected to name any.

For me, the most inadequate treatment is of Native organizations. They are frequently all that stand between Native people and government, industry, and anybody else who, for one reason or another, wants something that Indians happen to have. To give them such short shrift is to distort the nowday lives of the People. The statement that AIM (American Indian Movement) is "willing to use violence and conflict to get recognition of their goals" is particularly misleading. This group has been involved in violent incidents, but the violence has generally been on the part of those who oppose AIM's goals. To say that "some tribal leaders approve of AIM and its methods, but many do not," may be true, but it leaves out essential information. Many of the "tribal leaders" have been government-backed, elected under highly dubious circumstances. Some of these people have enriched themselves, or abused their positions at the expense of the people they were supposed to serve. Often, there has been liaison between members of AIM and tribal Elders, who approve of the stand taken against violations of Native rights and the mistreatment of Indian people.

To point out the inadequacies of this book is in no way to negate its many excellences. While this is not the book a Native author would have written, I cannot help wondering what of Hirschfelder's work was left on the editorial "cutting room floor." I am familiar with her earlier writing in this field, and feel that what she actually wrote may have been a better book. As it is, *Happily May I Walk* is good, and could be used in conjunction with resource materials containing more in-depth discussions.

Hudson, Jan

Sweetgrass

Tree Frog Press
1984; grades 5-up
Siksika/Blackfeet

Sweetgrass is the only daughter of Shabby Bull, member of the Blood Division of the Blackfeet Nation. Told in the first person, the first half of the book mainly concerns Sweetgrass's obsession with getting married.

Pretty Girl couldn't know how I would've sacrificed a finger [somehow, I doubt that] to be in her place. I was fifteen, and she was thirteen—but she was the one whose parents had announced her marriage.

This girl is self-absorbed to a degree that would be far more believable of a 20th century upper middle class American girl than of a young 19th century Blackfeet woman: "Father gives me all the little things I want...Grandmother is one person who cares about *me*...I get my own way most of the time" and so on. If this is the author's attempt to make Sweetgrass seem just like

themselves to young white girls, then she has succeeded.

About halfway through the book, the baby dies of smallpox; this is the beginning of a terrible epidemic. Sweetgrass is not stricken, and must tend the members of her family, some of whom live. This is supposed to have caused her to grow up, although there isn't much evidence of that. In the end, the one whom she constantly refers to as her "boyfriend" returns. Although they don't exactly ride off into the sunset together, we know that Sweetgrass is going to get her own way this time, too.

It is a little difficult to know what the author's intention was in writing this book. Certainly, she seems to have little understanding of the patterns of tribal life, and she says some truly extraordinary things: "Aside from my obnoxious almost-brother Otter...there have been only babies in our tipi. And when they die young, they don't count....But as I brewed the tea, I cried. All I wanted to do was leave all these sick people, go out on the clean snow and puke them all away." Sweetgrass's friend, Pretty Girl, is given to Five Killer, a man her father's age, to be a "slave wife," because her father needs the horses. (For those who don't know, it was not the custom of the People to sell their daughters...)

It took me a while to figure out that, when the smallpox strikes, Sweetgrass's family are camping alone. Granted, bands might split up during the winter, but no family, unless they had been banished, would choose to go off alone. That would be death.

Although none of the characters are too appealing, the portrayal of the women is appalling. "Bent-Over-Woman always walked like she was tired...with graying hair sticking out from her braids like dirty feathers, she looked just like a crow." "My aunt waddled toward us, panting from the heat. Her buckskin underclothes must have been sticking together." (Buckskin underclothes, eh? Oh, well.) The women have to be married off young, so that the men will have someone to "tan the buffalo robes for trading."

Sweetgrass may lack the overt racism of the *Little House* books, say, or *The Matchlock Gun*, but it is demeaning and inaccurate in so many ways, that I would not consider it, even as an alternative.

It might be of interest to note that this book received the Canada Council's Children's Literature Prize for 1984, and was the Canadian Library Association Book of the Year for children. And to think that I was told recently by a Canadian: "We treat our Indians better..."

Hungry Wolf, Beverly

The Ways of My Grandmothers

Morrow
1980; grades 8-up
Siksika/Blackfeet

Beverly Hungry Wolf, a young woman of the Blood Division of the Blackfeet Nation, has written about the lives of Native women, as experienced by her people during the recent past. The book grew out of her interest, as an adult, in learning about the traditions of the women of her people and in living a more traditional life herself. She also wanted to set down what the Grandmothers have to say while they are still with us and to provide some guidance for the young people coming along, many of whom "have a very confused idea of what it is to really be an Indian."

The book is a compilation of history, social life and customs, religious observances, "household hints," recipes, etc. There are stories, taped by the author, about the lives of her mother and Grandmother, and others of her Elders, as well as accounts of some of her own experiences in learning how to live in the traditional manner.

There is a section called "Myths and Legends of My Grandmothers" plus two groups of photographs collected from family albums, museums and other sources. Apart from its content, which is extremely valuable, one special quality of this work is its depiction of Native people living a happy, normal and fulfilling existence—here are *anybody's* Grandmothers, yours, mine, human beings.

Beverly Hungry Wolf is a very good writer. Her book is interesting, moving, and, here and there, pretty funny. Although an adult title, this is so readable that it could easily be used by and with older students. A lot of nonsense has been written about the women of Native America, past and present. *The Ways of My Grandmothers* is a good antidote. This book is not to be missed.

Johnston, Basil and Del Ashkewe

How the Birds Got their Colours/Gah w'indinimowaut binaesheenhnyuk w'idinauziwin-wauh

Kids Can Press
585 Bloor St. West
Toronto, Ontario M6G 1K5
1978; grades 3-5
Anishinabe/Ojibway/Chippewa

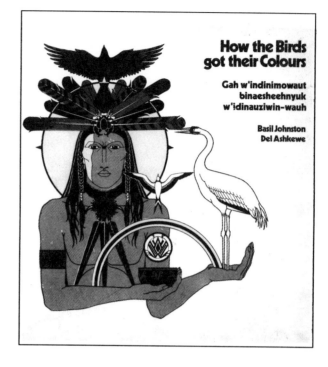

This is one of the best books made from a Native story that I have ever seen. Papeekawiss invites the birds to his Thanksgiving feast (no, not that Thanksgiving). The birds were all very plain in those days, and, envious of the animals' finery, they ask Papeekawiss to give them fine clothing. He agrees, and the next day, all the birds line up to get painted. To tell what happens would spoil the story. Suffice it to say, the Crow distinguishes himself, as usual. The pictures are wonderful; the story is very funny. Text in Anishinabe and English.

Katz, Jane

This Song Remembers: Self-Portraits of Native Americans in the Arts

Houghton Mifflin
1980; grades 8-up
various Nations

The title says it. Apart from providing an introduction and background information, the editor lets the artists speak for themselves. The book is divided into three parts: Visual Arts, Performing Arts, and Literature. There are the well-known names—R.C. Gorman, Allan Hauser, Grace Medicine Flower—and some that will be unfamiliar to the non-Native reader. There are photographs of contributors, and samples of the art. Songs and quotes from the words of the People are used in appropriate places. They come from all over, and speak of their lives as well as the work. Some of them have made rapprochement, to an extent, with white society, others remain "close to the source of tribal traditions."

"Art is a fundamental activity in tribal cultures, an integral part of the daily life of ordinary people. It is an expression of the basic need of people in all times." The people in this book "affirm the inviolability of the tribal consciousness, of the human spirit." A beautiful book, sensitively produced.

LeSueur, Meridel

SPARROW HAWK

Meridel Le Sueur

DRAWINGS BY ROBERT DESJARLAIT
FOREWORD BY VINE DELORIA, JR.

Sparrow Hawk

Holy Cow! Press
5435 Old Highway 18
Stevens Point, WI 54481
1950 (reprinted 1987); grades 6-up
Mesquakie/Sauk

The background for this book is the so-called Black Hawk War. The events of the story are seen through the eyes of Sparrow Hawk, a young boy who becomes as a son to Black Hawk.

The year is 1832, and it is the last of the time the Mesquakie People will have together in their homeland on the Fox River. By the end of the novel, their land has been taken from them by treachery and outright theft. Many of the people, including Sparrow Hawk's mother, Evening Star, are dead. Sparrow Hawk, although seriously wounded, survives. He and his white friend, Huck, will go on with their "cornbuilding, their work on herbs and the seeds and the flowers, putting the white man's knowledge and red man's knowledge together."

There are many wonderful things about *Sparrow Hawk*. Not the least amazing, is that it was written by a non-Native person, in 1950, the year in which, as Vine Deloria, Jr., says in his foreword, "Americans were just beginning to embark on a witch hunt...the book definitely takes an Indian slant...which must have been a distasteful concept at that time."

One of the best things is the friendship between the two boys, Sparrow Hawk and Huck, one Indian, one white. There is no condescension in it at all. It is a friendship of equals, as is that of their two families, with respect on both sides.

LeSueur's writing can be strongly evocative. Sometimes it is hard to remember that the author is a white woman. There is a wonderful scene in which, watching a river boat loaded with soldiers and cannon coming closer and closer, Black Hawk and his people pretend to be white men, trying to talk to Indians.

> "A beautiful spot. Too good for them." said one. "Try out some of your Sauk on these," another young brave laughed, and the first one spoke to Sparrow Hawk, in the foolish way white men spoke to Indians, "Fish much good here? Fish. Fish…" and he went through the motions of fishing. Sparrow Hawk drew into his blanket like an Indian pretending to be dumb, as if he did not understand. They all laughed. "A stupid people…They deserve to lose their land."

Then there are the things that mark *Sparrow Hawk* as, in some ways, a book of its time, the use of the word "brave," for example. Throughout the text, LeSueur refers to the people as Sauk. The name by which they know themselves is Mesquakie; surely at that time, this is how they would have called themselves.

And there is at least one real howler. Huck's family has a book, out of which he reads to Sparrow Hawk about how corn was developed from "a tiny grass bending in the wind, way down in South America." That the son of a farm family in 1832 would have been able to read, and that such a family would have such a book, seems quite unlikely. That Sparrow Hawk would need to have corn explained to him is probably pretty unlikely, too…

The illustrations, by Robert DesJarlait, a well-known Ojibway artist, are a powerful addition to the story. They would be called, I guess, stylized. In any case, DesJarlait's work is unlike anyone else's. His drawings are strong, and unexpected, about as far from either savage or romantic stereotype as it is possible to get.

The weakest part of the book is the last chapter. It seems completely tacked on, and its optimism for the future completely out of keeping with what has gone before. In the preceding chapter, Sparrow Hawk has been wounded, apparently mortally, and has sung his death song.

> He thought of moving now into the great stream so the father river in the evening would deliver him to the white shores of Saukenuk, and he stood and moved toward it, but then darkness came over him and he knew no more.

Despite its flaws, *Sparrow Hawk* remains a powerful indictment of a disgraceful episode in the history of America. Meridel LeSueur has been a writer and social activist all her life; during the McCarthy years, she was blacklisted as "a radical from a family of radicals." *Sparrow Hawk* contains nothing of which such a woman needs to be ashamed.

Lyons, Grant

Pacific Coast Indians of North America

Messner
1983; grades 3-6
Northwest Coast Nations

The people who inhabited the Northwest coastlands of the American continent prior to the coming of the whites developed one of the most complex societies to be found north of Mexico, but Grant Lyons has given us an extraordinarily superficial and insensitive account of their history. Although the title says "Pacific Coast," the book has almost nothing to say about anyone living below the Columbia River:

> Many other groups of Indians, speaking many languages, lived to the south...In general, these southern villages were smaller and the Indians' lives were simpler.

So much for them.

Lyons touches superficially on the destruction of the Native economy, culture and society. He says nothing of the current struggles of the Coastal Peoples to preserve their fishing rights, tribal lands (what's left of them) and just about every other aspect of their existence, saying only that "the Indians learned to adapt to the changes" and "there was no better lumberjack than a Tlingit Indian."

In fairness, I do not think the author is unsympathetic to "Indians" (just *once*, couldn't he refer to them as "people"?). I think the book's flaws are due not to malice, but to ignorance. Unfortunately, that does not seem to make a great deal of difference to the end result.

Maher, Ramona

Alice Yazzie's Year

Coward
1977; grades 3-up
Diné/Navajo

In January, *Yas Nilt'ees,* "snow covered the world." Snow heaps around and covers the hogan. The day is cold and still; the smoke rises straight up from the chimney. The sound of the horses pawing the snow for graze carries a long way. Their breath is white smoke, frosting their noses. You know all these things from Stephen Gammell's breath-taking illustrations. When the strip-mining machines tear up the earth, the shattering roar of their destruction is nearly audible.

The words of the story seem to come out of the pictures, in such a perfect whole that either would be less than half without the other. Alice's Grandfather, Tsosie, looks out at us from the light and shadow of the hogan at night. Alice rides her horse in the barrel race, and the gritty feel of clouds of dust is on our tongues and in our eyes.

There is not a page of this book that is not beautiful. There is not a time that I have read it, that I am not satisfied anew by its balance and rightness. Alice and her Grandfather are so real that, as many times as I have read this book, it is always with a sense of loss that I close it. Surely they are my friends, and someday I will go to Dzilijiin, and they will stand in the doorway of their hogan, and smile with their eyes, and say, "What took you so long?"

In *Nilch'itsoh*, December,

Grandfather's tobacco is under the tree...He's made her a bracelet, she's almost sure. Blue and silver—the way the world is. Silver snow lies on Black Mountain, hiding the gorges.

An afterword by Carl Gorman, "Notes About the Navajo Country and Ways of Life," completes the book. In beauty it is finished.

Of all books, why does *this* one have to be out of print?

Martin, Bill, and John Archambault

Knots on a Counting Rope

Holt
1987; grades 3-6
Diné/Navajo

Scenario: Two children's book authors and an illustrator, whose recent work has received critical acclaim, are discussing possibilities for their next work.

"Well," says one, "I want this one to be about a boy." "O.K.," says another, "—and let's have him blind!" "Great, that's good, but there's a lot of stuff about blind kids—we need another hook...."

"I know! I know! He's an Indian! A *blind* Indian!"

"Oh, wow, perfect!...But won't we hafta do a lot of research? I mean, I don't know very much about Indians, do you?"

"Oh, sure, I've got all these rugs my old man bought from the Navajos back in the forties—said he got them for a song."

This, of course, is probably not how it happened, but judging from the results, it might just as well have been.

A boy—he looks to be about ten—sits with his Grandfather beside a small fire, in the early evening. "Tell me the story again, Grandfather," he asks. "Tell me who I am." The story is told, entirely in the dialogue created by the boy's constant interruptions— the circumstances attending the boy's birth, his first horse, and the race in which he rode her, thus "crossing dark mountains." For anyone, this form makes it almost impossible to read the book aloud, with any degree of comprehension on the part of the

child audience. For the Native reader, *Knots on a Counting Rope* is repulsive, in its deliberate pandering to the romantic mythology about "Indians" in the minds of a certain kind of white adult purchaser.

To begin with, the conversation is embarrassingly overwrought:

A wild storm came out of the mountains...crying, "Boy-eeeeeeee! Boy-eeeeeeeee!" [yes, nine e's—I counted them]...and your mother said "I hear it in the wounded wind. A boy child will be born tonight."

And,

"Blue?...blue? Blue is the morning...the sunrise...the sky...the song of birds...O, I see it! Blue! Blue! Blue is happiness, Grandfather! I feel it!...in my heart."

And,

"You have raced the darkness and won! You can now see with your heart, feel a part of all that surrounds you. Your courage lights the way."

Storms are not *wild*; they just are. And, excuse me, but what the hell is a "wounded wind"? Is this how the authors think their readers expect Indians to talk—all primitive and poetical? I don't know anybody who talks like that. I don't even know any *white* people who talk like that.

Now, what Nation is this? You won't know from the text. Only in the advance publicity for the book, does it say: "The costumes (sic) are a mixture of Hopi and Navajo celebration garb. Because their reservations are so close to each other, the tribes usually participate together in ceremonies."

The illustrations might offer a clue: the setting is obviously Southwest, there is a lot of silver and turquoise around, and what may be a hogan in the background of one picture. On the other hand, the faces of the people are more Northern Plains than anything else. One guy, with a nice, bushy mustache, looks quite a bit like a Micmac/Métis friend I used to have.

The hair styles are certainly not Navajo. The women all wear braids; the men have their front hair braided, and the rest hanging loose down their backs. Mandan, Piegan, Blackfeet and Atsina peoples wore versions of this style. I wonder if the illustrator found it more attractive, or more obviously Indian-looking, than the clubbed and wrapped way of dressing the hair that is still worn by traditional Diné?

The men also wear pointed Tom Mix hats, with big concha bands. The Grandfather wears two eagle feathers sticking straight up out of the back of his hat; the little boy has one. Is this supposed to be a consolation for having been born blind? The book does not say what else he may have done, to be allowed this honor. The women wear little, round Cheyenne-style button earrings.

And, except under special circumstances, Native peoples do not "participate" in each other's ceremonies. They may attend tribal events of another Nation. Is it necessary to say that Hopi people would not be showing up at a Navajo horse race in sacred ceremonial gear?

The boy of the story is given the name "Boy-Strength-of-Blue-Horses" by his Grandfather, because when he was born—

too weak for crying—two great blue horses came galloping by...

"and they stopped, Grandfather. They stopped and looked at me..."

..."and you raised your arms to the great blue horse, and I said, 'See how the horses speak to him. They are his brothers from..."

..."from beyond the dark mountains. This boy child will not die.' That is what you said, isn't it, Grandfather?"

On my first reading of this book, I actually turned the page back, to see where the horses came from, before I realized that this is supposed (I think) to be an instance of "Native spirituality," and the closeness of Indians to the animal kingdom—or are the horses blue to show that they are spirit beings?

But, no matter where the blue horses came from, *nobody* gives a kid a name like that.

No Native person would be dumb enough to say of a child whose life was threatened, "this boy child will not die." That would be both an insult and a challenge to the spirits. Traditional Navajos would not hold a naming ceremony "after you smiled your first smile."

As in the old days, when a baby comes, they name it right away. To boys, they give names beginning with Haské, The Fierce One: Haské Yitah Deeya, Fierce One Who Walks Among Enemies.

Especially, with a frail baby, they'd name him right off, lest Someone might think they didn't want him.

And, finally, a child born blind does not have great, dark, glowing eyes. Nor would such a child ask a question such as, "Will I always have to live in the dark?" nor say, "I could see through the dark," nor would he be obsessed with finding out about colors. "Dark," "see," and colors are concepts of sighted people; they would have no meaning for a child who was born blind. Such a child might ask, "Will I always be blind?"

Most non-Native readers will have no way of knowing that there is very little of *Knots on a Counting Rope* that is true to any specific Native culture. Even the relationship between the boy and his Grandfather, which had the potential for being the one genuine thing about the book, is marred by the authors' ignorance:

- A child would *never* constantly interrupt an Elder, even if he'd heard the story a hundred times. He would just sit quietly and listen.

- No one would say, "I love you. That is better than a promise." We have learned too bitterly and too well that our love for our children is no protection for them against anything.

- Grandparents do not tire of repeating stories, or admonish children for

asking for them, or tell them that "this may be the last telling."

- What is this "counting rope" business anyway? Did the authors get the idea from the ancient Peruvian quipu? Or is this another of those "old Indian customs" of which none of us have ever heard?

Of some white people who write about Indians, it can probably be said that at least they meant well, despite the end results. Of some, it can be said that they knew better, and did it anyway. Unless they walked around with a bag over their heads, these guys have to know that what they have created has nothing to do with any Native reality. The romantic imagery of this book is no less a white fantasy than the bloody savages of more overtly racist titles. *Knots on a Counting Rope* has nothing of respect for any Native People. It is a crass, and deliberate, rip-off—an insult to all of us, and most of all to the people of the Navajo Nation.

Martinson, David

Real Wild Rice

Shemay, the Bird in the Sugarbush

Anishinabe Reading Materials
Duluth Indian Education
Advisory Committee
1975; grades 1-2
Anishinabe/Ojibway/Chippewa

Real Wild Rice is one of the less than few books to deal decently on a beginning-to-read level with *anything* to do with American Indians.

In a short story poem, a boy talks about going for rice. "I run with the rabbit/I jump and play/Today isn't Monday/It's wild rice day." Young readers will feel the teller's delight in the "Real wild/wild rice" that "grows tall and free/and tastes real nice," and in the pleasure of the day.

Illustrated with line drawings that are embellished with designs from the Great Lakes tradition, this is a light-hearted, humorous, and deeply satisfying little book.

In *Shemay*, Liza, an Anishinabe girl, goes out with her family for sugaring season. Liza loves to listen to the birds, but she hears one that sounds unhappy. So her grandmother tells her the story of how this little bird got its sad song.

The warmth between child and grandmother is conveyed by both text and illustrations. The People are dressed as they normally would be—no skins, no feathers. An excellent beginning reader.

Mathers, Sharon,
Linda Skinner
and Terry Tafoya

*The Mamook Book:
Activities for Learning
about the Northwest Coast
Indians*

Daybreak Star Press
1979; grades 4-6
Northwest Coast Nations

The Mamook Book deals with several Peoples, rather than concentrating on one Nation. Well-presented, authentic material makes for an attractive and appealing book. There are directions for a longhouse, transformation masks, a mobile and a salmon game that follows the life cycle of this most important of fishes. I particularly like the inclusion of both historical and contemporary scenes. *The Mamook Book*, as all Daybreak Star books, can definitely be recommended for use with Native and non-Native children.

Mayne, William

Drift

Delacorte
1985; grades 6-10
Nation unspecified

Although his work is not much read by children, William Mayne is a respected English children's book author. His forte is the odd and the offbeat, which he writes about in a vivid, evocative style. His child characters are quirky, and very real. It would be fascinating to know what led him to write *Drift*.

Rafe Considine is lured from the bosom of his family by an "Indian" girl, Tawena, who wants to show him a hibernating bear. This is Tawena:

> Tawena was throwing down little balls of suet from a lump of fat she had in her hand. Now and then she ate some herself. She had a fatty face...and brown eyes deep in the fat. He was sure she had stolen the suet.

This is how she talks:

> "Indian womans come...They kill Indian girl right off...Tawena go away, you ever see Tawena again, ever see Tawena, ever.

This white boy fire. Tawena ever at village."

You may be pardoned for not being sure what this means.

Unfortunately for both of them, the bear is very much awake, and, by a process too complicated to go into here, is the cause of their being swept away on an ice floe. The rest of the book is a chronicle of their adventures, together, trying to get home.

Neither setting, character nor plot have much to do with reality. Although Tawena has spent her entire life around the whiteman fort, she has all the skills necessary to survive in the northern forest.

> Tawena's instincts were working. [Because Indians, like animals, do have instinct, rather than intelligence...]. She saw and heard many more things than Rafe did, looking and listening, watching and being aware, sniffing and smelling,

feeling the wind and weather, searching the sky.

The ability of the Native people to communicate, either with each other or with Rafe and his people, is but a little up from that of animals. They do not, of course, have an identity, other than "Indians."

On the way home, Tawena encounters a herd of buffalo, a pack of wolves, Bigfoot, and Wendagoo (Mayne's spelling). When one of the women who capture/befriend Rafe is shot, it is Rafe who knows what to do about it, even though he is so incompetent in the woods that it is clear he would have died without their help.

Tawena's family lives in the white's village because

> The rules [of the "tribe"] were too hard for them to obey. The rule they had broken was to let Tawena live. There were too many girls in the tribe, and baby girls were not to live. Tawena had lived...Because of that she was not marked with the cheek-cuts of those allowed to live, so Indian women, and men too, would kill her if she was found in the wilderness.

This white fantasy seems to be as ubiquitous as those of old people thrown out like so much trash, and the brutal treatment accorded to those who are less than perfect physical specimens, whether by birth or accident.

All this is very much too bad, because, as always, Mayne's writing is richly visual, with scenes of both real humor and beauty.

Since this book came out, I have thought, off and on, of writing to Mayne to ask him what he thought he was doing. I might do it yet.

McGovern, Ann

If You Lived with the Sioux Indians

*Scholastic
1976; grades 1-4
Lakota*

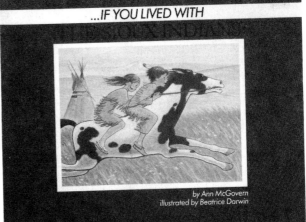

Ann McGovern's intent to deal sensitively with her material is marred by errors of fact and omission, and the bizarre impressions created by the ways in which she describes some aspects of Lakota life. Just imagine what a child totally unfamiliar with the realities of 19th century Plains existence will make of this:

> What would you eat? Buffalo, buffalo, buffalo, and more buffalo...and sometimes raw buffalo. You would even drink the blood of buffalo!

(McGovern consistently uses exclamation points for things she apparently thinks odd.) Here's more: "To boil buffalo blood, the women threw hot stones into the stomach of a freshly killed buffalo!"

This whole thing is going to seem pretty yukky (you know the sound; I think "Yyyyyeeeuuuuww..." is how it's usually written) to young children who think beef grows at McDonald's. But if they knew that life on the Plains, although immeasurably rewarding, was also very difficult, that physical survival depended on a high-energy diet, and that blood is what carries a body's nutrients, it then becomes possible to see that blood would be a very important, not-to-be-wasted food source.

As with blood, so with religion. "As part of the [Sun Dance] ceremony," McGovern writes, "a few of the men would perform acts of pain upon themselves. They believed that would please the spirits. Then they asked the spirits to take pity on them." I should think so. This statement makes nonsense of a concept central to Lakota religious belief. Piercing at Sun Dance is for the purpose of giving. You make sacrifice, for the well-being of the People, as a thank-offering for blessings received, as prayer for the fulfillment of needs. Children *can* understand this. The idea of sacrifice is at the heart of most of the "major" religions; why not make that analogy? The only possible conclusion to be drawn, as this stands, is that Indians are both barbaric and silly.

By talking only about the past, and by comparing the Lakota people with "you" (the unstated norm of white, middle-class America), McGovern further distances non-Native children from Lakota children (yes, they still exist; lots of them).

In some ways, a book such as this one has more potential for reinforcing misconceptions about Native Americans than one that is out-and-out racist. Because the author does not use derogatory terms such as squaw, brave, savage; because she writes positively about Lakota family life, the reader's inclination may be to assume that all of the material may be accepted as accurate and well-developed. This makes it all the easier for people to believe that there is some basis of truth for the stereotypes. "The Sioux were the most famous of all the Plains Indians," living in "exciting times when [they] rode horses to hunt the buffalo." "The name 'redskin' came from the red paint the Indians used on their faces when they went to war."

All in all, the impression is of a book written by someone who knows a little—but only on the most superficial levels. Either that, or possibly, the author felt that the material must be simplified for young readers. If so, there are ways of doing this without trivializing a whole culture. And, for everyone's information, "Lakota" was *not* "another name for the Sioux." Sioux was, as are so many of the names by which the People are known today, a derogatory term given to the Lakota peoples by enemies.

Here is a perfect example of the insufficiency of good intentions.

Miles, Miska

Annie and the Old One

> Little, Brown
> *1971; grades 2-up*
> *Diné/Navajo*

When this book came out, it was, for its time, unique, a picture story for young children that was neither overtly racist, nor condescendingly indulgent toward the quaint and curious customs of a "primitive tribe." The people in the story are not generic Indians, they are Navajo. The pictures are by Peter Parnall, and the lovely sweep of line for which his art is noted make every book he illustrates seem richer, slightly mysterious, and more accomplished. *Annie and the Old One* is a very beautiful book to look at. The intent of the story is to portray a People living in harmony with the land and its cycles, of birth and death, endings and beginnings. That Annie should learn to come to terms with the impending death of her beloved Grandmother, is essential to the rhythm of being. It is only as one looks more closely into both story and illustrations that a sense of doubt is born.

Briefly, the story is that the "Old One," Annie's Grandmother, tells her family that when the weaving Annie's mother is now doing comes off the loom, she will "go to Mother Earth." After various stratagems to delay the work have failed, Annie begins, each night, to pick out the weaving her mother has done during the day. On the third night, the Old One sees Annie, and the next morning she takes her granddaughter to "the small mesa." There, she tells Annie that all things must return to earth: "Earth, from which good things come for the living creatures on it. Earth, to which all creatures finally go." The continuity of life is established when Annie returns and tells her mother that she is now ready to learn to weave, "as her mother has done, as her grandmother had done."

I get the feeling sometimes, that non-Native writers think we ought to be grateful to them for taking an interest—particularly so, if they have made some attempt to treat their material in a non-racist manner. I can see their point, but it's hard to be grateful if they don't get it *right*. Here are some of the things that are not right with *Annie and the Old One*:

- There is no feeling of tribal life. This seems like a nuclear family, transposed into a Navajo setting. Is there really only one child?

- The language is halting and stiff—to sound "primitive"? People don't talk that way. And no one, in any culture, would call a Grandmother "the Old One"—they would call her "Grandmother."

- There is a hogan and sheep corral—where are the out-buildings? The summer house, or shelter for the weaver? Where is the pickup, or at least a wagon? You have to get the water and the groceries...

- The traditional dress is not accurate: the hair styles are wrong, the moccasins are wrong. The blanket designs are wrong, the design of the weaving on the loom is not Navajo—or even "Indian." The design on the pot is not authentic.

- "God's dog" is not a Navajo name for coyotes, and they do not "guard" the hogans. In fact, a coyote hanging around is a matter of unease.

- When Annie and her Grandmother are walking through the corn, they are carrying nothing, but when they get to the mesa, there is a blanket for the Grandmother to wear.

- The Grandmother would not sit "crossing her knees."

- The faces are wrong; the bone structure is all wrong. These are not Navajo faces.

- When the Grandmother calls her family together, they all stand in the door of the hogan, which is completely bare, except for a small rug, and a New England-style straight-backed chair, in which she is sitting. What kind of living arrangements are these? An open fire is built directly on the floor—no rocks, not even a fire-pit. Nobody does that, unless they're planning to burn the place down.... Open fires are built outside. For inside, you have a stove. The family would sit quietly at first, and then maybe make a little talk before they got to the serious stuff. There would probably be food.

- I am confused about this business of having each of the family choose only one thing of Grandmother's to have. Is there more family, somewhere? If she has other things, what happens to them? They cannot be given to anyone after she is gone.

- Mostly, only Elders wear traditional clothes for everyday, and Indian kids—anywhere—do not wear them to school.

- Finally, but no less importantly, it is difficult to believe that a child raised in such a traditional environment would react so badly to the idea of a death. And it would be unthinkable for her to deliberately act up in a way that might require her mother to come to the school. Acting out is, in general, a very non-Native way of dealing with stress. Rather, for Indian children, there is a tendency to close in and shut down. It also is just not realistic to show no adult reaction to Annie's behavior for three days.

I am glad that Miles has tried to show the gentleness of Native parents with their children, and the special relationship that can exist between a child and her Grandmother. It is good that the lifeways of the People should be treated with respect. It would have been better, if the author and illustrator had consulted Navajo people about their work. In that way, they might really have made it a first-rate book.

Munsch, Robert and Michael Kusugak

A Promise is a Promise

Annick Press, Ltd.
1988; grades 2-up
Inuit

On the first warm day of spring, Allashua says,

'I'm going to go fishing in the cracks in the ice.' 'Ah Ah,' said her mother, 'Don't go fishing on the sea ice. Under the ice live—allupilluit. They grab children who aren't with their parents...go fish in a lake.' 'Right,' said Allashua, 'I promise to go fishing in the lake and not in the ocean and a promise is a promise.'

Well, you know and I know where she goes. That isn't her worst mistake, though...

Allashua catches six fish in a row. "I'm the best fisherman in the world!" she yells. "And from behind her something said with a voice that sounded like snow blowing over ice, 'The best you may be, but the smartest you are not.'" Oh my gosh. There they are. With their blue and green hair, and their long white fingers, and their long, long green fingernails.

"Have you seen the child who yelled, '—allupilluit, —allupilluit can't catch me?'"

"Oh, no..and besides, my mother says that you can catch whatever you want to."

"Right," said the —allupilluit. "We catch whatever we want to and what we want to catch right now is you."...

Allashua let out her breath and yelled, "My brothers and sisters...I'll bring them all to the sea ice."

Well, a promise is a promise, but never fear. Allashua's mother is more than equal to any —allupilluit, and it all ends just fine.

A Promise is a Promise is a delight, a perfect blend of modern and traditional. Allashua lives in an ordinary house; she has her books and her teddy bear. There is a wonderfully warm and loving family to offset the scary parts, and the story is done with a light hand and great good humor. The illustrations, by Vladyana Krykorka, are a perfect match for the words, full of lovely colors; the round-faced, rosy-cheeked children are adorable.

And nowhere in this book is the word "Eskimo" used.

Nabakov, Peter, editor

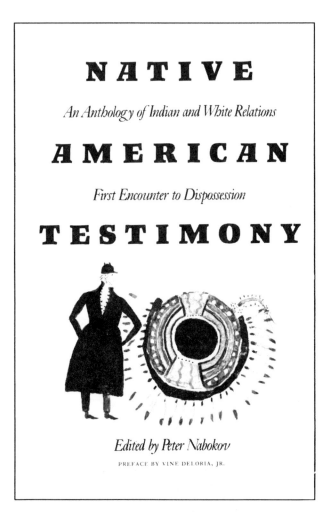

NATIVE

An Anthology of Indian and White Relations

AMERICAN

First Encounter to Dispossession

TESTIMONY

Edited by Peter Nabokov

PREFACE BY VINE DELORIA, JR.

Native American Testimony

Crowell
*1978; grades 7-up
all Nations*

This collection of primary source material is not always easy reading—although it is done for older children—but it is such a good, honest, truth-telling book, that it is important to use with them. An "anthology of Indian-white relations, first encounter to dispossession," this book is required reading for anyone interested in teaching American history as it actually happened. And it conveys one essential truth: "Even at his lowest point, the Native American's sense of his own traditional identity, and his search for new forms of tribalism, were not destroyed."

New Mexico People and Energy Collective

Red Ribbons for Emma

New Seed Press
P.O. Box 9488
Berkeley, CA 94709
1981; all grades
Diné/Navajo

For most Americans, knowledge of conflict between Native peoples and power companies is probably limited to a vague familiarity with the words "Big Mountain." For Emma Yazzie, it is every day. "Emma and the other rural Navajos look different from heroes we usually read about who are mostly...white men." But she is a hero, and this is her story.

Emma's hogan is completely surrounded by

> many different kinds of energy development. Coal trucks rumble along the road in back...The blue sky (is dirty) with chemicals and soot...When you walk under the power lines, they tower over you and your body shakes from all the electric energy in the air.

As of this writing (1981), Emma Yazzie had been fighting the power companies for 15 years. She had been to court to stop the plant and the mine, a case she lost.

> Inside her hogan, Emma has red ribbons hanging on her wall. They are not the fancy kind people win at state fairs, and nobody gave them to her. She took them!

She took them off the wooden stakes the company stuck into the land. Emma knows very well that the stakes are survey markers to show where the company plans to build more power lines and more mines.

One morning, men come to tell her to quit dong that. They threaten her with the police. Does that scare Emma Yazzie? Not so you'd notice. "It is not company land," she says,

> "it is the land where my mother and my grandmother herded sheep. It is not your land. I never gave it to you...I don't care if you hang me up and kill me. I'm ready to die for my land."

The writing does not romanticize the difficulty and poverty of Emma Yazzie's life; neither does it allow pity. Emma's indomitable spirit and sense of humor demonstrate clearly why we so value our Elders, and why the men say no Nation is defeated, so long as the hearts of the women are strong.

The photographs are good. This is an honest book.

Norman, Howard

Who-Paddled-Backward-With-Trout

Little, Brown
1987; grades k-3
Cree

It is possible to forget that Howard Norman is not Indian. (This is not something that happens every day.) He is one of the few non-Native writers who gets the stories right. He is one of the even smaller number who get our humor right. *Who-Paddled-Backward-With-Trout* is a very funny book.

"In one Cree village lived a boy who kept bumping into things...Each thing he bumped into flattened his nose a little more." An old man in the village dreams of a trout who keeps bumping into things. "That sounds just like our son," the parents say, and ask the old man's permission to name their child after his dream. So the boy becomes known as "Trout-With-Flattened-Nose." Trout, of course, is somewhat unhappy with his name. "I want a name I can be proud of," he tells his parents. One choice is "Who-Paddles-A-Canoe-Better-Than-Anyone." That's not the way it works, his father tells him, "You can't just have

whichever name you want. You have to earn a new name."

It would be absolutely unfair to reveal any more of the story. The book should appeal strongly to young children's sense of the ridiculous, and to their fascination with names. That appeal is greatly enhanced by Ed Young's black-on-white illustrations, which suit the story perfectly.

Norman tells us that the story was told to him by George Wesukmin, who lived near Gods Lake in Northern Manitoba. "In his village," Norman says, "if you were not happy with the name your parents chose for you, you could try to earn a new name." Norman has spent a lot of time with the Swampy Crees, speaks Cree, and has translated their stories. He has published two collections of these translations, *The Wishing Bone Cycle*, and *Where the Chill Came From: Cree Windigo Tales & Journeys*.

This is one story for younger children that I recommend unequivocally.

North American Indian Travelling College

Legends of Our Nations

North American Indian
Travelling College
R.R. #3, Cornwall Island
Ontario K6H 5R7
1984; grades 5-up
Various Nations

Perhaps it is only possible to truly appreciate this book after having read hundreds of stories set down by non-Native "writers," in stilted, flat, pseudo-"primitive" prose, "adapted" for white audiences, or so de-natured, to conform to what is considered suitable for white children, as to have lost nearly all of their original meaning. Nothing could be more sharply contrasted to the mangling of our literature than the stories in *Legends of Our Nations.*

There are 26 legends here, that tell how things came to be as they are in the world, or carry lessons for us. They come as close, in their written versions, to actual telling as anything I have seen. Pick up and read anywhere, and see how easily the words come to be said. In these stories, the reality is still there, the mystery is still there. If you want to know something of the power of Native stories, to understand something of what they mean to us, this is as good a place to start as any, short of actually hearing them told.

The drawings are wonderful.

O'Dell, Scott

Black Star, Bright Dawn

Houghton Mifflin
1988; grades 5-7
Inuit

Bright Dawn lives with her mother, Mary K., and her father, Bartok, in Womengo, Alaska. When Bartok is trapped on an ice floe, he loses his courage, as well as some fingers, and can no longer stand the sight of the ocean. So the family moves inland, to Ikuma. When some of the influential men of the town see how good Bartok is with a dog team, they ask him to represent Ikuma in the Iditarod, the 1,000-mile Anchorage-to-Nome dogsled race. But Bartok breaks his shoulder in a practice run, and Bright Dawn takes his place. She does not come close to winning, but receives the $2,500 Sportsmanship Award, for going out of her way to help other "mushers."

One might well wonder why an elderly white man would choose to write from the point of view of a teenage Inuit— "Eskimo"—girl. There are writers able to put themselves into the mind and heart of another culture, or even sex, and make it believable. They are few, and Scott O'Dell is not one of them. He never has been. His characters are not living people, with all their complexities: they are "Eskimos." Oteg, for example, was

> an Eskimo from Fox Island...He was short and broad and when he walked he looked like a bear.

> Oteg did a dance in the snow. He shook the bundle of knives above his head and muttered, "Wind, who blows cold from the north, we've had enough of you... Speak to your sister, South Wind. See that she replies."

"'Water,' he said, 'is bad. It washes you away, bits at a time. Not good.'" "Bartok frowned. 'If that happens you will be a white girl, not an Eskimo girl. This, I do not like much. What are you now, Eskimo or white? One thing or the other?' 'Eskimo,' I said, to please him." "Mr. Weiss...was half Eskimo and half Tlingit Indian. It was the Tlingit part that made him rich."

Although Bartok is called "chief man of our village...the one that everyone listens to," he is a stubborn, impatient man. His character is so one-dimensional that it is hard to see what might have made him such a leader. The behaviors given to him are unbelievable for someone who is described as "the best hunter in our village." For example:

> remembering the winter when we were coming home and, just on the other side of Salmon Creek, Black Star pulled up and wouldn't move. My father took the whip to him and still he wouldn't move. Then my father walked out on the frozen creek and fell through the ice up to his neck.

Not a good way to achieve long life in the sub-Arctic.

The plot turns on a series of implausible events: Bright Dawn loses half her team when they run off to join a band of wolves, one of whom, she is sure, is Black Star's father, because he, like her lead dog, is white with a black face. She is attacked by moose, who, with "blazing eyes," lurk in wait for her at a bridge. Her dogs kill the male. She becomes stranded on an ice floe, luckily not too far from her home town, because it is her father who overcomes his fear of the ocean and comes to get her—and the seven dogs, and the sled—in a skiff.

O'Dell has made a career of writing books about "minorities." He has done very well from it. He has received the Newbery Award, the Jugendbuchpreis, twice, the Hans Christian Andersen Author Medal, and been a Newbery runner-up three times. *Island of the Blue Dolphin* and *The Black Pearl* were made into movies.

Maybe we could guess why he decided to write this book....

Okanagan Tribal Council

How Food Was Given
How Names Were Given
How Turtle Set the Animals Free

Armstrong, Jeannette

Neekna and Chemai

Theytus Books
P.O. Box 218
Penticton, B.C. V2A 6K3
1984; grades 3-up (younger for read-aloud)
Okanagan

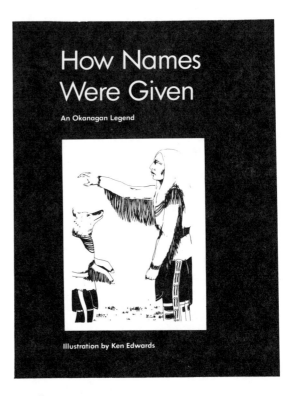

As part of the Okanagan Curriculum Project, the Okanagan Tribal Council has produced the *Kou-skelowh* (We Are the People) series. These four books were written for that project. Three are traditional stories; the fourth, *Neekna and Chemai,* is, in a sense, the context in which to place them, a way of showing how the lives of the People are lived according to the beliefs embodied in the stories.

How Food Was Given tells that, in the time before this world, the chiefs of the Animal and Plant People met together to decide how the People-To-Be would live and what they would eat. Skimgheest (Bear) said, "I will give myself and all the animals that I am chief over, to be food for the People-To-Be." The chiefs of the things that live in the water, of the roots under the ground, and the good things that grow above ground each said, "I will do the same."

"Chief Skimgheest was happy because there would be enough food...He said, 'Now I will lay down my life to make these things happen.'" So he did.

Simply written, simply illustrated, with line drawings more full of light and beauty than seems possible, this is a heart-shaking story. It shows clearly, and in a way even quite young children can understand, why no traditional Native person will ever kill *anything* without thanking the Life that is given so that she or he may also live.

How Names Were Given is a Coyote story. Coyote is determined to be first in line on the day of name-giving. All for naught, because the Great Spirit has plans for him, and when Coyote wakes up, he finds that all names but one have been given. He is heartbroken. "'Poor Coyote,' thought the Great Spirit, 'I can not let him feel so bad.'" And so he reveals the special job he has in mind.

How Names Were Given is funny, and very touching. It shows the love of Creator for all of his creatures, even—maybe especially—Coyote, that less-than-perfect perpetrator of a thousand sneaky tricks and deceits. It shows that there is a place for each of us, whether we understand it or not, and that each of us, for all of our lives, will walk in both light and shadow.

> Eagle was very fast. He raced all the Animal People and beat them...All...who lost...became Eagle's slaves. Eagle was chief of all the animals, except for Turtle who lived with his partner Muskrat. They were free because they were the only ones who did not race Eagle. They knew they could not run very fast, but one night Turtle had a dream. He was told, "You must race Eagle tomorrow to free the Animal People. They must be free when the People-To-Be come."

How Turtle Set the Animals Free is a deceptively simple story, carrying more meanings than may at first appear.

Neekna and Chemai are best friends, living in the Okanagan Valley, before the coming of the Europeans. Neekna tells of the four seasons of her people's year. Always, they follow the ways that have allowed them to survive upon the land.

> My people, remember this always...We must honor our relatives, the animals, the fish and the plants...If we...forget how important they are to us, we begin to destroy them. If their lives are in danger, so is ours, that is the law of the giver of Life. Remember that always.

For Neekna and Chemai, secure in the love and warmth of their People, all the world is a beautiful adventure. They learn the stories and lifeways from mothers, grandmothers, little mothers. They are at home in the world in a way that is inconceivable to modern, non-Native society. I think many non-Native children will envy them.

The drawings for all four books were done by Ken Edwards, and they add dimensions of both spirit and understanding to the stories.

The Okanagan Curriculum Project was designed to "create a better understanding between the Native and non-Native community." I don't see how it could help but be so. These stories are the gift of the Okanagan People to a world in sore need of what they have to offer. (Curriculum kits are available from the En'Owkin Centre, 257 Brunswick St., Penticton, B.C. V2A 5P9.)

Ortiz, Simon J.

The People Shall Continue

Children's Book Press
*1977; all grades
all Nations*

The People Shall Continue is the single best overview of Native History for younger children that I have ever seen. Ortiz is Acoma, and a poet, and it shows. In the words of Harriet Rohmer, the series editor, this is

> an epic story of Native American People …from the creation to the present day…it speaks in the rhythms of traditional oral narrative. Essentially, this is a teaching story, as are most Native American stories. Its purpose is to instill a sense of responsibility for life…the words of the story transmit the spirit of the People.

Just so. With simplicity, without polemic, Ortiz gives the true story of how it was, how it is, and—with hope and a little luck—maybe how it will come to be, for all of us.

Ortiz tells the names of heros—Popé, Tecumseh, Black Hawk, Crazy Horse, Osceola, Joseph, Sitting Bull, Captain Jack. He speaks of the constant betrayal, broken treaties, broken promises, the children taken away.

They took the children to boarding schools far from their homes and families. The children from the West were taken to the East. The children from the East were taken to the West. The People's children were scattered like leaves from a tree.

> Even so,

All this time, the People remembered. Parents told their children, "You are Shawnee. You are Lakota. You are Pima. You are Acoma. You are Tlingit. You are Mohawk. You are all these Nations of People."

Native life before the conquest is not romanticized:

> Nevertheless, life was always hard. At times, corn did not grow, and there was famine. At times, winters were very cold and there was hardship. At times, the winds blew hot and rivers dried.

Nor does Ortiz say that Indians are the only true Americans:

> The People looked around them and they saw Black People, Chicano People, Asian

People, many white People and others who were kept poor...The People saw that these People...shared a common life with them. The People realized they must share their history with them...they said..."We must make sure that life continues. We must be responsible to that life. With that humanity and the strength that comes from our shared responsibility for this life, the People shall continue."

The illustrations by Sharol Graves, who is Shawnee, Chippewa, and Sisseton, are vivid and stately, and perfect. If you give only one book about Native Americans to your young children, let this be the one.

Paige, Harry W.

Johnny Stands

Warne
1982; grades 5-7
Lakota

Johnny Stands is sitting on the front steps ("Some might call it a prairie shack, but he called it home.") when the social worker drives up. Miss Brady tells Johnny that his grandfather is too old to "provide" for him, and he's going to have to go live with his aunt in the city. When the grandfather, Stands Alone Against the Enemy, gets home, he and Johnny decide to "run away." This leads them into a variety of adventures.

None of it is exactly convincing, but never mind. It certainly does give the author the opportunity to show that he knows a lot about Indians, what their goals ought to be and what behaviors are appropriate to achieve them. Since Paige has been kind enough to give us the benefit of his expertise, it might be instructive to examine the things that can be learned from reading his book—about the Lakota in particular, and by inference, about Indians in general:

- They always refer to each other as "Indians," never as people, as in "Indians, including women and small children, sat on the rolled rugs lining the room."

- Real Indians, as opposed to militants, "mixed bloods" and other malcontents, talk and think in a sort of Early Jawbreaker. They say "It is good," and "hau!" all the time.

- "Mixed bloods" and militant people are not real Indians. They don't "speak Sioux." They talk like this: "Don't be chicken. We're modern warriors, and this is a fight... Sometimes people get hurt..."

- Medicine men are charlatans: "Old Enos Two-Feathers would give money to the 'yuwipi man' to tell him things that were not as true as his grandfather's words..."

- Native ceremonies are strange, savage rites: "The drums grew louder, and the singing rose to an ear-splitting pitch. The younger children screamed, frightened by the darkness and the wild cries of the singers."

- Real Indians can only be happy down on the reservation: "A Lakota in the city is a Lakota lost—I can see that now. He is only half-alive...you must go home again if you want to find your strength."

On the other hand,

- It is only in the white man's world that Indians can learn "the right things to do." In the end, Johnny Stands realizes that "he couldn't go home again...You couldn't step in the same river twice." [Honestly. It really does say that]. Johnny had to "learn what was right and good, and he would come back and tell his people." But Native people cannot solve their own problems anyway. It has to be done for them by members of the white power structure.

The book as a whole seems to have been written from a position of near-total ignorance and with a complete lack of sensitivity. It is also very badly written. There is no attempt at consistent characterization, only stereotypes and clichés. The text is peppered with the 38 Lakota words the author knows, some used in a fashion that must surely be unique. And there is always an immediate "translation"; some of these are unique, too.

**Patacsil, Sharon,
   and Colleen Neal**

*Daybreak Star Preschool
Activities Book*

Daybreak Star Press
*1979; grades ps-2
all Nations*

The Activities Book is a teacher's guide, to provide children with the opportunity to learn from materials that are reflective of the cultures of all children. The Native American child is provided the opportunity to develop a positive self-image...At the same time...[use of] these kinds of materials builds in the non-Indian child an awareness and sensitivity towards a culture that is different from her/his own.

There are instructions and clearly drawn designs for number cards, puzzles, lotto games and a variety of other materials. Excellent.

Poatgieter, Hermina

Indian Legacy: Native American Influences on World Life and Cultures

Messner
1981, grades 7-up
all Nations

U.S. history books, particularly those for children, frequently have a chapter on "our" Indian heritage. That is essentially what Indian Legacy is about. The standard acknowledgements are made—foods, medicines, sports, the influence of the Iroquois League on the formation of the U.S. government, etc. The chapter "Lessons in Conservation from the First Americans" attempts to deal with the spiritual relationship with the Earth that was central to pre-conquest civilizations in the Western hemisphere—and its importance for the survival of modern humanity.

The writing is an odd mixture of honesty and insensitivity. Many statements show a respect for Native peoples and cultures. The author speaks of Indian leaders with respect and notes that "most... Indian peoples...held democratic beliefs that were not common among English colonists... This love of liberty eventually began to rub off on the colonists." The Europeans are named as invaders who completely disrupted a way of life that had been successful for millennia.

But contemporary tribal leaders are most notable for their absence; also missing is any discussion of the pressures to which Native peoples are now being subjected in both North and South America. The primary focus remains on those things that have been of material benefit to whites, and the book reinforces the notion that Native people are for the most part no longer a vital presence in the Americas.

There is a great deal of information here of the kind frequently sought for traditional school assignments, and the book is temptingly easy to use. It contains nothing, however, that cannot be searched out in other sources. Those concerned about the attitudes children learn from books might be advised to help them to do so.

The author has dedicated her book "to the American Indian children, who should know the great gifts that their people have given the world." If we really were incapable of telling our children the things that they need to know, this would not be my first choice of a book to hand them.

Rock Point Community School

Between Sacred Mountains: Navajo Stories and Lessons from the Land

Rock Point Community School
Chinle, AZ 86503
Grades 3-up
Diné/Navajo

Between Sacred Mountains

If I had to pick one book to act as an antidote to all the garbage that has been printed and said about the Diné, this would be it. The book has history, culture, stories, pictures, maps—the works, even a satellite photo of Diné Bikéyah, Navajo Country. The chapter headings are: Land, Plant Watchers, Hunters, Anasazi, Ancestors, Spaniards, War and Reservation, Peace and Livestock, Stock and People, Navajos and Hopis, Modern Times, Remember the Land, and The Future.

The book is dedicated to

the young people of Diné Bikéyah, who will decide its future...Look on all the land as our land. All things on it and all people that are on it are in our care. Our songs and ceremonies call us caretakers of this land for all people. We have been taught to take care of this land in this way so that all people will benefit and all living things.

Rohmer, Harriet, Octavio Chow and Morris Viadure

The Invisible Hunters/Los Cazadores Invisibles

Children's Book Press
1987; all grades
Miskito

Rohmer, Harriet and Dorminster Wilson

Mother Scorpion Country/La Tierra de la Madre Escorpión

Children's Book Press
1987; all grades
Miskito

Children's Book Press, which publishes "Fifth World Tales, stories for all children from the many peoples of America," is noted for its high quality bilingual stories, and is strongly recommended for its sensitivity and lack of racism. Publisher and author Rohmer's latest are two Miskito stories, authenticated by travelling into the war zone in Nicaragua and seeking out Miskito Elders.

Invisible Hunters chronicles the crucial first moment of contact between indigenous peoples and the outside world. Three Miskito brothers encounter the magical Dar vine, which gives them the power of invisibility, on the condition that they always use hunting sticks and never sell what they catch. They soon become famous hunters, and all goes well, until they meet the strangers, who talk the hunters into using guns and selling the wari meat. Soon, the brothers are hunting with guns, selling the meat and refusing it to those who

cannot pay, and disrespecting their Elders. By following the strangers' ways, and forgetting their own, they break their promise to the Dar, which exacts its own suitable revenge.

In *Mother Scorpion Country*, a legend reflecting the matriarchal traditions of pre-Christian Nicaragua, a young and grief-stricken husband, Naklili, follows his wife, Kati, to the land of the dead, Mother Scorpion country. Even though Mother Scorpion takes pity on him and allows him to stay, he belongs to the land of the living and cannot share Kati's paradise. The trees that Kati sees as filled with golden bananas and ripe coconuts, Naklili sees only as "the skeletons of trees that had died centuries before." He must go back.

Because Naklili has been forbidden to tell about the land of the dead, the people become suspicious of him. More and more lonely, he thinks of the string of beads in his doorway that Kati has promised him he need only touch in order to return to her.

His relations gasped in horror. Coiled above Naklili's fingers was a poisonous snake. 'Naklili,' they cried. But Naklili did not even feel the snake bite him. He heard Mother Scorpion call his name...he knew that Kati was waiting for him.

Both *The Invisible Hunters* and *Mother Scorpion Country* are moving legends of the People. The illustrations are brilliant and beautiful, and both books, as well as the others in the Fifth World series, belong in every library collection. Write for a catalog.

Roth, Susan L.

Kanahéna, a Cherokee Story

St. Martin's Press
1988; grades 2-3
Cherokee

When you see that this book is praised by a professor of anthropology, you sort of know where it's going to go...

An old woman is stirring a pot over an open fire. A little girl asks her what she's up to. Kanahéna, real kanahéna, is the answer.

> "No one makes it now, no one but me...Kanahéna is the real food of the Cherokees. Come sit with me, child...I'll tell you a story about Kanahéna and Terrapin. It's an old Cherokee story, about an old Cherokee food. Hominy, you call it, or cornmeal mush, the oldest old Cherokee food."

I guess we know she's Cherokee. And old.

Terrapin and Possum are out looking for persimmons. Possum is throwing them down, but Bad Wolf comes along and jumps in front of Terrapin and eats them all. But he chokes on a really big one, and Terrapin cuts off his ears for Kanahéna spoons. "'Strange,'

thought Terrapin's friends, 'strange.'" I guess.

Well, the wolves get wind of all this, and come after Terrapin.

> "We'll throw you into the deepest part of the river where you will drown," said the Other Wolves [No, I don't know why it's capitalized] "Oh, no, not THAT!" begged Terrapin. "Not the deep, deep water! Not the..."

Well, you know how it goes.

> "Did you like the Cherokee story?" asked the woman. "Yes," said the child, "but did Bad Wolf die?" "Maybe he just lost his ears, that old Bad Wolf [This is a non-violent story...]." "What about your Kanahéna? It's ready to eat now." "Alright," said the little girl. "But I want to eat with a regular spoon."

"A beautiful job of retelling a traditional Indian story in a way accessible to modern children but without compromising the essential Indianness of the original," the professor of anthropology says—some real new material, here.

The illustrations here are collages, using "natural materials," and they are ugly. The old woman looks like a superannuated hippy, with long fuzzy cotton hair, a brown ("leather"?) mini-skirt, and a headband. The possum looks just exactly like a cat.

Corn meal mush is not exactly a rarely cooked food in the U.S., and it is not the same thing as hominy. Hominy is made by soaking kernels of corn in lye, until they are soft and white.

Oh, yes. There is a recipe. I tried it; what you get is instant glue. This is a terrible book.

Siberell, Anne

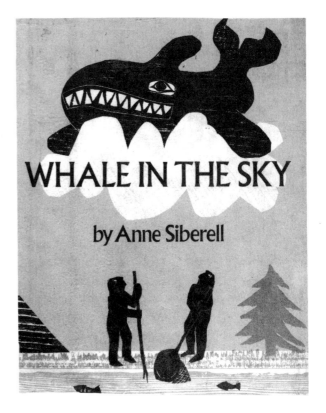

Whale in the Sky

Dutton
1982; grades ps-1
Northwest Coast Nations

This is a loose retelling of a "Northwest coast story," Nation unspecified. I always wonder, when writers don't happen to mention where they got their stories, whether they are afraid we might go back and check up on them. Anyway, there are not "Northwest coast stories," any more than there are "Indian" stories. There are Haida, Tlingit, Tsimshian, Kwakiutl, etc., stories. Siberell says, "Sometimes a chief would hire an artist to carve a story in pictures on the trunk of a giant tree...the carved tree (was) called a totem pole." As a piece of information, this is so grossly over-simplified as to be meaningless. Carving was done for a variety of reasons. There were house, ancestor and funeral poles, and since these cultures suffered the same fate as all other Native ones, not even the People themselves can always say now what they mean. For Siberell to say that *"Whale in the Sky* is such a story," makes me wonder if she didn't see a "totem pole" some place, and make the whole thing up.

This is the story: Thunderbird sees Whale gobbling up Salmon in the river, which makes Frog afraid. Frog tells Raven, who tells Thunderbird, who grabs Whale and drops him on top of a mountain. Whale promises to keep out of the river, so Thunderbird lets him go back to the sea. "The chief of the people told this tale to the carver. The carver made the story into a totem pole. Thunderbird holds Whale, while Raven watches over Salmon and Frog." The end.

The book is illustrated with colored woodcuts, which bear a *very* superficial resemblance to the art of Coastal peoples. The human beings in the pictures look vaguely Hawai'ian (forgive me, my Kamaaina sisters and brothers) and the final cut, of the finished totem pole, is worthy of gracing any tourist-trap "Indian" trading post. The Thunderbird is clearly not a Thunderbird, but a bald eagle. The "chief" is walking around with a mask on *top* of his head. The Frog, as with many creatures who live in more than one world, has a special significance, and for the Haida People at least, a generative force that would make its shape on the pole one utterly different than the one given to it by Siberell.

It is not that non-Native people should *never* try to do Native stories. It is that, if they are going to, they should at least learn enough so that they are not going to trash someone else's culture.

Speare, Elizabeth George

The Sign of the Beaver

Dell
1983; grades 4-7
Nation unspecified

It is 1768. Matt's father must return to Massachusetts for Matt's mother, sister, and the new baby. Until they arrive, Matt will be alone at the new Maine cabin. After Matt encounters a series of disasters, culminating in an attack by a swarm of angry bees, Saknis and his grandson, Attean, come to Matt's rescue. When Matt offers Saknis his only book—*Robinson Crusoe*—in return for all they have done for him, Saknis asks Matt to teach Attean to read. The boys become friends, although not easily.

I do not know whether Speare feels that she has broken new ground; her approach is the standard one for "Indian" adventure novels, since *Last of the Mohicans*.

The relationship between the two boys is uneven from the start. Attean and his grandfather save Matt's life, befriend him, give him gifts, teach him everything he needs to survive, and even invite him to go north with them for the winter hunt. When they leave, Attean even gives Matt his beloved dog. In return, Matt gives Attean his grandfather's silver watch—"His father would never understand"—and, "probably, Matt thought, Attean would never learn to use it." In the end, Saknis, Attean and their people fade conveniently into the sunset, never to return, driven from their ancestral lands by the encroaching whitemen. And Matt never does manage to teach Attean to read. But it doesn't matter: "'What for I read? My grandfather mighty hunter. My father mighty hunter. They not read.'"

At no point in the book are the Native characters allowed to speak in other than this grade-B movie pidgin. "'That our way. All Indian understand.'" Attitudes toward women are those usually drawn by white writers.

Matt's weeding is "squaw work." Attean's sister says of herself: "'Attean think squaw girl no good for much.'" And, when Attean kills a bear: "'Belong squaw now,' he said. 'I go tell.' 'You mean a squaw is going to carry that heavy thing?' 'Cut up meat, then carry. Squaw work.'"

The feast following the bear killing is a wild and barbaric event, half terrifying, half silly. Attean comes for Matt.

> With an ugly chill against his backbone, Matt stared at the hideously painted face. Then he recognized Attean..."What's the war paint for?" he demanded. "Not war paint...Squaws make feast with bear. My grandfather say you come."

They arrive at the village. "Then he was aware of Indians. They sat silently on either side of the fire, their painted faces ghastly in the flickering light." Matt is welcomed. "In a sudden terrifying yell the rows of Indians echoed the greeting. 'Ta ho,' they shouted." Attean acts out the killing of the bear, and the "savage rites" begin.

> Then began a sound that sent a tingle, half dread and half pleasure down Matt's spine. A lone Indian leaped to the head of the line...He strutted and pranced in ridiculous contortions, for all the world like a clown in a village fair.

And so on. This scene bears little relationship to the leisurely feasting, and ceremonious dancing, that would actually have occurred on such an occasion. The only thing that Speare has gotten half right is the teasing and good humor with which the story of Matt's part in the killing of the bear is received.

There is evidence that Speare has done some research; but her use of the words she has learned is often inappropriate. "E'he," for instance, is not a word of acquiescence, as in "'E'he,' Attean agreed," but of approbation, of congratulations, of honoring.

One scene is quite disturbing. The boys come upon a fox, caught in an iron trap. Although Attean agrees that it is a cruel way to trap an animal, he will not free the fox, because

the trap is set on the "hunting ground" of another clan.

> "We can't just let it suffer," Matt protested. "Suppose no one comes for days?"

> "Then fox get away."

> "How can he get away?"

> "Bite off foot."

> Indeed, Matt could now see that the creature had already gnawed its own flesh down to the bone.

> "Leg mend soon," Attean added..."Fox have three leg beside."

How could a child think anything except that the speaker of such words really is a savage at heart? This is absolutely contrary to all Native teachings. To cause an animal unnecessary pain was—and is—an unforgivable violation of the compact between the humans and the four-leggeds.

Stories of Indians, of living with Indians, of friendships between Indians and whites, have strong appeal for children. Unless the writing is truly godawful, a book based on such a theme is assured a wide readership, and critical acclaim.

The author who chooses to write on a topic of compelling interest to children has, I believe, a more than ordinary obligation to write the most honest and revealing book of which she is capable. The popularity of *The Indian in the Cupboard* cannot have been lost on Elizabeth Speare, because children's book authors all do know about each other's work.

I feel that Speare has succumbed to the temptation to deal in sure-fire American Indian stereotypes, rather than to risk the controversy of portraying the Native People of Maine as they really were, and their lives, as they actually lived them.

One last thing: in Speare's book, the People have no name. But they did not go away. They are still here. I know this to be true, because I have friends among them.

Steltzer, Ulli

A Haida Potlach

University of Washington Press
1984; grades 4-up
Haida

Ulli Steltzer's invitation read:

You are invited to witness the naming of xa. adaa 7laa git'lang 7isis (children of the good people) and the adoption of Joe David to the t'sa.ahl 7laanaas Tribe. November 6 & 7 1981, George M. Dawson School, Masset, B.C.

As a family friend, Steltzer asked how she could help. "You could take the photographs," Robert Davidson said. And so *Haida Potlach* was born.

There have been many misconceptions about potlaches, among anthropologists and historians, as well as "laypeople." The potlach has been interpreted as the willful wasting of goods and resources in the quest for personal aggrandizement, and a major cause of the "downfall" of Northwest Coast societies. In actuality, of course, potlaches are ceremonials of great meaning for Coastal Peoples. This fact was very clearly understood by the white governments which made them illegal.

The word "potlach" is not a Haida word. It derives from a similar sounding word...meaning 'to give'...and was... applied to any ceremonial distribution of property...A potlach may be the creation of one person, but it requires the participation, the help, the goodwill of many others to carry it out.

Robert Davidson, grandson of Florence Edenshaw Davidson, and a well-known artist, gave his first potlach in 1969, on the occasion of the raising of the village totem pole. It took "about a year and a half" to prepare for his second one. This book is the story of that period of time, as well as of the event itself.

Although in no way meant to be a children's book, *A Haida Potlach* is one of those books that can speak to all ages. The photographs are wonderful, and, with their captions, give a very clear idea of what is going on. The text, taken mostly from videotapes made on the two nights of the potlach, and later interviews with the participants, is simply and clearly written. A knowledgeable teacher could easily use this book with children from about grade four and up.

On the first night of the potlach, Susan Davidson says,

> I am the mother of two Haida children, and I am proud to be with you now. When I hear different speakers say, tonight, the Haida people have only their culture and their heritage, I want to say that the Haida people have their children. I am proud to be part of this Haida family that comes together to celebrate all of their children. We are here to remember the strength and the sharing of our family and we do it for ourselves and for our children.

This beautiful book can teach, perhaps better than the most detailed lesson plan, about a complex Native society, its traditions—maintained and reborn against all-but-impossible odds—and the humanity of its People.

St. Paul Community Programs in the Arts and Sciences

Angwamas Minosewag Anishinabeg—Time of the Indian

Indian Country Press
292 Walnut
Irving Park Offices
St. Paul, MN 55102
*1977; grades 5-up
various Nations*

The Red School House, in Minnesota, has published a number of titles through Indian Country Press. This one is a collection of writings by young people, ages 9 to 18, with one longer poem by Edward Benton-Banai, director of the school. There are some wonderful photographs of children, and line drawings.

> The people were created
> sacred.
> There was a gift within them.
> A sound to make.
> A song.
> A praising to the creator of All
> Things.
> A voice of Thanksgiving.

> The centers within them were
> very strong.
> When they spoke
> they addressed the Creator.
> When they spoke
> they spoke to All things.
> The vibration of voice was
> Powerful.

> This is language.

Dorene Day, age 17

That's what it's about. If you truly have an interest in knowing what real Native peoples—as opposed to Anglo fantasies—are about, this beautiful book is a good place to start.

Staheli, Julie West

Kachinas: Color and Cut-Out Collection

Troubador Press (Price/Stern/Sloan)
1984; grades 1-4
Hopi

The idea of "Indian" coloring books seems a little too much like genuine Big Chief Indian headdresses made in Hong Kong, YMCA Indian Princess programs, and all the other similar rip-offs of Native American cultures with which we are familiar. *Kachinas* ("adapted from Hopi originals") comes close to being in that category, not so much because of what it includes, as in what it leaves out. The only information about Kachina dolls and their meaning for Hopi people appears in a four-sentence paragraph on the title page. The figures themselves—to be colored and cut out—are of course simplified; the illustrations give the name of the doll, coloring instructions and, occasionally, a brief additional "explanation" ("Sip-ikne is a reminder of ancient wars" reads one).

Kachina dolls are used to teach Hopi children about their people's beliefs: this is very different from using them to provide recreation for the children of another culture.

Steptoe, John

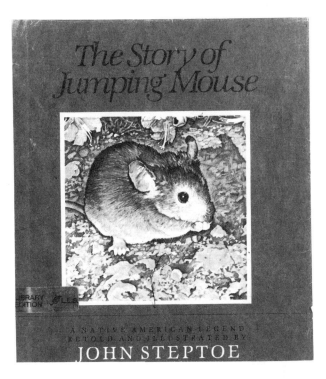

The Story of Jumping Mouse

Lothrop
1984; grades ps-3
Northern Plains Nations

A young mouse, although warned that the journey would be long and perilous, sets off to find the "far-off land." On the way he meets various beings in need, and gives pieces of himself away, until, arriving at the far-off land, he can neither see nor smell. For his unselfish and loving spirit, he is given a new name: "You are now called Eagle, and you will live in the far-off land forever."

John Steptoe is a wonder. From his first *Stevie*, written at age 16, each of his books has been a beautiful and original work of art. He grows. *Jumping Mouse* is his version of a Northern Plains story that he heard many years ago. "It has haunted me...I know that I've included many things that are my own...that is what a storyteller does in the oral tradition. I owe a debt of gratitude to the original storytellers. I think they would have understood me." I think he is right, because Steptoe has understood the spirit of this story. Although he has made no attempt to achieve an anthropological exactitude, this is an honorable book. The pictures, in black and white, are completely different from anything Steptoe has ever done before. From the first little mouse, in his minute world of flowers and grasses, to the last, of the newly-created, soaring eagle, silhouetted blackly against the fiery sun, they are so luminous that they raise the hair on the back of my neck. They add immeasurably to the wondrousness of the story.

The heart that is not moved by *Jumping Mouse* is made of stone. Thank you, John.

Strete, Craig Kee

When Grandfather Journeys into Winter

Greenwillow
1979; grades 4-6
Nation unspecified

The Bleeding Man and Other Stories

Greenwillow
1977; grades 8-up
Nation unspecified

Craig Strete has written a number of stories that, for want of a better term, might be called science fiction. That seems appropriate, since so much of the Native American story is surreal, to say the very least. Many of them are bitter and painful; the writing is wonderful. "A Sunday Visit with Grandfather" is one of the funniest stories I have ever read, and "When They Find You," one of the saddest. *The Bleeding Man* was brought out as a children's book, with a forward by Virginia Hamilton, but it really isn't—or at least is not just for children. Anyone reading Strete's stories will know something of what it can feel like to be Indian in America, right now.

Grandfather is more directly a children's story. Little Thunder's beloved Grandfather rides the unridable horse at the Horsebreaking, to win him for his grandson. It is Tayhua's last ride, and Little Thunder must come to terms with the fact that his Grandfather is going to die. Tayhua helps the boy, to do that just as he has with so many other things. This lovely book is a little marred, for me, by the way Little Thunder and Tayhua talk about the boy's mother, Elk Woman.

> There was a shrieking noise. It was somebody female yelling for Tayhua and Little Thunder...it sounded like a loose fanbelt on a '57 Chevy...Tayhua covered his ears..."One of these days my two-legged screech owl of a daughter is going to call us for supper and her yelling will make the whole house fall on her head."

This is funny; there are people who sound like that, but maybe Strete was too young when he wrote it to realize that this lady doesn't have any easy road with these two guys. Not all of her is this negative.

The huge plus of *Grandfather* is that it is about the lives of Native people, now, as they are lived. It shows that, despite real hardships, Native values have been retained, and have meaning and viability, even in the 20th century. The author's tribal affiliation is not given.

TallMountain, Mary

Green March Moons

New Seed Press
1987; grades 5-up
Koyukon

mary tallmountain

Tashyana is an 11-year-old Koyukon girl, just coming into her womanhood. The whiteman's flu has taken her father, along with many other people. Before, "there was lots of laughing in their house." Tash has an uncle, Vaska: "Uncle didn't smile much, but when he did, it wasn't really a smile. There were cold lights behind his eyes. Tash always felt a chill when he grinned at her."

Tash is a skilled trapper, and at first things do not go badly. But in December, her mother starts losing her appetite. "She's lost too many, your three brothers. You don't remember," Aunt tells Tash. When Rayu dies, Tash is at the mercy of Uncle Vaska:

> He gave her a brash, bold glance that traveled down her body and lingered upon her newly forming breasts and round thighs. She was frightened. No one had ever looked at her so.

After a night of drinking, Uncle Vaska comes to Tash's cabin and rapes her with great brutality. In the morning, Aunt comes, knowing what has happened, saying nothing, but thinking much: "My little girl...For what she has endured...I must not let her know I see how she has been hurt." Aunt will arrange for Tash to live with "old Philomena."

> Seeing it was almost day, they went outside...It was silent all around, and the world was made of moving light. Full out to the edges of the land, snow shimmered in waves of metal fire...They gave quick little indrawn breaths of wonder. Then Aunt groaned. "Oh, it's been a terrible winter."

This is a tragic story. One's first reaction is to say that it is not for children, but things like this happen to them all the time. Because we hate it, we want to say that writing about it on their level is not suitable. But when a terrible thing has happened, attention must be paid. The very least we can do, is not to turn away.

Because the writing in *Green March Moons* is so beautiful, its effect is all the more devastating. I think every adult who must work with a child who has been so brutalized, should be required to read this book, to understand.

Here is Tash before:

She appeared older than her years because her mouth sloped naturally down at the corners...She was serious and dreamy most of the time, and she wore such a dignified air that Rayu and Kobayo laughingly called her Little Old Woman. But sometimes when she was bursting with joy her eyes were shining blackberries under her thick shaggy bangs.

And here is Tash after:

She stood up. Her steps were small. She bent stiffly to the water bucket and poured water into a pan...With a rough cloth she scrubbed herself all over. Her face dripping, she kept scrubbing until she was sure she was clean. She... wrapped herself in an old dress of Rayu's...she hugged Rayu's dress closer. Then she rested her head on her arms.

The telling of Tashyana's story is powerful in its simplicity, and the illustrations, by Joseph E. Senungetuk, suit it perfectly. With great poignancy, Mary TallMountain tells us that awful things happen to people, especially the innocent.

Sometimes, nothing can be done about it, and we have to keep going, just the same. In the real world, in which children live, that's often the way it is.

Tapahonso, Luci

A Breeze Swept Through

West End Press
P.O. Box 27334
Albuquerque, NM 87125
1987; grades 6-up
Diné/Navajo

These are lovely poems, both lyrical and strong. They reflect a life so deeply rooted that, reading them, it is almost possible to believe what the Elders say—that the last 500 years is only a time, and that the Navajos, at least, will be here long and long after the white man, with all his machines, has blown himself to glory.

These poems would be good to use with non-Native young people, because there is no "hostility" and little of the anger of which young—and not-so-young!—Native writers are so often accused. Just the beauty that comes from knowing who you are forever. There is much love in these poems, as to say, "Oh, yes. This is how it was supposed to be."

Did I forget to say that Luci Tapahonso is a very accomplished writer?

Tohono O'odham Tribal Council

Tohono O'odham: Lives of the Desert People

Tohono O'odham
Education Department
P.O. Box 837
Sells, AZ 85634
1984; grades 3-up
Tohono O'odham/Papago

Tohono O'odham are the people that most of us know as Papago. This book begins, properly enough, with the Creation story. Land, farming, gathering, hunting, dress and lifeways are discussed. Both past and present are considered.

One really nice thing is that songs are included: Song of the Elder Brother After He Had Created the Spirits of Men, Song After Emerging from Ashes Hill, songs for hunting, for success in a race, songs for singing up the corn, a lullaby. Song is an integral part of all Native ceremonials, and so here, the context is given.

Tohono O'odham are a people who have lived for a very long time in right relation to a place that most of us would consider difficult, at best. This book reflects that relation, beautifully. A powerful symbol of the People is The Man in the Maze:

> The figure, like the O'odham, seeks the deeper meaning of life...the center of the circle stands for that deeper meaning... the figure, like the O'odham, must struggle and work hard...This book is about the O'odham journey...it is about how the people lived long ago. It is also about the stories, songs and ways of doing things which the older O'odham still teach their children.

Their book is a first choice for use with young children.

Trimble, Stephen, and Harvey Lloyd

Our Voices, Our Land

Northland Press
1986; all grades
Southwestern Nations

Northland has published a number of attractively produced books on aspects of Native American history and culture. Most are outside the scope of this work. *Our Voices, Our Land* was designed as a "thirty-minute, continuously-running, multi-screen, multi-media production" to serve as an introduction to the Heard Museum's permanent exhibit, "Native Peoples of the Southwest."

Apart from the introduction, and various afterwords, the entire text is in the words of Native people who live in this part of the country. That is what makes the book so good to use with children. The words are clear, and give a better sense of the people who speak them than do a thousand pages of anthropological expertise. There are seven sections: The Land, Sustenance, Family, Community, Ceremony, Artists, and Continuity. The photographs are beautiful and of high quality.

One word of caution: *Our Voices, Our Land* would be an easy book to misuse. Do not, because of its great beauty, romanticize the people who are speaking. There is something to be learned here, if you allow yourself to listen to what they are saying.

Troll Associates

Fleischer, Jane

Pontiac: Chief of the Ottawas

Ottawa

Sitting Bull: Warrior of the Sioux

Dakota

Tecumseh: Shawnee War Chief

Shawnee

Jassem, Kate

Chief Joseph: Leader of Destiny

Nez Percé

Pocahontas: Girl of Jamestown

Pamunkey

Sacajawea: Wilderness Guide

Shoshone

Squanto: The Pilgrim Adventure

Patuxet

Oppenheim, Joanne

Black Hawk: Frontier Warrior

Mesquakie/Sauk

Osceola: Seminole Warrior

Miccosukee/Seminole

Sequoyah: Cherokee Hero

Cherokee

All published in 1979; grades 3-5

Troll Associates has published a series of easy biographies of Native Americans who come up more or less routinely in school assignments.

Good material on any or all of these people would be more than welcome, but what we have here is formula non-fiction. Their lives, and the circumstances surrounding them, have been so sanitized, so white-washed, as to have lost all meaning. All of these books are filled with made-up conversations; in the case of *Pocahontas*, *Sacajawea* and *Squanto*, most of the rest is made up, too. Practically the only hint of authenticity is—one more time—Joseph's "I will fight no more forever" speech.

I can understand that an author might want to spare young children some of the grislier aspects of the history of Indian-white relations. But to refer, as Fleischer does in *Sitting Bull*, to the murder of more than 200, mostly unarmed, people in the following way, is just plain dishonest:

> Not long afterward, the Indian war drums were silenced at the Battle of Wounded Knee.

It is clear that some effort has been made to show the ways in which Native Peoples have suffered at the hands of white governments. But there is no sense that what was done to the Native population of America was *wrong*. Their inevitable defeat by superior numbers and "civilization" is a strong underlying theme. Even when Indians fight back, their fight is made to seem foolish, and their defeat is a foregone conclusion. In *Osceola* :

> By the summer of 1836, Osceola held most of Western Florida. But he felt no joy. His people were growing tired of war. They no longer had homes. Their families were gone.
>
> Many Seminole Indians had died. Many more were sent west of the Mississippi to live.

Would it have been too much to add that, on this journey hundreds died, because they were denied food, clothing, medical attention, and rest?

The illustrations, for the most part, suit the texts. In *Pocahontas*, for instance, "Powhatan" wears a full Plains-style eagle-feather bonnet—all the time. And although there are enough photographs of both Joseph and Tatanka Iotanka ("Sitting Bull"), none of the drawings bears even superficial resemblance to the real people.

These books feed directly into the myths of superiority and infallibility of white American institutions, myths that are force-fed to children in school. They are not recommended.

Wallin, Luke

Ceremony of the Panther

Bradbury Press
1987; gr. 7- up
Miccosukee/Seminole

Moses Raincrow has killed a panther—a rare, endangered, protected, and very much illegal, Everglades panther. He has done this because Grandmother Mary is severely ill with the deer sickness, and only the medicine of the panther will cure her. His son, John, is with him, because, "without John's vision, they never would have found him." The Endangered Species Task Force agent knows that Moses has been looking for a panther, and he and his assistants are waiting for him. Moses is arrested.

It is within this framework that Luke Wallin sets his story of John Raincrow's uncertainty about himself—who he is, and what his future may be. Told in the form of a long flashback to the events leading up to Moses Raincrow's arrest, it is a story of conflict—between white and Indian, between John and his father. Moses wrestles alligators for tourists as a living, and John can't stand the idea. He sees no future for himself, because he is both poor and Indian, so he uses the drugs, and drinks the beer that his friend, Max Poor Bear, provides for him. Max is Coyote for John. He has a power about him that John cannot resist, and all of it is bad. After a night of crisis, Moses takes John back to the reservation and leaves him with his Great-Grandmother. Both Moses and John have some things to work out.

Luke Wallin writes well, but for a Native reader, the rhythm is off. The title is misleading, there is no ceremony here. The author does not allow time for it. Although it is easy to tell that Wallin's sympathies lie with the Miccosukee people, there are jarring notes: "The old Miccosukee world was a dangerous place [compared to what, I wonder], full of spirits and enemies and magical warfare." He tells us that Grandmother Mary "had been a great medicine woman," and refers to her "spells." Native rites are no more "spells" than are the ceremonies of the Judeo-Christian tradition.

Faces are "wide" and "bronze": Grandmother Mary's face is "wide and copper-colored, a classic Miccosukee face." Does Wallin *really* know any copper- or bronze-colored Indians?

Moses says of Grandmother Mary:

"But when she starts up about her soul wandering...and wants those old songs... that's a lot more complicated. Takes time. I can't just snap my fingers and dance around the fire like some witch doctor in a movie!"

It is very hard to believe that a traditional medicine person would talk about sacred things in such a flip way.

Wallin is careful to draw the line between killing from need—"when we need meat...when we need medicine"— and "killing everything that moves." The Endangered Species guy is a fool—no other word for it—who, through his inept attempts to tag the male panther, manages to kill his pregnant mate. Nevertheless, Wallin writes so beautifully about the animals that the young reader can only feel that Moses has indeed done great wrong to kill the panther. He puts the stamp on the "wrongness" of what he has done, when, even though the great stag has come to him, John Raincrow chooses not to shoot it. In Native traditions, this is a great violation of

the compact between humans and the four-leggeds. John has been given the dream; he has been given a song. "At the thought of the buck, he imagined a strange whistling sound that seemed important." If Wallin knows this much, how does he not also know that you cannot turn away from such a Giving? It is, perhaps—who knows?—time for a new compact, but that is not for me, nor for Luke Wallin, to say.

Many young Indians *do* go through periods of rebelliousness and questioning, particularly under pressures from the dominant society. The family relationships that Wallin delineates seem more contrivances to further his plot than the result of any inner necessity. Grandmother Mary does not seem believable, for a medicine woman of her years. She is petulant and demanding, with none of the inner light such Elders have: "Grandmother Mary wasted no time in bringing up tribal traditions," but she does not so much teach John, as nag at him.

And finally, many Native people will know that *Ceremony of the Panther* is strongly based on a true incident. I believe that the author should have said so—he could have done that easily, without naming names—rather than saying, "any references to historical events; to real people... or to real locales are intended only to give the fiction a setting in historical reality." Luke Wallin may indeed have "shared...a long struggle... to participate correctly in another spiritual tradition." For this reader, he has attempted to draw contrasts between modern and traditional ways of living, without being able to give the spirit and feel of it.

Wallin, Luke

In the Shadow of the Wind

Bradbury
1984; grades 6-up
Creek

It is 1835. Caleb McElroy is white, living a hardscrabble life with his mother and Grandfather in the Nation (the area that became Alabama). Pine Basket is Creek, living with her mother June Duck Moon, her brother Six Deer and her Grandfather Brown Hawk. Caleb and Pine Basket are both 16. By the end of the novel, they have lost nearly everything except each other; Pine Basket, because of the white greed for Indian lands, Caleb because he is naive enough to believe that justice should be the same for all. The working out of their interwoven destinies is a complicated story, firmly set in the historical context and drawing in all societal elements of the time.

After Caleb and his family have moved to "the Judge's" plantation, he and his Grandfather do some work with a young slave, Big Robert. When Caleb finds Six Deer near death in a blizzard (a *bit* unusual for Alabama), his Grandfather asks Big Robert to hide the boy. The Judge finds out: Caleb

and Six Deer flee, Caleb returns, after seeing Six Deer safely home, to learn that Robert has been tortured but did not "tell on" the whites. To what purpose, one wonders, since the Judge *knows* Caleb was the one who brought Six Deer in.

Often, one is conscious of the heavy hand of the writer, manipulating plot and character. Here, I think Wallin's intent was to contrast Robert's strength, his sense of himself and the realities of life, with Caleb, who at this point in the novel has a road yet to go. One senses a beautiful reality about Robert, however, that seems to come through almost by accident. I want to know what became of him. Did he survive? Did he escape? He has the spiritual strength for it, as well as the physical. Robert didn't "tell," not because he was "mighty loyal," but for his own honor. I wish this had come across a little more clearly, and that it didn't seem so much as though this Black character was created only in order to make some sort of statement.

There are some other problems. "Bad" Indians still tend to be those who are hostile to whites. On the other hand, the novel gains as it goes, and there are moments of real beauty. The Native peoples have an identity—Creek—and a town and culture of their own; they are not just "the Indians." The pain in the book is real, and when Caleb and Six Deer finally catch up with the men responsible for the abduction and terrible suffering of Pine Basket and her mother, there is no nonsense about "forgiveness." Retribution is swift, just and final.

In the Shadow of the Wind is one of those odd books that is better than it deserves to be. It is also better than many so-called "historical" novels about the Native-white experience. What is really different is that the author, although not from a Native background himself, makes no excuses for the whites' behavior.

Weeks, Rupert

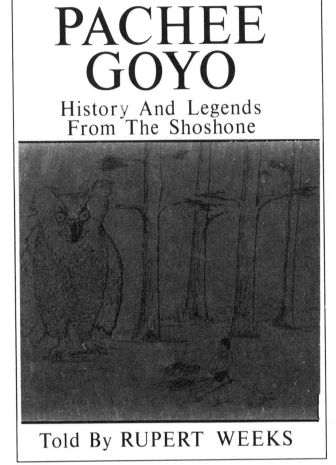

PACHEE GOYO

History And Legends
From The Shoshone

Told By RUPERT WEEKS

Pachee Goyo, History and Legends from the Shoshone

Jelm Mountain Press
209 Grand Avenue
Laramie, WY 82070
1981; grades 3-7
Shoshone

Pachee Goyo is a young Shoshone boy. He is staying in the Moobeech Oiquai, Owl Creek Mountains, with his grandfather and older brother. Givee Wee Hee, Short Knife, has "taken the task of tutoring his grandsons to be great hunters and brave warriors." The older brother, Beya Wee Hee, is "as smart and cunning as his grandfather," and takes care of his brother, "keeping (him) out of mischief." That's good, because Pachee Goyo needs all the help he can get. He wants the world, and he doesn't plan to wait on getting it.

This is how he talks:

"What do you see up there, uh? What's up there? Has the snow and wind quit, uh?...Do you think the weather will clear up tomorrow, Brother? Do you hear me, dear Brother, uh? Maybe we will go and hunt the great white buffaloes Grandfather told us about, uh? Hey, you hear me?"

Who could *help* it?! There's another thing about Pachee Goyo—he messes up every time.

At first, Weeks seems to be making little more than a setting for some stories, but there is more than one thing going here. As Givee Wee Hee tries to teach this kid something—and keep him in one piece until he learns it—the author weaves in Shoshone tribal customs, history and religious beliefs. As we read on, the meanings deepen, and the patterns become more complex.

Pachee Goyo stands for all of us when young—how we have to learn to listen, to give up our selfishness, to see what others need—to grow up. Each of his escapades becomes more serious, until at last his foolishness puts his life in jeopardy. Now, he must do it right, no more games. Pachee Goyo does finally learn some things; he does finally *get* it. Always, he has help, from his family, from the animal people, from some who may be spirit beings. At the end, he is ready to take his place as a responsible member of his Nation.

This is not to say that Rupert Weeks has written a bit of moral uplift, a sort of "Native American bibliotherapy." He is an accomplished storyteller, and his book is imaginative and entertaining. It is funny, scary and moving, by turns—good listening for any child. I *would* be tempted to edit out terms such as "braves," "howling painted warriors," "savage," and "squaw," even though they are the author's own choice of words.

Yue, Charlotte and David

The Pueblo

Houghton Mifflin
1986; grades 4-7
Pueblo Peoples

The Tipi: A Center of Native American Life

Knopf
1984; grades 4-7
Plains Nations

The Pueblo examines housing of the Pueblo Peoples. Structure, as well as family and community life, history and culture, are discussed.

Pueblo people have been building villages, cultivating crops, and making beautiful pottery since the time of Christ. And their hunter-gatherer ancestors were living in the Southwest thousands of years before that. Long before Columbus arrived, civilizations flourished and elegant stone masonry cities were constructed high in the walls of sheer cliffs.

The Yues make clear the continuum of Pueblo being, from ancient times to the present. The authors' respect for, and admiration of, the people they are writing about is evident in their treatment of the material.

The Tipi is a long way from the usual construction manual. Instead, this book is an intelligent discussion of "a sophisticated dwelling designed and built with enormous skill to meet the demands of life on the Great Plains." To begin with, it is hard to blow over a cone-shaped tipi. In addition, the structure is not perfectly symmetrical (the back is steeper). This makes an adjustable smoke-hole possible and acts as a further brace against the wind. In a land of high winds, bitter cold in winter and scorching heat in summer, the tipi is a "practical, livable home: well lighted, well ventilated, cozy... sturdy...and dry in heavy rains."

Raising the tipi is discussed in some detail, as are furnishings, good tipi manners, camp circles and the spiritual importance of the tipi. The authors conclude that "the tipi offered safety and comfort as well as beauty and luxury." Their approach is one seldom taken in writing for children about Native Americans, stressing, as it does, the degree of success achieved by the People in their adaptations to their environment—and the general felicity of their lives.

An afterword tells "What Happened to Tipis"—how the land was lost, and how, under white domination, Native people "were issued drafty, cheerless, uncomfortable housing that had no medicine." Exactly. Nevertheless, the book notes, many still try to "keep their culture and traditions alive. Camp circles are still being formed for special ceremonies and events."

This is a short book and easy to read, but it is written and illustrated with sensitivity and humor, and a child can learn more things from it that are true than from many works three times its length. *The Tipi* is a good example of what can be produced by authors of intelligence and good will, even though they may not know absolutely everything. It is recommended as an excellent corrective to a lot of the nonsense non-Native children "know" about the Plains peoples.

The Pueblo and *The Tipi* together are among the most informative and intelligently written books currently available for children.

Zitkala-Ša

Old Indian Legends

University of Nebraska Press
1985; grades 4-up
Dakota

First written down in 1902, these stories of the Dakota peoples have been reissued with an introduction by Agnes M. Picotte, professor of history at the University of South Dakota. There are 14; most are about Iktomi. Iktomi is the Spider, who embodies some of our less attractive characteristics. He is lazy, sneaky, selfish and vain. He never listens when people tell him things, so he is always in some kind of trouble. He works twice as hard to avoid work, and the person he outsmarts is usually himself. This is Iktomi coming up on something he isn't sure about:

> He lifted his foot lightly and placed it gently forward...From shoulder to shoulder he tilted his head. Still further he bent from side to side, first low over one hip and then over the other. Far forward he stooped, stretching his long thin neck like a duck, to see.

Iktomi is both a man, and something else.

Zitkala-Ša's life, in some ways, stands for what was happening to her people. A Yankton-Nakota woman, she was born in 1876, and spent the first eight years of her life on the reservation. Then she was sent away to school, first to a Quaker missionary school, called "White's Manual Labor Institute." ("During this time," the introduction says, "the government was anxious to save the Indians through Christianity and civilization.") Among other things, she attended the Boston Conservatory of Music, became an accomplished violinist, and taught for a time at Carlisle. "Whether she knew it or not," the introduction continues, "she was being formed into a cultured, Christian lady...."

Her writing reflects that, and is very much a product of the times. She calls Iktomi a Spider "fairy," for instance, and says things like, "the old legends of America belong quite as much to the blue-eyed little patriot as to the black-haired aborigine." Picotte tells us that,

> Although she identified strongly with her Indian roots, Zitkala-Ša could never return to a grassroots Nakota stage again. She used her knowledge of both the Indian and the white culture mainly to help other Indian people. Sadly, her motives were distrusted many times by both sides due to her tenuous bi-cultural condition.

It is easy to see why from these stories. They would have been much too "Indian" for white readers of that time, and too white in the method of telling for many Indians. But, if you can set aside the turn-of-the-century phraseology, these are really wonderful tales, easily used with children—with some judicious editing. (Eliminate, for instance, "fairy." Iktomi is not a fairy—nor anything like.) They have, after all, been told and retold forever, and are written down in "an easy, engaging style with a certain dramatic power." Some are laugh-out-loud funny—"Iktomi and the Coyote," for one—and all can teach us something. Iktomi is part of all of us.

Agnes Picotte sets the stories within the context of the period, in her excellent introduction, and brief biography of the author. Zitkala-Ša's own preface, read today, is painfully moving. She says,

> And when they are grown tall like the wise grown-ups may they not lack interest in a further study of Indian folklore, a study which so strongly suggests our near kinship with the rest of humanity and points a steady finger toward the great brotherhood of mankind... of the American aborigine as in any other race, sincerity of belief...demands a little respect... After all he seems at heart much like other peoples.

I wish I could tell Red Bird that I like her book.

How to Tell the Difference

Beverly Slapin, Doris Seale, and Rosemary Gonzales

Since the realities of Native lifeways are almost completely unknown to outsiders, it is often very difficult for them to evaluate children's books about American Indians. For this reason, we have compiled this list of criteria in the hope that it will make it easier for a teacher, parent, librarian or student to choose non-racist and undistorted books about the lives and histories of the People.

As you may immediately notice, some of the choices in our checklist are blatant; others are more subtle. Few books are perfect. When looking at books about Native peoples, then, perhaps the most important questions to ask are: Does this book tell the truth? Does the author respect the People? Is there anything in this book that would embarrass or hurt a Native child? Is there anything in this book that would foster stereotypic thinking in a non-Indian child? We hope this checklist is useful to you.

Look at Picture Books

In ABC books, is "E" for "Eskimo"?

Eskimo

Figure 1

In ABC books, is "I" for "Indian"?

Indian

The **Indian** wears bright colors.
He likes to live outdoors.

Figure 2

Look at Picture Books

In counting books, are "Indians" counted?

Are children shown "playing Indian"?

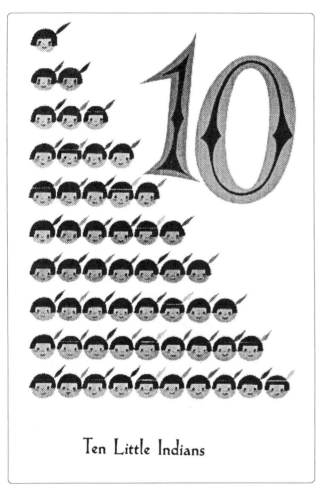

Ten Little Indians

Figure 3

Well, I'm an Indian, and Indians can ride.

Figure 4

Look at Picture Books

Are animals dressed as "Indians"?

Do "Indians" have ridiculous names, like "Indian Two Feet," or "Little Chief"?

Imitating Indians

Figure 5

Figure 6

Look for Stereotypes

Are Native peoples portrayed as savages, or primitive craftspeople, or simple tribal people, now extinct?

She was shot and scalped.   Figure 7

or

Are Native peoples shown as human beings, members of highly defined and complex societies?

Figure 8

Look for Stereotypes

Are Native cultures oversimplified and generalized?
Are Native people all one color, one style?

> And what would America have been without the Indians themselves, with their magnificent feathered headdresses, their colorful blankets, their bows and arrows and wampum belts, their wigwams and moccasins and birch-bark canoes that cut through the water like steel ploughs—their poetry and their history.

Figure 9

or

Are Native cultures presented as separate from each other, with each culture, language, religion, dress, unique?

> The People of the many Nations visited each other's lands. The People from the North brought elk meat. The People from the West gave them fish. The People from the South brought corn. The People from the East gave them hides. When there were arguments, their leaders would say, "Let us respect each other. We will bring you corn and baskets. You will bring us meat and flint knives. That way we will lead a peaceful life. We must respect each other, and the animals, the plants, the land, the universe. We have much to learn from all the Nations."

Figure 10

Look for Stereotypes

Is the art a mishmash of "generic Indian" designs?

Figure 11

or

Is attention paid to accurate, appropriate design and color; are clothes, dress, houses drawn with careful attention to detail?

Figure 12

Look for Loaded Words

Are there insulting overtones to the language in the book? Are racist adjectives used to refer to Indian peoples?

> A huge Indian came forward. He was over six feet tall, his half-naked body superbly muscled. His long black hair hung loosely to his waist. His brutal face gleamed with malice and under his low brows shone eyes like a wolf's.

Figure 13

or

Is the language respectful?

> My grandchildren, I am glad that you, the young Ojibway of today, are seeking to learn the beliefs, the customs, and the practices of our people, for these things have too long been alive only within the memories of the Old Ones. I am glad that you are asking, for it has always been the custom for us to tell what must be passed on so that our ways will be known to the Ojibway children of the future.

Figure 14

Look for Tokenism

Are Native people depicted as stereotypically alike, or do they look just like whites with brown faces?

Figure 15

or

Are Native people depicted as genuine individuals?

Figure 16

Look for Distortion of History

Is there manipulation of words like "victory," "conquest," or "massacre" to justify Euro-American conquest of the Native homelands? Are Native Nations presented as being responsible for their own "disappearance?" Is the U.S. government only "trying to help?"

> Vast, dark, unknown, the land lay for thousands of years, hardly used at all by men and women, for the few Indians never knew how to use it and never cared to learn. The wolf, the bear, the panther, and the bison flourished and increased faster than people. The land waited for a master who did not come for a long, long time.

Figure 17

or

Is history put in the proper perspective: the Native struggle for self-determination and sovereignty against the Euro-American drive for conquest?

> Soon, the People saw the destruction of their Nations. They soon found out it was the aim of the English, French, and Dutch to take their lands. The rich and the powerful of these men formed an American government. They wanted the land because it was fertile with forests and farmland and wealthy with precious minerals. And they wanted the People to serve them as slaves. When the People saw these men did not respect them and their land, they said, "We must fight to protect ourselves and the land."

Figure 18

Look for Distortion of History

Does the story encourage children to believe that Native peoples accepted defeats passively?

One hundred years after the Captain's visit, most of the Indians were gone from the Potomac. The white men had taken their lands. Unable to resist, the Indians fled west into the mountains. Many of them died. Nacotchtank and all the other villages disappeared, for their buildings were only bark-covered huts.

Figure 19

or

Does the story show the ways in which Native peoples actively resisted the invaders?

Most of the [settlers]...merely took what land they wanted. By the 1660s the Wampanoags were being pushed back into the wilderness. A chief named Metacom believed the Indians were doomed unless they united to resist the invaders [and] began to form alliances with the Narragansetts and other tribes in the region.

In 1675, Metacom led his...confederacy in a war against the colonists...But after months of fighting, the firepower of the colonists nearly exterminated the tribes. Metacom was killed and his head exhibited at Plymouth for 20 years. His father had been Massasoit, great chief of the Wampanoags, one of the four Indians who had kept the first colonists alive in the New World.

Figure 20

Look for Distortion of History

Are Native heroes only the people who, in some way or another, are believed to have aided Europeans in the conquest of their own people?

Pocahontas had done much for Jamestown. It was her help that enabled the struggling colony, the first permanent settlement in America, to survive. It was Pocahontas who planted the seeds of friendship that linked the Old World with the New World.

* * * * * * *

It is believed that Squanto died about a year after this first Thanksgiving Day in the new land. But his help to the Pilgrims will long be remembered. Bradford wrote that Squanto was a special instrument sent by God for the Pilgrims' good.

* * * * * * *

Sacajawea was the first woman to cross the Rocky Mountains. With Lewis and Clark, she had helped to open the way west. She did not know that she always would be remembered for these things.

Figure 21

or

Are Native heroes those who are admired because of what they have done for their own people?

That young man's name was Many Deeds,/And he had been a leader of a band of fighters/Called the Redstick Hummingbirds, who slowed/The march of Cortez' army with only a few/Spears and stones which now lay still/In the mountains and remember./Greenrock Woman was the name/Of that old lady who walked right up/And spat in Columbus' face. We/Must remember that, and remember/Laughing Otter the Taino who tried to stop/Columbus and who was taken away as a slave./We never saw him again.

Figure 22

Look at the Lifestyles

Are Native cultures presented in a condescending manner? Are there paternalistic distinctions between "them" and "us?"

> In our half of the world, which we call the Western Hemisphere, there was no civilization five hundred years ago except in Mexico and Peru, where people built cities with houses of stone and knew how to carve statues and paint pictures.

Figure 23

or

Is the focus on respect for Native peoples and understanding of the sophistication and complexity of their societies?

> Long before the white man came, civilizations flourished in the American Southwest. Elegant stone masonry cities were built high in the walls of sheer cliffs, and adobe villages clustered along rivers and next to mesas and hills. The Pueblo people had learned how to farm the dry land of the region. They made beautiful pottery and baskets in which to serve and store the food they grew. They had mastered their environment and lived in harmony with it.

Figure 24

Look at the Lifestyles

Are Native peoples discussed in the past tense only, supporting the "vanished Indian" myth? Is the past unconnected to the present?

Now, in all of Georgia and Alabama, there is nothing left of the nation that had lived there for a thousand years before the white man came. The Cherokees are gone, pulled up by the roots and cast to the westward wind.

They are gone like the buffalo and the elk which once roamed the mountain valleys. They have disappeared like the passenger pigeons which once darkened the sky as great flocks flew over the river routes from north to south and back again. Like wayah, the wolf, and like the chestnut trees, the Cherokees are no longer found in the mountains of Georgia.

Now only the names remain: Dahlonega, Chattahoochee, Oostenaula, Etowah, Nantahala, Tennessee, Ellijay, Tallulah, Chatooga, Nacoochee, Hiawassee, Chickamauga, Tugaloo, Chattanooga.

Figure 25

or

Is the continuity of cultures represented, with values, religions, morals, an outgrowth of the past, and connected to the present?

There was a knock, and Oona turned and saw a small girl in the doorway. The child stood with eyes cast down just as Oona had stood before her grandmother. Oona said, "Come in, my child, and speak if you wish to do so." The child said, "My name is Mary in the English way, but in the language of our people, I am called A-wa-sa-si." "And what is your wish, my child?" asked Oona. "I should like," said the child, "to hear the stories of our people." Oona felt a joy in her spirit and a light on her face. She knew that the Ojibway ways would forever be known in future years. "My name is Ni-bo-wi-se-gwe," said Oona, "and I shall tell you of our people."

Figure 26

Look at the Lifestyles

Is a culture portrayed in a distorted or limited way? Are religions described as "superstitions," with backward or primitive connotations?

> The most famous ceremony was the Sun Dance. It took place every year, before the big buffalo hunt. It lasted many days. Everybody took part to ask the spirits to bring them plenty of buffalo. As part of the ceremony, a few of the men tortured themselves. They believed that would please the spirits. Then they asked the spirits to take pity on them.

Figure 27

or

Are Indian religions and traditions described accurately, in the context of their civilizations?

> The land we live on has many stories. The stories tell us about things that happened long ago. These things make us, and our community, what we are today. The stories tell us where we came from, and how our ancestors lived on the land. Our elders tell us that by knowing these stories, we will have strength. The stories from the past help us solve problems today. They help us plan for the future. They help our community.

Figure 28

Look at the Lifestyles

Is there an ethnocentric Western focus on material objects, such as baskets, pottery, rugs?

> The old and new Indian crafts are found to be well suited for modern home decoration. In the living room, the den, or a child's room, one or more Navajo rugs create warmth and color. A pair of kachina dolls hung on the wall or standing on the mantel, or a fine piece of pottery on a bookshelf, adds much charm to a room. A painting made by an Indian artist has an interesting subject, and its soft earth colors blend with almost any decor. Large baskets, serving as wastebaskets, are a unique touch, and since those from different tribes rarely clash, they may be mixed in the same room.

Figure 29

or

Does the writer show any understanding of the relationship between material and non-material aspects of life?

> Art is a fundamental activity in tribal cultures, an integral part of the daily life of ordinary people. It is an expression of the basic need of people in all times and environments to communicate with others, to record experience and impressions, to cope with a finite existence by passing on something of oneself and one's heritage to future generations...The "art object" is valued not only for aesthetic reasons, as it is in Western society, but also for its utilitarian and religious functions. A Navajo basket is used in healing ceremonies. A Pueblo pot is treasured because the clay comes from Mother Earth and contains "the spirit of those who have gone before."

Figure 30

Look at the Lifestyles

Are Native peoples shown as "relentlessly ecological"?

What would you eat? Buffalo, buffalo, buffalo, and more buffalo. Buffalo boiled, buffalo broiled, dried buffalo, and sometimes raw buffalo. You would even drink the blood of buffalo! To boil buffalo blood, the women threw hot stones into the stomach of a freshly killed buffalo!...

The muscles along the buffalo's backbone...were used as thread in sewing. Twisted sinew made strong bows. Spoons and cups were made from the horns of the buffalo. The stomach of the buffalo was cleaned out and made a fine pot...The tongue of the buffalo was special. It was saved for important ceremonies...Dried buffalo droppings were used for fuel for camp fires. Buffalo hair was used for making ropes, fancy belts, and decorations. Buffalo ribs made sleds for winter fun.

Figure 31

or

Are Native societies described as coexisting with nature in a delicate balance?

Grandmother Woodchuck opened Gluskabi's game bag and looked inside. There were all of the animals in the world. "Oh Gluskabi," she said, "why must you always do things this way? You cannot keep all of the game animals in a bag. They will sicken and die. There will be none left for our children and our children's children. It is also right that it should be difficult to hunt them. Then you will grow stronger trying to find them. And the animals will also grow stronger and wiser trying to avoid being caught. Then things will be in the right balance."

Figure 32

Look at the Dialogue

Do the People speak in either a sort of "early jawbreaker" or in the oratorical style of the "noble savage"?

> She nodded fiercely. "Woman see. Soldier come village. Braves fight. Soldier make fire in house. Kill many. Take prisoner. Braves chase. Out, out—far! Bright Stars hide. See Little Bear fall. See soldier—" She mimed shooting again. "Bright Stars run, catch pony, bring Little Bear home to village. All fire! Dead Brave! Woman cry! I shut eyes, not see. Whoosh!" She made a strange noise like a rush of wind. Opened her eyes—and pointed at Omri with a look of acted surprise.
>
> "And suddenly you were here."
> She nodded. "Spirits bring. You save."

Figure 33

or

Do the People use language with the consummate and articulate skill of those who come from an oral tradition?

> We had no word for the strange animal we got from the white man—the horse. So we called it sunka wakan, "holy dog." For bringing us the horse we could almost forgive you for bringing us whiskey. Horses make a landscape look more beautiful.

Figure 34

Look for Standards of Success

In modern times, are Indian people portrayed as childlike and helpless? Does a white authority figure—pastor, social worker, teacher—know better than Native people themselves what is "good for them?" Are Indian children "better off" away from their families?

> "You know what I wish?" Mary Beth tried not to cringe when Melody's fingers combed quickly through her hair. "I wish we could have another Indian mother. Why do you s'pose Indian people don't adopt all the Indian children like us who need homes?"
>
> "You know perfectly well why not," retorted Melody. "They're too poor, and they have no nice place to live, and not enough food." She listed all the reasons Miss Perry, the social worker, had mentioned when they asked.

Figure 35

or

Are Native adults seen as mature individuals who work hard and make sacrifices, in order to take care of their families, and for the well-being of the people?

> The next day Father called the people together. He told them that they must all agree either to move to the big Ojibway village or to stay in their forest place.
>
> The people were afraid of the sickness in the big village. Every time of cold the sickness was there. "We have been favored," they said, "because we did only what we have always done." They did not want to leave the old place. Father said, "If this is your wish, then we will stay."
>
> Grandfather said, "Each ricing time the man will come for the children. If they live in the longhouse of the school they will never know our ways. Our strength will be lost. If we move close to the big village, the children will stay home at night and we can still teach them the old ways. We must decide—shall we stay separate and not see the children from ricing to planting, or shall we speak to them each night about the good of our people?"
>
> The people said, "We shall go to the big village."

Figure 36

Look for Standards of Success

Do Native people and their communities contrast unfavorably with the "norm" of white middle-class suburbia?

"You know what I wish?" Mary Beth tried not to cringe when Melody's fingers combed quickly through her hair. "I wish we could have another Indian mother. Why do you s'pose Indian people don't adopt all the Indian children like us who need homes?"

"You know perfectly well why not," retorted Melody. "They're too poor, and they have no nice place to live, and not enough food." She listed all the reasons Miss Perry, the social worker, had mentioned when they asked.

Figure 37

or

Are Native people and their communities seen as their own cultural norm?

When I was small my life was totally an Indian life... I learned about the religion of my people, about the Mountain God Dancer, from my grandmother and from elders of the tribe who teach children about those things...Four times a year we would go to the sacred place for my group near the base of Sierra Blanca for ceremonies. There would be prayers for the people and for the land and things in nature...

I don't know yet what the Washington [D.C.] experience will mean to me. I've met Indians here, ones who have worked here a long time, who don't seem much like Indians...I don't think that would ever happen to me, no matter how long I stayed away. I have the language of my tribe. I have the religion. I have the years of growing up on the land inside me. I have lived the customs of my people. I know who I am. No matter where I am, I am an Apache.

Figure 38

Look for Standards of Success

Does it take "white" standards for Native people to get ahead?

> "What you got to do," David would start out telling him, "is keep going to school. Whatever happens, just keep going. Because let me tell you, you're no 'dumb Injun.' When you graduate high school, you go to college. And when you get out of college, you'll have your eyes open. You'll tell the white man things he doesn't even know about. He will look amazed and think to himself, 'Man, this guy has really got something on the ball.' And pretty soon he'll be thinking, 'I'd better be careful because this Injun Benjamin may get ahead of me!'"

Figure 39

or

Are Native values of hard work, sharing, honesty, and courage seen as integral to growth and development?

> We sometimes shared our one room with others who had no place, so that there might be nine or ten of us. We could not let friends be out on the street without bed or board...we helped and gave a place to other Ojibway people.
>
> Our paydays were on different days and so whoever had money lent carfare and bought meat and vegetables. Stew was our daily fare because we had only a hot plate and one large kettle.
>
> I mention this practice because I know other Indian people did the same thing, and sometimes whole families evolved from it. This was how we got a toehold in the urban areas—by helping each other. Perhaps this is the way nonmaterialistic people do. We were a sharing people and our tribal traits are still within us.

Figure 40

Look at the Role of Women

Are women completely subservient to men? Do they do all the work, while the men loll around, waiting for the next hunt?

> Originally, the travois had been drawn by squaws or by dogs. The Spaniards introduced the Indians to the horse, and horsepower proved superior to dog or "squaw-power."

Figure 41

or

Are women portrayed as the integral and respected part of Native societies that they really are?

> Among the Cherokee, there was a women's council, as there was among the Iroquois, which could override the authority of the chiefs. Other seaboard tribes probably had similar councils. The Cherokee council was made up of one woman from each clan, chosen by the clan members. The head of this assembly was called the Beloved Woman and she spoke for the women at all meetings of the chiefs. It was said that she represented and spoke for the Great Spirit.

Figure 42

Look at the Role of Elders

Are Elders treated as a dispensable burden upon their People to be abandoned in times of trouble or famine; querulous, petulant, demanding, nagging, irritating, and boring?

> "Try everything. Deer songs, rabbit songs, maybe the horse songs, too. That stuff I can handle...But when she starts up about her soul wandering...and wants those old songs...that's a lot more complicated. Takes time. I can't just snap my fingers and dance around the fire like some witch doctor in a movie!"

Figure 43

or

Are Elders treated as loved and valued custodians of a People's history, culture, and lifeways? Are they cherished in the words of the writer as they were and are in the reality of the lives of the People?

> Every evening, after a day of playing, exploring, and learning, Oona returned to the lodge of Grandfather and Grandmother. She sat before them, and they said, "Our daughter, what has been done today? Can you ask in truth and peace, 'Have I done enough today to earn the right to live tomorrow?'" Oona would count and think about the things she had done that day. Grandmother would touch her fingers to the back of Oona's hand, and Grandfather would place his hand on her head in blessing.

Figure 44

Look for the Effects on a Child's Self-Image

Is there anything in the story that would embarrass or hurt a Native child?

> She saw two naked, wild men coming... They were tall, thin, fierce-looking men. Their skin was brownish-red. Their heads seemed to go up to a peak, and the peak was a tuft of hair that stood straight up and ended in feathers. Their eyes were black and still and glittering, like snake's eyes... The naked wild men stood by the fireplace...she smelled a horribly bad smell.

Figure 45

or

Are there one or more positive role models with which a Native child can identify?

> Emma Yazzie is a hero who is living right now in the Navajo Nation of New Mexico. She is a hero in our modern age—the time we all live in. Emma is brave and strong and courageous. And she is not alone. Many of her people work and struggle with her. They are brave, strong, and courageous heroes, too. They are the rural Navajo people. They call themselves "grassroots" people because, like the hardy grass on their reservation, they have to be tough to survive. Grassroots means that, like the grass, they have their roots in the land.

Figure 46

Look at the Author's or Illustrator's Background

Is the background of the author and illustrator devoid of the qualities that enable them to write about Native peoples in an accurate, respectful manner? Is there an ethnocentric bias which leads to distortions or omissions?

> Betty Baker, the author who delighted many young readers with *Little Runner of the Longhouse*,...writes, "I love the Southwest, its history, and the people who once roamed its haunting countryside..." Only through Betty Baker's imagination could it have become such a delightful story about Indians old and young, wise and frolicsome, stubborn and willing.

Figure 47

or

Is there anything in the author's and illustrator's background that qualifies them to write about Native peoples? Do their perspectives strengthen the work?

> Ellen White, whose Salish name is Kwulasulwut, which means "Many Stars," lives in Nanaimo, British Columbia, where she teaches Native Studies and the Coast Salish language. The five tales which make up *Kwulasulwut: Stories from the Coast Salish* have been adapted from the stories which Ellen uses to teach her students at Nanaimo area elementary schools about Native traditions and culture. The cover painting and illustrations for this book are by Nootkan artist Vincent Smith, from Nuchatlitz on Nootka Island.

Figure 48

Footnotes

Figure 1. Reed, Mary, and Edith Osswald, *My Little Golden Dictionary* (Simon and Schuster, 1949).

Figure 2. Eastman, P.D., *The Cat in the Hat Beginner Book Dictionary* (Random House, 1964).

Figure 3. Seiden, Art, *Counting Rhymes* (Grossett and Dunlap, 1959).

Figure 4. Paterson, Diane, *Hey, Cowboy!* (Alfred A. Knopf, 1983).

Figure 5. Sendak, Maurice, *Alligators All Around* (Harper & Row, 1962).

Figure 6. Hoff, Syd, *Little Chief* (Harper & Brothers, 1961).

Figure 7. Morris, Richard B., *The First Book of the Indian Wars* (Franklin Watts, 1959).

Figure 8. Chee, Hosteen Clah, and Franc Johnson Newcomb, *Navajo Bird Tales*, illustrated by Na-Ton-Sa-Ka (The Theosophical Publishing House, 1970).

Figure 9. Commager, Henry Steele, *The First Book of American History* (Franklin Watts, 1957).

Figure 10. Ortiz, Simon, *The People Shall Continue* (Children's Book Press, 1977).

Figure 11. Esbensen, Barbara Juster, *The Star Maiden*, illustrated by Helen K. Davie (Little, Brown and Company, 1988).

Figure 12. Tehanetorens, *Tales of the Iroquois*, illustrated by Kahionhes (Akwesasne Notes, 1976).

Figure 13. Daugherty, James, *Trappers and Traders of the Far West* (Random House, 1952).

Figure 14. Broker, Ignatia, *Night Flying Woman, an Ojibway Narrative* (Minnesota Historical Society Press, 1983).

Figure 15. Fritz, Jean, *The Good Giants and the Bad Pukwudgies*, illustrated by Tomie dePaola (G.P. Putnam's Sons, 1982).

Figure 16. Kahionhes, *Mohawk Family*.

Figure 17. Johnson, Gerald W., *America is Born* (William Morrow & Company, 1959).

Figure 18. Ortiz, Simon, *op. cit.*

Figure 19. Holland, J., *They Built a City: The Story of Washington, D.C.* (Charles Scribner's Sons, 1953).

Figure 20. Brown, Dee, *Wounded Knee: An Indian History of the American West*, adapted for young readers by Amy Ehrlich from Dee Brown's *Bury My Heart at Wounded Knee* (Holt, Rinehart and Winston, 1974).

Figure 21. Jassem, Kate, *Pocahontas, Girl of Jamestown; Squanto, the Pilgrim Adventure; Sacajawea, Wilderness Guide* (Troll Associates, 1979).

Figure 22. Durham, Jimmie, *Columbus Day* (West End Press, 1983).

Figure 23. Johnson, Gerald W., *op. cit.*

Figure 24. Yue, Charlotte and David, *The Pueblo* (Houghton Mifflin Company, 1986).

Figure 25. Bealer, Alex W., *Only the Names Remain: The Cherokees and the Trail of Tears* (Little, Brown and Company, 1972).

Figure 26. Broker, Ignacia, *op. cit.*

Figure 27. McGovern, Ann, *If You Lived With the Sioux Indians* (Scholastic, Inc., 1972).

Figure 28. Title IV-B Materials Development Project, *Our Community—Yesterday and Today, Book Two* (Navajo Curriculum Center, 1983).

Figure 29. Hofsinde, Robert, *Indian Arts* (Morrow Junior Books, 1971).

Figure 30. Katz, Jane, *This Song Remembers: Self-Portraits of Native Americans in the Arts* (Houghton Mifflin Company, 1980).

Figure 31. McGovern, Ann, *op. cit.*

Figure 32. Bruchac, Joseph, "Gluskabi and the Game Animals," from *The Wind Eagle and Other Abenaki Stories* (Bowman Books, 1985).

Figure 33. Banks, Lynne Reid, *The Return of the Indian* (Doubleday & Company, 1986).

Figure 34. Erdoes, Richard, *Lame Deer, Seeker of Visions* (Simon & Schuster, 1972).

Figure 35. Warren, Mary, *Walk in My Moccasins* (Westminster, 1966).

Figure 36. Broker, Ignacia, *op. cit.*

Figure 37. Warren, Mary, *op. cit.*

Figure 38. Ashabranner, Brent, *To Live in Two Worlds: American Indian Youth Today* (Dodd, Mead & Company, 1984).

Figure 39. Cone, Molly, *Number Four* (Houghton Mifflin, 1972).

Figure 40. Broker, Ignacia, *op. cit.*

Figure 41. Sutton, Felix, *The How and Why Wonder Book of North American Indians* (Price/Stern/Sloan, 1985).

Figure 42. Gridley, Marion E., *American Indian Women* (Hawthorne, 1974).

Figure 43. Wallin, Luke, *Ceremony of the Panther* (Bradbury Press, 1987).

Figure 44. Broker, Ignacia, *op. cit.*

Figure 45. Wilder, Laura Ingalls, *Little House on the Prairie* (Harper & Row, 1971) (first published 1935).

Figure 46. New Mexico People & Energy Collective, *Red Ribbons for Emma* (New Seed Press, 1981).

Figure 47. Baker, Betty, *The Shaman's Last Raid* (Harper & Row, 1963).

Figure 48. White, Ellen, *Kwulasulwut: Stories from the Coast Salish* (Theytus Books, Ltd., 1981).

Resources

Native educators are concerned with creating materials that give Indian children pride in themselves and their cultures, and are also intent on helping all children appreciate Native peoples. And they are determined to wipe out the stereotypes that offend Native peoples and cheat non-Native people of information that may enrich their lives.

In response to the need for accurate learning materials about Native cultures, groups of Indian educators have developed and published units, books, audio-visual material, games, and teacher's guides that range from preschool through high school levels. These culture-based materials can be used to round out and add perspective to social studies, language arts, music, arts and crafts, mathematics, physical education, and other classes.

The following groups, listed alphabetically, show a representative selection of materials and ordering addresses.

Akwesasne Notes
Mohawk Nation via
Rooseveltown, NY 13683

This group publishes and distributes an assortment of materials written and illustrated by Mohawk writers and artists that can be used in classrooms. For example, it offers a variety of posters; *Legends of Our Nations*; *Mohawk Coloring Book* for grades k-2; *Coloring Book of Our Nations* for grades 2-5; and many other books. Akwesasne Notes also publishes a newspaper by the same name, which covers issues and articles about indigenous peoples in North and South America. Resources, books, posters, and records are listed in each issue. Of further interest to teachers are book reviews in each issue, and articles about schools and educational programs. Akwesasne Notes is published six times per year.

American Indian Curricula Development Program
c/o United Tribes Technical College
3315 University Drive
Bismarck, ND 58501

This group has developed Plains Nations curricula and teacher's guides relevant to the needs of all Indian and non-Indian students in grades k-12. The elementary units deal with traditional lifestyles, junior high materials with turn-of-the-century issues, and high school with contemporary Native American studies. The k-5 social studies materials include eight units: Indian Family, Dwellings, Communities, Education, Foods, Values, Animals, and Birds; as well as booklets, overhead transparencies, activity cards, and a teacher manual. There are 18 correlated slide cassette/tape programs that run from 3-15 minutes (for sale individually), with grade levels suggested.

There are five junior high Plains Nations units (kit or available individually): Circle of Life; Peace Pipe; Arts and Crafts; Indian Country; and A Feather to Each, which includes biographies of past and present leaders and 14 portrait posters. There is a teacher's guide with discussion questions and activities. There are five slide cassette/tape shows that run between 11 and 15 minutes. The 9-12 curriculum features two units on contemporary Native studies: Social Conflicts and Fine Arts.

American Indian Studies Center
University of California, Los Angeles
405 Hilgard Ave.
Los Angeles, CA 90024

In 1968, in response to the needs of American Indian students at UCLA, a group of Indian students met with representatives of the Los Angeles Indian community and formed a grassroots movement that resulted in the development of the American Indian Cultural Center, now the American Indian Studies Center. Since its inception, the AISC has developed an extensive collection of Native materials, and, more recently, has begun developing Native curricula at UCLA. Besides providing student services,

lectures, conferences, and workshops, the AISC offers a wide range of print and audio material, including the Native American Literature Series: *Thunder-Root: Traditional and Contemporary Native American Verse* by Judith Volborth, *My Horse and a Jukebox* by Barney Bush, *Shadow Country* by Paula Gunn Allen, *Eclipse* by Linda Hogan, *Migration Tears* by Michael Kabotie, and *The Light on the Tent Wall: A Bridging* by Mary TallMountain.

Anishinabe Reading Materials
Duluth Indian Education Advisory Committee
Independent School District #709
Lake Avenue and Second Street
Duluth, MN 55802

This group has developed four small booklets and teacher's guide entitled *Real Wild Rice; Cheer Up, Old Man; Shemay, the Bird in the Sugarbush;* and *Manabozho and the*

Bullrushes. In addition, *Aseban (Raccoon), an Ojibway Legend* and *A Long Time Ago is Just Like Today,* both with teacher's guides, are available.

Canadian Alliance in Solidarity with Native Peoples
P.O. Box 574
Station P
Toronto, Ontario M5S 2T1

CASNP is an organization of Native and non-Native people working together to spread awareness of issues vital to indigenous peoples. Their publications include *The Phoenix*, their newsletter; the *Resource Reading List*, an annotated bibliography by and about Native peoples; *All My Relations: Sharing Native Values through the Arts*, a resource kit for teachers and group leaders; and *Indian Giver: A Legacy of North American Native Peoples.*

Canyon Records and Indian Arts
4143 North 16th Street
Phoenix, AZ 85016

Canyon offers a huge selection (literally hundreds) of albums and tapes, including traditional music, stories and legends recorded by Native artists and storytellers. Especially noteworthy is *American Indian Music for the Classroom*, by Louis W. Ballard (Cherokee-Quapaw). This music education package contains four albums or cassettes, and presents Native music for classroom study and listening, including song analyses and diagrams, a teacher's guide, 20 study photographs, a bibliography, and a set of spirit masters for duplication. The music and dances represent 35 societies, along with cultural information on more than 50 Nations.

Choctaw Heritage Press
Mississippi Band of Choctaw Indians
Route 7, Box 21
Philadelphia, MS 39350

The Choctaw Heritage Press specializes in materials of an authentic nature that deal with the Mississippi Band of Choctaw Indians. Besides print materials, video tapes entitled, "By the Work of Our Hands" and "Choctaw Tribal Government" are available for rental or purchase.

Costo, Rupert, and Jeannette Henry, editors
Textbooks and The American Indian
Indian Historian Press, 1493 Masonic Ave.
San Francisco, CA 94117

This highly informative book, edited and published by noted Indian scholars Costo and Henry, evaluates over 150 textbooks in use in both the public schools and the Bureau of Indian Affairs schools. American history, geography, state and regional history, and world history are among the textbooks evaluated. A comprehensive list of criteria for evaluating textbooks and their treatment of Native peoples is included.

Council on Interracial Books for Children
Unlearning "Indian" Stereotypes
CIBC
1841 Broadway
New York, NY 10023

This teaching unit for elementary teachers and children's librarians contains a study of stereotyping in popular picture books; a filmstrip with a script and lesson plans; ten classroom "don'ts" for teachers; guidelines for publishers, illustrators, and writers; role-playing strategies; and Native American perspectives on Thanksgiving, Columbus Day, and Washington's Birthday. This book can be purchased separately from the filmstrip, but both are a "must" for concerned educators.

CIBC also publishes *Chronicles of American Indian Protest*, a comprehensive collection of documents that vividly recounts the struggle from 1622 to 1978. Each document is prefaced by a brief historical introduction. The selections include: Popé's Uprising against Spanish rule in Taos (1680), Pontiac's Rebellion against the British (1763), "We Shall Not Be Moved," the Cherokee removal (1823 and 1836), the Lakota struggle in defense of the Black Hills (1876), Wounded Knee (1973), the Geneva Conference (1977), and The Longest Walk (1978). This is a "must" textbook for the older grades (9-up), as well as an important teacher resource.

Cross-Cultural Education Center
P.O. Box 66
Park Hill, OK 74451

This center publishes materials about Cherokee culture and history, as well as about the Creek, Chickasaw, Choctaw, and Seminole peoples. There are biographies of Cherokees Elias Boudinot and Joe Thornton for elementary students plus *Traditional Cherokee Foods* and *Changing Fashions — Five Tribes*. Also available is a filmstrip entitled "Historical Sites within the Old Cherokee Nation," *Cherokee Enrichment Guide* and *Culture Through Concept—Five Tribes*, which contains teaching units about the history and culture of the Oklahoma Five Tribes.

Davids, Dorothy W., and Ruth A. Gudinas
Student Activities and Teacher Materials for Use During the Thanksgiving Season
Developed for the Department of Human Relations
Madison Metropolitan School District
545 West Dayton Avenue
Madison, WI 53703

This unbound packet was created for Madison teachers who were concerned that "simplistic, stereotypical approaches to the teaching of history and human relationships are neither appropriate nor necessary...they are aware that the closer we come to the truth about this country's history—all of it—the closer we are to a true appreciation for the American people and their respective traditions—all of them." Included are writings by Native peoples, student resource sheets, and student activities. A very good resource for

teachers who throw up their hands in disgust around this time of year.

Daybreak
P.O. Box 98
Highland, MD 20777-0098

Daybreak is a news magazine dedicated to indigenous cultures and issues. It is published quarterly by Five Rings Corporation in association with Eagle Eye Communications Group, a Native collective "dedicated to the preservation of Mother Earth and recognition for the cultural diversity of her inhabitants. Eagle Eye serves as a vehicle for

the dissemination of information, resources and arts of indigenous people from around the world. Our goal is to provide a voice, articulate opinions for community development and to empower people to solve their problems using their own initiatives."

Daybreak Star Press
P.O. Box 99100
Seattle, WA 98199

This press offers materials ranging from preschool through high school level. For the youngest, there is the *Daybreak Star Preschool Activities Book*. For the elementary grades, there are *Chief Sealth and His People* plus teacher's guide and *The Mamook Book*. For junior high and high school level, there is

Our Mother Corn and teacher's guide; *Tribal Sovereignty: Indian Tribes in U.S. History* and teacher's guide. Daybreak Star also offers video materials (Beta or VHS), learning aides such as board games, and *Native Americans of Washington State: A Curriculum Guide for the Elementary Grades*.

Eagle Wing Press, Inc.
P.O. Box 579 MO
Naugatuck, CN 06770

Eagle Wing produces a newspaper by the same name, which is published six times per year. Most of its articles are devoted to North American Indian peoples, although articles on South American Indian issues are

sometimes covered. Each issue includes a craft corner, articles on Native foods, book reviews, editorials, regional announcements, and news.

Featherstone Productions, Inc.
P.O. Box 536
Agency Village, SD 57262

Featherstone is an Indian-owned and -operated company, featuring cassettes of traditional, contemporary, cultural/ historical, and special presentation music and stories,

such as *Gordon Bird Sings Traditional/ Contemporary American Indian Songs* from the Mandan, Hidatsa and Arickara Nations of North Dakota; *Dakota Songs* by Wahpe Kute,

12 songs of the Dakota Nation, including Honor songs, Grass Dance songs and other traditional songs; *Assiniboine Singers—Live at Dakota Tipi*, 11 songs recorded at Chief Gall Honor Celebration, Dakota Tipi Portage La Prairie, Manitoba, Canada; *Lakota Wiikijo Olowan* by Kevin Locke, Lakota flute music;

All Nation Singers—Flandreau Indian School, 12 traditional songs from various Nations; and *Songs of the People* by Georgia-Wettlin Larsen, ten traditional songs of the Lakota, Ojibway, Navajo, Caddo, Kiowa, and Zuni Nations.

Four Worlds Development Project
The Univesity of Lethbridge
4401 University Drive
Lethbridge, Alberta T1K 3M4

The Four Worlds Development Project, a non-profit Native education and development group, was founded in December 1982 by Native Elders, cultural leaders and professionals from various communities, who came together to address the root causes of Native alcohol and drug abuse and to develop human and community healing strategies. In addition to providing technical support and training to Native communities, the Project produces written and audio-visual curriculum material including: *The Sacred Tree*, which presents Native teaching concerning the nature, purposes and possibilities of human existence; *Unity in Diversity*, a social studies curriculum for high school students that deals with the roots and dynamics of prejudice and the skills needed to overcome it; and *Walking with Grandfather*, a video series of semi-animated Native stories which teach positive, life-enhancing values. Write for a catalogue.

Greenfield Review Literary Center
R.D. #1
P.O. Box 80
Greenfield Center, NY 12833

The Greenfield Review Literary Center is a non-profit organization devoted to contemporary literature, with a special emphasis on multi-ethnic writing. Its activities include the Native American Authors Distribution Project, which sells books by Indian writers at pow-wows and through mail order; The Greenfield Review Press, which has published a number of books by American Indians; and Good Mind Records, which produces cassette tapes by Native storytellers.

Among the selections from Good Mind, a superb set of stories recorded by Native storytellers, are: *Indian Wisdom Stories* as told by Jay Silverheels (dramatized legends recorded with authentic Salish language chants, drum songs and sound effects; legends included are "Beginning of the World," "Owl and Chipmunk," "Coyote and the Frost Giant," and "Buffalo and Coyote."); *Iroquois Stories* as told by Joseph Bruchac (includes "The Creation Story," "Turtle's Race with Bear," and "How Buzzard Got His Feathers," and two long stories about Iroquois women: "The Wife of Thunderer" and "The Brave Woman and the Flying Head"); *Reflections* by Tsonakwa (stories include "The Porcupine," "The Salmon," "Kuloscap Stories," and "My Brother the Bear"); *White Buffalo Calf Woman* as told by Martin High Bear (this Lakota spiritual leader narrates the moving story of the White Buffalo Calf Woman, the sacred being who brought special gifts to the People).

Hirschfelder, Arlene B.

American Indian Stereotypes in the World of Children: A Reader and Bibliography
Scarecrow Press
52 Liberty Street, Box 4167
Metuchen, NJ 08840

This anthology presents evidence from a variety of sources—toys, pageants, misrepresented "history," and advertisements—that demonstrates the pervasiveness of Indian stereotypes. The articles spell out the prevalent attitudes of children, detail the images of Indians in children's stories and textbooks, analyze toy Indian imagery, describe the misuse of Indian religion and customs in YMCA programs, and report on sports teams with Indian names and derogatory mascots. For more information, see Book Review section.

Hirschfelder, Arlene B., Comp.

American Indian Authors: A Representative Bibliography
Association on American Indian Affairs
95 Madison Ave.
New York, NY 10016

This bibliography was compiled to inform people about the extensive body of oral and written literature authored by Native peoples. It is followed by two supplementary sections: a selection of anthologies of American Indian oral and written literature, and a list of periodicals published by Native organizations.

Indian Historian Press

1493 Masonic Ave.
San Francisco, CA 94117

This all-Indian educational publishing house was organized by the American Indian Historical Society "in order to develop an accurate and authentic body of literature in the culture, history, lifeways, and current affairs" of Native American peoples, "for the use of the educational community." Among their many excellent books are: *A Thousand Years of American Indian Storytelling, Give or Take a Century: An Eskimo Chronicle* (grades 10-up), *The Pueblo Indians* (grades 10-up), and *Legends of the Lakota* (grades 10-up). Sourcebooks for teachers, which are expected to be published, include: *Textbooks and the American Indian*, and *Natives of the Golden State: The California Indians*. The press has published *The Missions of California: A Legacy of Genocide*, and is working on *A Child's History of the American Indian* (grades ps-up, including teacher's guide). Write for their catalogue; their books are a must for all school resource shelves.

Indian Image Productions
P.O. Box 3621
Evansville, IN 47735

Indian Image Productions offers a variety of calendars, signed prints and posters, and note cards reproducing paintings in a diversity of styles practiced by contemporary Native American artists. Accompanying each painting is an informative story line, which provides unique insights from each artist's perspective.

Indian Reader
P.O. Box 59
Strawberry Plains, TN 37871

The Indian Reader is an "international indigenous journal featuring current personalities and news," and presents issues "that concern the commonality of all earth-dwellers...Indian, 'earth-dwelling' values and ethics are needed at a world level." This newspaper, a publication of the Native American Indian Media Corporation, with primary support provided by the Tennessee Indian Council and the Indian Historical Society of the U.S., is published three times yearly.

Indian Rights Association
1505 Race Street
Philadelphia, PA 19102

Indian Truth, published since 1924, is the bimonthly newsletter of the Indian Rights Association. It covers major Indian rights news from Indian country, the courts, and the government. Subscription to *Indian Truth* is automatic with an annual membership contribution.

Minneapolis Public Schools
Planning, Development, and Evaluation Department
807 Northeast Broadway
Minneapolis, MN 55413

A staff of Native curriculum writers, housed within the Minneapolis public school system, has produced an array of materials ranging from language arts to arts and crafts. There are seven legends from the Lakota, Ojibway/Chippewa, and Winnebago Nations for grades 1-3, two legends available as filmstrips with cassette tapes; an oratory unit entitled *Ojibway People Speak Out* (grades 4-6); *The Making of a Treaty* (grade 5); *Native Americans of the Twentieth Century* (biographical sketches, ten leaflets); *Beadwork for Children/Birch Bark* (two-part unit for elementary grades); *Winnebago Basketry* (upper elementary and junior high); *Maple Sugar Harvesting/Wild Rice Harvesting* (two-part unit for grades 1-6); and *Tree Ties* (card game for junior/senior high school).

Minnesota Chippewa Tribe

P.O. Box 217
Cass Lake, MN 56633

This group distributes ten mini-lessons for elementary school on Native contributions, history, math, maps, calendar, etc.; *Legend of Nett Lake* (with teacher's guide); *History of* *Kitchi Onigaming: Grand Portage and Its People* (middle school); *Against the Tide: The Story of the Mille Lacs Anishinabe* (high school); and *Time of the Indian*, poetry by Indian students.

Montana Council for Indian Education

P.O. Box 31215
Billings, MT 59107

This organization has some 50 booklets (for first grade through high school) for its Indian Culture Series. There are biographies, histories, arts, crafts, and skill books, legends and folk stories, and contemporary accounts. Write for complete list.

Native American Center for the Living Arts, Inc.

25 Rainbow Mall
Niagara Falls, NY 14303

Native American Center for the Living Arts, Inc., is a non-profit organization dedicated to the presentation of tradition, creation of public awareness, and the development of artistic expression. Its magazine, *Turtle Quarterly*, explores various Native American arts, histories, cultures, philosophies, and athletics.

Native American Materials Development Center

407 Rio Grande Blvd., N.W.
Albuquerque, NM 87104

NAMDC was established in 1976 and is sponsored by the Ramah Navajo School Board, Inc. Curricula available include: reader texts, workbooks, teacher's guides, booklets, posters, and dictionaries. Most of the materials are bilingual (Navajo and English).

Native Indian/Inuit Photographers' Association

124 James Street
South Hamilton, Ontario L8P 2Z4

The Native Indian/Inuit Photographers' Association is a non-profit organization maintained by photographers from across Canada. The main goal of NIIPA is to set up an Indian/Inuit photographic educational network and to encourage as well as promote the usage of photography as a medium of the fine arts. The only such organization in North America, NIIPA's objective is to "promote a positive, realistic and contemporary image of Native Indian/Inuit people...By using photography as a visual element, other people will be encouraged to look at the real image of Native Indian/Inuit people as they live and work in today's world." Write for catalogue, newsletters, and posters.

Navajo Curriculum Development and Production Center
Box 587
Chinle Unified School District No. 24
Chinle, AZ 86503

This curriculum center has available a variety of materials: posters, stories, English as a Second Language, games, coloring books, plays, flash cards, and teacher's guides. The main focus is upon accurate, relevant materials about the Diné people.

New York City Board of Education
Native American Heritage and Culture Week Resource Unit
Office of Bilingual Education, Native American Education Program
234 West 109th St., Room 507
New York, NY 10025.

The all-Indian staff of the Native American Education Program has done a superb job in presenting this 135-page overview of Native American cultures. Included are information, activities, and lessons about Stereotypes About Native Americans, Social Studies, Language Arts, Science, Food, and Recreation/Health. This is an important resource for teachers.

North American Indian Travelling College
R.R. #3
Cornwall Island
Ontario K6H 5R7

The Travelling College publishes *Tewaarathon (La Crosse) Akwesasne's Story of Our National Game*, which represents the Native perspective of a sport which originated in North America. Other materials include: Posters, "Leaders and Elders of the Past" and "Leaders and Elders of the Present," *Wampum Belts*, and *Seven Generations*, a history of the Kanienkehaka (Kahnawake Survival School). This book includes a creation story, quotes from historical documents, legends, and reproductions of early maps.

OHOYO Resource Center
c/o Mozelle Cherry
4712 Florist
Wichita Falls, TX 76302

Ohoyo Ikhana ("learned woman...growing in knowledge") is a tool for teachers to incorporate into school curricula a broader image of Native peoples from both historical and contemporary perspectives. The work, containing 1,200 entries, is arranged into four sections: Curriculum Materials, Resource Materials, Bibliographies, and Periodical Articles; and is a must for every teacher serious about presenting non-biased material by Native peoples. *Ohoyo One Thousand: 1983 Location Update*, contains updated address and phone number listings for entrants as of October 1983; a vital supplement to the 1982 Resource Guide, due to the mobility of Indian contemporary society. *Ohoyo One Thousand: Resource Guide of American Indian-Alaska Native Women, 1982*, contains biographical and expertise entries of 1,004 notable Native American women, and includes a comprehensive skills index. *Words of Today's Indian Women: Ohoyo Makachi*, the 1981 Conference Volume of Ohoyo's regional conferences presented at Tahlequah, Oklahoma, contains presentations of 32 women from 15 states.

Oyate
2702 Mathews St.
Berkeley, CA 94702

Oyate is a group of Native Elders, artists, activists, educators, and writers who, from increasing concern for the future of our children, have come together to bring the real histories of the indigenous peoples of this continent to the attention of all Americans. Our purpose is to deal with issues of cultural and historical bias as they affect the lives of all our children. Our work includes evaluation of texts and resource books as well as fiction, workshops to help educators deal in a positive way with the literature about American Indians, and the distribution of children's books written and illustrated by Native people. For our own children, whose need is great, our intent is that they may know what they came from, who they are, and that their lives need not be such as they are now. Oyate is a non-profit organization. Write for a list of our materials.

Pemmican Publications, Inc.
412 McGregor St.
Winnipeg, Manitoba R2W 4X5

Pemmican Publications was established in 1980 as a Métis publishing house, to provide opportunities for Métis and Native peoples to tell their own stories. Although Pemmican also publishes some books by non-Native writers, the group is committed to publishing books which depict Métis and Native lifeways in a positive light, and which address historical, social, and contemporary issues. Pemmican has established itself as a leading publisher of children's books, many of which combine modern teaching methods and traditional Native storytelling skills. For younger students, some of our favorites are *Murdo's Story* (in Cree and Ojibway), *I Can't Have Bannock But the Beaver Has a Dam, Eagle Feather—An Honour, The Birth of Nanabosho, Nanabosho Steals Fire*, and *The Big Tree and The Little Tree*; for older students, *Honour the Sun, Where the Rivers Meet*, and *April Raintree*.

Red School House
643 Virginia St.
St. Paul, MN 55103

The Red School House is an Indian-controlled alternative school serving k-12 students. Content, approach, and format are designed from an Indian perspective by staff members of the school. Materials are developed with the goal of changing attitudes by presenting accurate images of Indian peoples. Among their publications are *The Mishomis Book: The Voice of the Ojibway*, stories which have their foundation in the teaching of the Midewiwin, and provide the reader with an accurate account of Ojibway culture and history; *With Yesterday, We Learn for Tomorrow*, values teaching posters; *The Sounding Voice*, a collection of poetry; and *Un Gi Dah So Win—Counting*, an Ojibway language counting workbook for elementary students.

Rising Wolf, Inc.
240 North Higgins Ave. #4
Missoula, MT 59801

Rising Wolf publishes *Stories from the Old Ones*, as told to Walter A. Denny, Ojibway-Cree storyteller, edited by Harold E. Gray, Siksika-Cree, and Patricia Scott.

Rough Rock Press
RRDS Box 217
Chinle, AZ 86503

This press publishes a wide variety of materials designed to preserve the artistic and cultural heritage of the Diné/Navajo Nation. For all grades, there is a flashcard set entitled *Navajo Landmarks Flashcards* (12 cards); *Grandfather Stories of the Navajos, vol. 1*; *Navajo Music* (cassette and booklet). For older readers, there are *Navajo History, vol. 1*; *Navajo Biographies, vol. 1*; and *Navajo Biographies, vol. 2*.

Sinte Gleska College
Bookstore
Rosebud Sioux Reservation
P.O. Box 156
Mission, SD 57555

The college has published two sets of books and musical recordings appropriate for secondary music, religion, and language arts classes. *Lakota Ceremonial Songs* (recording and publication) contains a collection of songs sacred to the Lakota People. *Songs and Dances of the Lakota* contains a collection of many of the most popular songs and dances known among the Western Lakota. For younger grades, there is *Buckskin Tokens, Contemporary Narratives of the Lakota*, stories told for generations.

Theytus Books, Ltd.
Box 218
Penticton, British Columbia V2A 6K3

Theytus, a Coastal Salish word which translates as "preserving for the purpose of handing down," is Canada's first Native Indian-owned and -operated publishing house. Theytus covers such diverse areas as adult and children's novels, Native history, culture, politics, and education. Especially notable are their "Kou-skelowh" ("We are the People") series of Okanagan legends:

How Turtle Set the Animals Free, How Names Were Given, How Food Was Given; and *Neekna and Chemai*, an Okanagan story, for very young readers. Under the auspices of the En'Owkin Centre (257 Brunswick Street, Penticton, B.C. V2A 5P9), Theytus is working on the Okanagan Indian Curriculum Project, which will soon be available to teachers.

Tillicum Library
100-1062 Homer Street
Vancouver, Canada V6B 2W9

Tillicum Library was founded by Alberni Band member Randy Fred in 1982 to publish books by both Native and non- Native people about Native history and culture, particularly in British Columbia. Tillicum's titles include: *Children of the First People*, a beautiful photo essay on Native children of Canada's west coast, along with narratives by ten Native Elders speaking about their own childhoods; *Resistance and Renewal:*

Surviving the Indian Residential School, a study of the Kamloops Indian Residential School that won the British Columbia Book Prize in 1989; *Stoney Creek Woman*, an award-winning biography of Carrier Elder Mary John; and *Ted Trindell: Métis Witness to the North*, a biography of a Métis Elder from the Northwest Territories. Write for a catalogue.

The Wicazo Sa Review
Indian Studies MS 188
Eastern Washington University
Cheney, WA 99004

Wicazo Sa Review, a bi-annual journal of Native studies, published under the auspices of the Native Studies Center of Eastern Washington University, Cheney, Washington, is devoted to the development of Native Studies as an academic discipline.

The journal contains interviews, profiles, literature, poetry, humor, and reviews of books by and about Native peoples. This is an excellent look at the concerns of Native people in the academic field.

A Selected Bibliography

These are books by and about Native people that we have read and recommend for use with children. Some of these books may be out of print, but many can be found in libraries, used book stores, and flea markets.

A note about grade levels: Native stories, whether they are creation stories or teaching stories, were and are, first of all, told. Often, stories are told, virtually unchanged, by an Elder to groups of adults and children together. Understanding, the reasoning goes, comes to people as they develop awareness, and adults and children each comprehend at their own individual levels. In fact, because they have heard the stories so often, children may have memorized the stories long before fully understanding them. Still, Elders never tire of telling stories, and children and adults never tire of hearing them.

"Good" stories — the ones we like best — get on the pages the same way they are told; they have the same style, rhythm and cadence as they would if an Elder were telling them. Imagine, if you can, a cold, dark winter's night, sitting by a fire or wood stove, mending some clothes or sharpening a weapon, or holding a sleepy child, and an Elder says, "Now we shall have a story..."

Grade levels are always somewhat arbitrary — a child may read on one level, for instance, but comprehend on a different level. Or stories meant to be read to children might be difficult for a child to read independently. Particularly, with Native stories, which are meant to be told, grade levels are practically meaningless. We have reluctantly graded the books we recommend here, since many find the idea of grade levels useful.

Along with approximate grade levels, we have identified Nations of the People, and indicated with an asterisk (*) those books written by Native authors. If we have made any mistakes, we apologize. We hope this list is useful to you.

Anishinabe Reading Materials, *Ojibwe Gikinomagewin: Chippewa Teaching* (teacher's guide). Duluth Indian Education Advisory Committee; 1985 (Anishinabe/Ojibway/Chippewa)*

Anishinabe Reading Materials, *Ojibwe Inaonewin: Chippewa Sharing* (teacher's guide). Duluth Indian Education Advisory Committee; 1985 (Anishinabe/Ojibway/Chippewa)*

Anishinabe Reading Materials, *Ojibwe Nibwakawin: Chippewa Wisdom* (teacher's guide). Duluth Indian Education Advisory Committee; 1984 (Anishinabe/Ojibway/Chippewa)*

Armstrong, Jeannette, *Entwhisteetkwa: Walk in Water*. Theytus, 1982; gr. 2-5 (Okanagan)*

Armstrong, Jeannette, *Neekna and Chemai*. Theytus, 1984; gr. 3-up (Okanagan)*

Armstrong, Jeannette, *Slash*. Theytus, 1985; gr. hs-up (Okanagan)*

Ashabranner, Brent, *Children of the Maya: A Guatemalan Indian Odyssey*. Dodd, 1986; gr. 6-up (Maya)

Ashabranner, Brent, *Morning Star, Black Sun*. Dodd, 1982; gr. 6-up (various Nations)

Ashabranner, Brent, *To Live in Two Worlds: American Indian Youth Today*. Dodd, 1984; gr. 6-up (Cheyenne)

Awiakta, Marilou, *Rising Fawn and the Fire Mystery*. St. Luke's Press, 1983; gr. 4-up (Choctaw)*

Baker, Olaf, *Where the Buffaloes Begin*. Warne, 1981; gr. k-4 (Siksika/Blackfeet)

Bales, Carol Ann, *Kevin Cloud, Chippewa Boy in the City*. Reilly & Lee, 1972; gr. 3-5 (Anishinabe/Ojibway/Chippewa)

Baylor, Byrd, *A God on Every Mountain Top: Stories of the Southwest Indian Sacred Mountains*. Scribner, 1981; gr. 4-6 (Southwest Nations)

Baylor, Byrd, *And It Still Is That Way: Legends Told by Arizona Indian Children*. Scribner, 1976; gr. ps-3 (Southwest Nations)

Benton-Banai, Edward, *The Mishomis Book: The Voice of the Ojibway*. Indian Country Press, 1988; gr. 5-up (Anishinabe/Ojibway/Chippewa)*

Bernstein, Margery and Janet Kobrin, *The Summer Maker: An Ojibway Indian Myth*. Scribner, 1977; gr. 1-5 (Anishinabe/Ojibway/Chippewa)

Bierhorst, John, ed., *The Girl Who Married a Ghost and Other Tales from the North American Indian*. Four Winds, 1978; gr. 5-up (various Nations)

Big Crow, Moses Nelson, *A Legend from Crazy Horse Clan*. Tipi Press, 1987; gr. 4-up (Lakota)*

Blakey, Sherry, and Edward Benton-Banai, *The Sounding Voice*. Indian Country Press; gr. 7-up (various Nations)*

Blood, Charles, and Martin Link, *The Goat in the Rug*. Four Winds, 1976; gr. ps-up (Diné/Navajo)

Brescia, Bill, ed., *Our Mother Corn*. Daybreak Star Press, 1981; gr. 5-up (Hopi, Pawnee, Seneca)*

Brand, Johanna, *The Life and Death of Anna Mae Aquash*. Lorimer, 1978; gr. hs-up (North American Nations)

Brewer, Linda Skinner, *O Wakaga: Activities for Learning About the Plains Indians*. Daybreak Star Press, 1979; gr. k-3 (Plains Nations)*

Broker, Ignatia, *Night Flying Woman: An Ojibway Narrative*. Minnesota Historical Society Press, 1983; gr. 5-up (Anishinabe/Ojibway/Chippewa)*

Bruchac, Joseph, *The Faithful Hunter: Abenaki Stories*. Bowman Books; 1988; gr. 3-up (Abenaki)*

Bruchac, Joseph, *Iroquois Stories* (tape). Good Mind Records, 1988; all grades (Haudenosaunee/Iroquois)*

Bruchac, Joseph, *Iroquois Stories: Heroes and Heroines, Monsters and Magic*. Crossing Press, 1985; gr. 5-up (Haudenosaunee/Iroquois)*

Bruchac, Joseph, *Return of the Sun: Native American Tales from the Northeast Woodlands*. Crossing Press, 1989; gr. 3-up (Northeast Woodlands Nations)*

Bruchac, Joseph, *Songs from this Earth on Turtle's Back: Contemporary American Indian Poetry*. Greenfield Review Press, 1983; gr. 6-up (various Nations)*

Bruchac, Joseph, *Stone Giants and Flying Heads: Adventure Stories from the Iroquois*. Crossing Press, 1979; gr. 5-7 (Haudenosaunee/Iroquois)*

Bruchac, Joseph, *The Wind Eagle and Other Abenaki Stories*. Bowman Books, 1985; gr. 5-7 (Abenaki)*

Cameron, Anne, *Raven Returns the Water*. Harbour Publishing Co., Ltd., 1987; gr. ps-up (Northwest Coast Nations)

Campbell, Maria, *Riel's People: How the Métis Lived*. Douglas & McIntyre, 1978; gr. 4-6 (Métis)*

Charging Eagle, Tom, and Ron Zeilinger, *Black Hills: Sacred Hills*. Tipi Press, 1987; gr. 4-up (Lakota)*

Clark, Ann Nolan, *In My Mother's House*. 1941; gr. ps-up (Diné/Navajo)

Clymer, Theodore, *Four Corners of the Sky*. Little, Brown, 1975; gr. 1-4 (various Nations)

Coatsworth, David, *Adventures of Nanabush: Ojibway Indian Stories*. Atheneum, 1979; gr. 5-7 (Anishinabe/Ojibway/Chippewa)

Collura, Mary-Ellen Lang, *Winners*. Dial, 1984; gr. 6-10 (Siksika/Blackfeet)

Cone, Molly, *Number Four*. Houghton Mifflin, 1972; gr. 4-7 (Northwest Coast Nations)

Cooper, Amy Jo, *Dreamquest*. Annick Press, 1987; gr. 5-up (Anishinabe/Ojibway/Chippewa)

Council on Interracial Books for Children, *Chronicles of American Indian Protest*. CIBC, 1979; gr. hs-up (North American Nations)

Crow, Allan, *The Crying Christmas Tree*. Pemmican, 1989; gr. 1-2 (Métis)*

Culleton, Beatrice, *April Raintree*. Pemmican, 1984; gr. hs-up (Métis)*

Culleton, Beatrice, *Spirit of the White Bison*. Pemmican, 1985; gr. 4-up (Plains Nations)*

Day, Michael E., *Berry Ripe Moon*. Tide Grass Press, 1977; gr. 4-6 (Penobscot)

DeArmond, Dale, *Berry Woman's Children*. Greenwillow, 1985; gr. k-6 (Inuit)

DeArmond, Dale, *The Seal Oil Lamp*. Little, Brown, 1988; gr. 3-6 (Inuit)

DePaola, Tomie, *The Legend of the Bluebonnet*. Putnam, 1983; gr. ps-3 (Commanche)

Dixon, Sarah, *Dennis*. Cypress, 1979; gr. 4-6 (Kwakiutl)

Dodge, Nanabah Chee, *Morning Arrow*. Lothrop, 1975; gr. 3-4 (Diné/Navajo)*

Durham, Jimmie, *Columbus Day*. West End Press, 1983; gr. 7-up (all Nations)*

Ekoomiak, Normee, *Arctic Memories*. Holt, 1990; gr. all (Inuit)*

Erdoes, Richard, *American Indian Myths and Legends*. Pantheon, 1984; gr. 6-up (various Nations)

Erdoes, Richard, *The Sound of Flutes and Other Indian Legends*. Pantheon, 1976; gr. 5-up (Plains Nations)

Evers, Larry, *Hopi Photographers, Hopi Images*. Suntracks, University of Arizona Press, 1983; gr. 7-up (Hopi)

Evers, Larry, ed., *The South Corner of Time*. University of Arizona Press, 1983; gr. hs-up (Hopi, Diné/Navajo, Tohono O'odham/Papago, Yaqui)

Falk, Randolph, *Lelooska*. Celestial Arts; gr. 9-up (Kwakiutl)

Franklin Northwest Supervisory Union Title IV Indian Education Program, *Finding One's Way: The Story of an Abenaki Child*. Abenaki Self-Help Association, 1987; gr. 4-6 (Abenaki)*

French, Michael, *The Throwing Season*. Delacorte, 1980; gr. 6-up (Cherokee)

García, Maria, *The Adventures of Connie and Diego/Las Aventuras de Connie y Diego*. Children's Book Press, 1981; all grades (Chicano)*

Goble, Paul, *Beyond the Ridge*. Bradbury, 1989; gr. 3-up (Plains Nations)

Goble, Paul, *Buffalo Woman*. Bradbury, 1984; gr. 3-up (Plains Nations)

Goble, Paul, *Death of the Iron Horse*. Bradbury, 1987; all grades (Cheyenne)

Goble, Paul, *Dream Wolf*. Bradbury, 1990; gr. 3-up (Plains Nations)

Goble, Paul, *The Friendly Wolf*. Bradbury, 1974; gr. 4-up (Plains Nations)

Goble, Paul, *The Gift of the Sacred Dog*. Bradbury, 1980; gr. 4-up (Lakota)

Goble, Paul, *The Girl Who Loved Wild Horses*. Bradbury, 1978; gr. 4-up (Plains Nations)

Goble, Paul, *The Great Race*. Bradbury, 1985; gr. 4-up (Plains Nations)

Goble, Paul, *Star Boy*. Bradbury, 1983; gr. k-up (Siksika/Blackfeet)

Goble, Paul and Dorothy, *Brave Eagle's Account of the Fetterman Fight*. Pantheon, 1972; gr. 3-up (Lakota and Cheyenne)

Goble, Paul and Dorothy, *Red Hawk's Account of Custer's Last Battle*. Pantheon, 1969; gr. 3-up (Lakota)

Green, Richard G., *Wundoa: I'm Number One*. Ricara Features, 1983; all grades (Mohawk)*

Haegert, Dorothy, *Children of the First People*. Tillicum Library, 1983; gr. 5-up (West Coast Nations)

Hathaway, Flora, *The Little People*. Montana Reading Publications; gr. 3-5 (Crow)

Hausman, Gerald, *Sitting on the Blue-Eyed Bear: Navajo Myths and Legends*. Lawrence Hill, 1975; gr. 5-up (Diné/Navajo)

Henry, Edna, Wechappituwen (Blue Star Woman), *Native American Cookbook*. Messner, 1983; gr. 5-up (various Nations)*

Henry, Jeannette, and Rupert Costo, *A Thousand Years of American Indian Storytelling*. Indian Historian Press, 1981; all grades (all Nations)*

Hirschfelder, Arlene, *American Indian Stereotypes in the World of Children: A Reader and Bibliography*. Scarecrow, 1982; gr. hs-up (various Nations)

Hirschfelder, Arlene, *Happily May I Walk: American Indians and Alaska Natives Today*. Scribner, 1986; gr. 5-up (all Nations)

Houston, James, *Ojibwa Summer*. Barre, gr. 7-up (Anishinabe/Ojibway/Chippewa)

Hungry Wolf, Beverly, *The Ways of My Grandmothers*. Morrow, 1980; gr. 8-up (Siksika/Blackfeet)*

Johnson, Basil, *How the Birds Got Their Colours/Gah w'indinimowaut binaesheenhnyuk w'idinauziwin-wauh*. Kids Can Press, 1978; gr. 3-5 (Anishinabe/Ojibway/Chippewa)*

Jones, Hettie, *Coyote Tales*. Holt, Rinehart, 1974; gr. 4-up (Assiniboine, Pawnee, Lakota)

Jones, Hettie, *The Trees Stand Shining*. Dial, 1971; gr. ps-up (poetry of various Nations)

Katz, Jane B., *This Song Remembers: Self-Portraits of Native Americans in the Arts*. Houghton Mifflin, 1980; gr. 7-up (various Nations)

Kleitsch, Cristel, and Paul Stephens, *Dancing Feathers*. Annick Press, 1987; gr. 5-up (Anishinabe/Ojibway/Chippewa)

Kleitsch, Cristel, and Paul Stephens, *A Time to be Brave*. Annick Press, 1987; gr. 5-up (Anishinabe/Ojibway/Chippewa)

Lacapa, Michael, *The Flute Player*. Northland, 1990; gr. k-3 (Apache)*

LeGarde, Amelia, *Aseban: The Ojibwe Word for Raccoon*. Anishinabe Reading Materials; 1978; gr. 2-4 (Anishinabe/Ojibway/Chippewa)*

LeSeuer, Meridel, *Sparrow Hawk*. Holy Cow! Press, 1987; gr. 6-up (Mesquakie/Sauk)

Lopez, Andre, *Pagans in Our Midst*. Akwesasne Notes, gr. 6-up (Mohawk)*

McLellan, Joseph, *The Birth of Nanabosho*. Pemmican, 1989; gr. 3-up (Anishinabe/Ojibway/Chippewa).*

McLellan, Joseph, *Nanabosho Dances*. Pemmican, 1989; gr. 3-up (Anishinabe/Ojibway/Chippewa).*

McLellan, Joseph, *Nanabosho Steals Fire*. Pemmican, 1989; gr. 3- up (Anishinabe/Ojibway/Chippewa).*

Maher, Ramona, *Alice Yazzie's Year*. Coward-McCann, 1977; gr. ps-up (Diné/Navajo)

Martinson, David, ed., *A Long Time Ago is Just Like Today*. Anishinabe Reading Materials, Duluth Indian Education Advisory Committee, 1976; gr. 7-up (Anishinabe/Ojibway/ Chippewa).*

Martinson, David, *Cheer Up Old Man*. Anishinabe Reading Materials, Duluth Indian Education Advisory Committee, 1975; gr. ps-1 (Anishinabe/Ojibway/Chippewa)*

Martinson, David, *Manabozho and the Bullrushes*. Anishinabe Reading Materials, Duluth Indian Education Advisory Committee, 1976; gr. ps-1 (Anishinabe/Ojibway/Chippewa)*

Martinson, David, *Real Wild Rice*. Anishinabe Reading Materials, Duluth Indian Education Advisory Committee, 1975; gr. ps-1 (Anishinabe/Ojibway/Chippewa)*

Martinson, David, *Shemay, the Bird in the Sugarbush*. Anishinabe Reading Materials, Duluth Indian Education Advisory Committee, 1975; gr. ps-1 (Anishinabe/Ojibway/ Chippewa)*

Mathers, Linda Skinner, and Terry Tafoya, *The Mamook Book: Activities for Learning About the Northwest Coast Indians*. Daybreak Star Press, 1979; gr. 4-6 (Northwest Coast Nations)*

Messerschmidt, Jim, *The Trial of Leonard Peltier*. South End Press, 1983; gr. hs-up (North American Nations)

Muñoz, Rie, *Andy: An Alaskan Tale*. Cambridge University Press, 1988; gr. k-3 (Inuit)

Munsch, Robert, and Michael Kusugak, *A Promise is a Promise*. Annick Press, 1988; gr. 2-up (Inuit)*

Nabakov, Peter, *Native American Testimony: An Anthology of Indian and White Relations*. Crowell, 1978; gr. 7-up (all Nations)

Nelson, Mary C., *Michael Naranjo*. Dillon, 1975; gr. 5-7 (Tewa)

New Mexico People & Energy Collective, *Red Ribbons for Emma*. New Seed Press, 1981; all grades (Diné/Navajo).

Norman, Howard, *How Glooskap Outwits the Ice Giants*. Little, Brown, 1989; gr. 4-up (Northeast Coast Nations)

Norman, Howard, *Who-Paddled-Backward-With-Trout*. Little, Brown, 1987; gr. k-3 (Cree)

North American Indian Travelling College, *Legends of Our Nations*. NAITC, 1984; gr. 5-up (various Nations)*

Okanagan Tribal Council, *How Food Was Given*. Theytus, 1984; gr. 3-up (Okanagan)*

Okanagan Tribal Council, *How Names Were Given*. Theytus, 1984; gr. 3-up (Okanagan)*

Okanagan Tribal Council, *How Turtle Set the Animals Free*. Theytus, 1984; gr. 3-up (Okanagan)*

Ortiz, Simon, *The People Shall Continue*. Children's Book Press, 1977; all grades (all Nations)*

Page, Suzanne, *A Celebration of Being*. Northland Press, 1990; gr. 6-up (Hopi, Diné/Navajo)

Parlow, Anita, *Cry, Sacred Ground: Big Mountain USA*. Christic Institute, 1988; gr. hs-up (Diné/Navajo, Hopi)

Patacsil, Sharon, and Colleen Neal, *Daybreak Star Preschool Activities Book*. Daybreak Star Press, 1979; gr. ps-2 (all Nations)*

Plain, Ferguson, *Eagle Feather*. Pemmican, 1989; gr. 2-up (Anishinabe/Ojibway/Chippewa)*

Pratson, Frederick J., *Land of the Four Directions*. Chatham Press, 1970; gr. 7-up (Passamaquoddy, Micmac and Maliseet)

Robinson, Tom D., *An Eskimo Birthday*. Dodd, Mead, 1975; gr. 2-6 (Inuit)

Rock Point Community School, *Between Sacred Mountains: Navajo Stories and Lessons from the Land*. University of Arizona Press, 1982; gr. 5-up (Diné/Navajo)*

Rockwood, Joyce, *Groundhog's Horse*. Holt, Rinehart, 1978; gr. 4-7 (Cherokee)

Rohmer, Harriet, Octavio Chow, and Morris Viadure, *The Invisible Hunters/Los Cazadores Invisibles*. Children's Book Press, 1987; all grades (Miskito)

Rohmer, Harriet, and Dorminster Wilson, *Mother Scorpion Country/La Tierra de la Madre Escorpión*. Children's Book Press, 1987; all grades (Miskito)

Running, John, *Honor Dance*. University of Nevada Press, 1985; gr. 7-up (various Nations)

Sawyer, Don, *Where the Rivers Meet*. Pemmican, 1989; gr. hs-up (Shuswap)

Scott, Ann Herbert, *On My Mother's Lap*. McGraw-Hill, 1972; gr. ps-1 (Inuit)

Scribe, Murdo, *Murdo's Story: A Legend from Northern Manitoba*. Pemmican, 1986; gr. 3-up (Anishinabe/Ojibway/Chippewa).*

Slipperjack, Ruby, *Honour the Sun*. Pemmican, 1987; gr. hs-up (Anishinabe/Ojibway/Chippewa)*

Sneve, Virginia Driving Hawk, *The Chichi Hoohoo Bogeyman*. Holiday House, 1975; gr. 4-6 (Lakota)*

Sneve, Virginia Driving Hawk, *Dancing Teepees*. Holiday House, 1989; gr. 2-up (various Nations)*

Sneve, Virginia Driving Hawk, *High Elk's Treasure*. Holiday House, 1972; gr. 5-up (Lakota)*

Sneve, Virginia Driving Hawk, *When Thunders Spoke*. Holiday House, 1974; gr. 5-up (Lakota)*

St. Paul Community Programs in the Arts and Sciences, *Angwamas Minosewag Anishinabeg—Time of the Indian*. Indian Country Press, 1977; gr. 5-up (various Nations)*

Steltzer, Ulli, *A Haida Potlach*. University of Washington Press, 1984; gr. 4-up (Haida)

Steltzer, Ulli, *Inuit*. University of Chicago Press, 1982; gr. 7-up (Inuit)

Steptoe, John, *The Story of Jumping Mouse*. Lothrop, 1984; gr. ps-3 (Northern Plains Nations)

Strete, Craig Kee, *When Grandfather Journeys Into Winter*. Greenwillow, 1979; gr. 4-6 (Nation unspecified)*

Strete, Craig Kee, *The Bleeding Man and Other Stories*. Greenwillow, 1977; gr. 8-up (Nation unspecified)*

TallMountain, Mary, *Green March Moons*. New Seed Press, 1987; gr. 5-up (Koyukon)*

Tapahonso, Luci, *A Breeze Swept Through*. West End Press, 1987; gr. 6-up (Diné/Navajo)*

Tappage, Mary Augusta, *The Big Tree and the Little Tree*. Pemmican, 1986; gr. k-3 (Shuswap/Métis)*

Tehanetorens, *The Gift of the Great Spirit: Iroquois Lesson Stories* (tape). Good Mind Records; 1988; all grades (Haudenosaunee/Iroquois)*

Tohono O'odham Tribal Council, *Tohono O'odham: Lives of the Desert People*. Tohono O'odham Education Department, 1989; gr. 3-up (Tohono O'odham/Papago)*

Trimble, Stephen, and Harvey Lloyd, *Our Voices, Our Land*. Northland Press, 1986; all grades (Southwestern Nations)

Walters, Anna Lee, *Ghost Singer*. Northland, 1988; gr. hs-up (Diné/Navajo)*

Weeks, Rupert, *Pachee Goyo, History and Legends from the Shoshone*. Jelm Mountain Press, 1981; gr. 3-7 (Shoshone)*

Weist, Tom, *A History of the Cheyenne People*. Montana Council for Indian Education, 1977; gr. 7-up (Cheyenne)*

Wheeler, Bernelda, *I Can't Have Bannock But the Beaver Has a Dam*. Pemmican, 1985; gr. k-3 (Cree/Salteaux)*

Wheeler, Bernelda, *Where Did You Get Your Moccasins?* Pemmican, 1986; gr. k-3 (Cree/Salteaux)*

White, Ellen, *Kwulasulwut: Stories from the Coast Salish*. Theytus, 1981; gr. 4-up (Coast Salish)*

Yellow Robe, Rosebud, *Tonweya and the Eagles*. Dial, 1979; gr. 2-up (Lakota)*

Yue, Charlotte and David, *The Igloo*. Houghton Mifflin, 1988; gr. 5-8 (Inuit)

Yue, Charlotte and David, *The Pueblo*. Houghton Mifflin, 1986; gr. 4-7 (Pueblo)

Yue, Charlotte and David, *The Tipi: A Center of Native American Life*. Knopf, 1984; gr. 4-7 (Plains Nations)

Zitkala-Ša, *Old Indian Legends*. University of Nebraska Press, 1985; gr. 4-up (Dakota)*

American Indian Authors for Young Readers:
An Annotated Bibliography

Compiled by
Mary Gloyne Byler

Well over 600 children's books were examined during a four-year period in the preparation of this bibliography. Roughly two out of three were rejected out-of-hand because the contents or illustrations were conspicuously offensive. A closer look at the remaining 200 or so books proved discouraging. The prevalence of more subtle stereotypes, misconceptions and clichés led to further rejections. Finally, it was decided to limit selection to American Indian authors.

While non-Indian authors may produce well-written and entertaining children's books featuring American Indians, there is little in their stories that tells us much about American Indians. We do learn what non-Indians imagine Indians to be, or think they should be.

There is more to being an American Indian—Apache, Seneca, Hopi, or whatever tribe—than can be acquired through an act of will, a course of study, or discovering an Indian ancestor somewhere in the family tree. It is not an intellectual choice. In short, being Indian is growing up Indian: it is a way of life, a way of thinking and being. Shaped by their own life experiences, non-Indians lack the feelings and insights essential to a valid representation of what it means to be an American Indian.

This bibliography is short. It is short because there are so few books for children written by American Indians. One reason for

this is that publishers have had little interest in developing American Indian authors.

Additionally, the oral tradition by which American Indians convey and perpetuate vast bodies of knowledge does not contain a section of literature that is exclusively for children. This oral tradition, free from the limits imposed by the written word, does not tailor its material to appeal to varying age groups.

Those "quaint" fables, myths and "animal stories" that have been "retold" for children often have many levels of meaning in the original versions—meanings that a child may grasp at varying stages of development and may come to fully understand only with the passage of time and an ever-growing experience of life.

This bibliography contains many books that would not ordinarily appear in a listing of books for children. But in the oral tradition, those who have information share it with those who do not. In this spirit then, it is up to those who can read to embrace the oral tradition and share what they read with those who cannot. At this point in time it is the only way very young children will be able to learn what American Indians are saying and writing about themselves.

[Editors' note: Mary's bibliography was originally published in 1973, and therefore, many, if not all, of these books will be found to be out of print. However, in our experience, haunting flea markets and used book stores can often turn up some very good titles; and this list can be used as a guide.]

Bennett, Kay, *Kaibah: Recollections of a Navajo Girlhood*. Western Lore Press, 1964; gr. 8-up (Diné/Navajo).
   Bennett presents Diné life as no outsider can. She writes of her years as a girl on the Navajo reservation during the years 1928-1935. Her people are depicted with love and understanding.

Black Elk, *Black Elk Speaks: Being the Life Story of a Holy Man of the Oglala Sioux*, as told to John Neihardt. University of Nebraska Press, 1961; gr. 10-up (Lakota).
   Originally published in 1932, this is a personal narrative by one of the great spiritual leaders of the Oglala. Black Elk, a holy man who was born in 1863, gives a moving account of his life from early boyhood to the massacre at Wounded Knee in 1890 and the gathering of the Oglalas on the Pine Ridge reservation in South Dakota.

Black Hawk, *Black Hawk: An Autobiography*, ed. by Donald Jackson. Peter Smith, 1955; gr. 10-up (Mesquakie/Sauk).
   In the story of his life, recorded in 1833, 70-year-old Black Hawk tells of his early battles with other tribes and ends with an account of his last flight from the United States Army and the merciless massacre of his people at Bad Axe, Wisconsin, in 1832.

Blue Eagle, Acee, *Echogee, the Little Blue Deer*. Palmco Investment Corp., 1971 (Flagship Air Gifts, P.O. Box 5188, Church Street Station, New York, NY 10049); gr. k-3 (Pawnee-Creek).
   Echogee (pronounced E-Joe-G), a little blue deer, bravely ventures away from his mother to explore the world. He encounters rabbits, skunks, turkeys and other animals who repeatedly caution him against straying too far. However, it is "dreadful noises" that finally send the little deer back to the comforting presence of his mother. There are 22 full-color illustrations in this 9" x 12" book.

Chief Joseph, *Chief Joseph's Own Story*. Montana Reading Publications, 1972; gr. 3-up (Nez Percé).
   In this oration delivered in Washington, D.C. in 1879, Chief Joseph traces the history of the Nez Percé contact with non-Indians beginning roughly in 1779, when French trappers traveled into eastern Oregon, to the time of his surrender, betrayal, and exile to Oklahoma Territory.

Clutesi, George, *Son of Raven, Son of Deer*. Gray's Publishing Ltd., 1967; gr. 5-up (Nootka).
   These 12 fables of the Tse-shaht people reveal various aspects of a rich culture. They are for teaching children the many wonders of nature, the importance of all living things, and to acquaint them with the closeness of people to all animals, birds and sea creatures. Good for reading aloud.

Cohoe, William, *A Cheyenne Sketchbook.* University of Oklahoma Press, 1964; gr. 4-up (Cheyenne).
  Cohoe, one of 72 warriors from the Great Plains taken as prisoners to Fort Marion, Florida, in 1875, sketched scenes from his past and from his life as a prisoner. The drawings are in three groups: life on the Plains, hunting; life on the Plains, ceremonies; life at Fort Marion, prisoners of war.

Crashing Thunder, *Crashing Thunder: The Autobiography of a Winnebago,* ed. by Paul Radin. Dover, 1963; gr. 11-up (Winnebago).
  A re-publication of a 1920 edition, this life story of a Winnebago man incorporates a great deal of information about the tribe's customs. It is a forthright account of a boy's growing to manhood.

Eastman, Charles Alexander (Ohiyesa), *Indian Boyhood.* Dover Publications, 1963; gr. 11-up (Dakota).
  Originally published in 1902, this is a first-person account of the everyday happenings in the life of a young Santee boy. The time is immediately prior to the reservation period. Woven into the story are the customs, traditions, and religious beliefs of the people as they were then. The sentiments expressed in the first paragraph of the dedication are unworthy of the rest of the book.

Eastman, Charles Alexander (Ohiyesa), *Wigwam Evenings: Sioux Folk Tales Retold,* with Elaine G. Eastman. Little, Brown, 1909; gr. k-up (Dakota).
  This collection of traditional Dakota stories is designed to be read or told to children of five and up.

Fadden, Ray, *Migration of the Iroquois.* White Roots of Peace (Mohawk Nation at Akwesasne via Rooseveltown, NY 13683), 1972; gr. 5-up (Mohawk).
  This story is about the Haudenosaunee or the People of the Longhouse, as recorded on a beaded belt which can be seen at the Six Nations Museum in Onchiota, New York.

Fredericks, Oswald White Bear, *Book of the Hopi,* ed. by Frank Waters. Viking, 1963; gr. 9-12 (Hopi).
  Drawings and source material recorded by Fredericks are the heart of this account of Hopi history, religion, customs, and ceremonies. Thirty members of the tribe tell of their experiences and of their efforts to maintain their spiritual beliefs.

Freuchen, Pipaluk, *Eskimo Boy.* Lothrop, Lee, 1951; gr. 3-up (Inuit).
  Ivik pledges to take on the job of finding food for his family after his father is killed in a hunting accident. Bad luck and inexperience finally force the young boy to undertake a long and hazardous journey across the ice to seek help on the mainland. The story of Ivik's long trek, his encounter with a polar bear, eventual rescue and triumphant return is told with unrelenting realism.

Geronimo, *Geronimo: His Own Story,* ed. by Steven Melvil Barrett. E.P. Dutton, 1970; gr. 7-up (Apache).
  In this story of his life, dictated while he was imprisoned at Fort Sill, Oklahoma Territory, Geronimo gives both a cultural and an historical account of his people.

Josie, Edith, *Here are the News*. Clark, Irwin, 1966; gr. 7-up (Loucheaux).
This book contains the newspaper columns of Edith Josie, which have appeared in the *Whitehorse Star* since the fall of 1962. She writes of the Indian village of Old Crow, located on the banks of the Porcupine River inside the Arctic Circle. Her accounts of trapping, fishing, incoming planes, and dogsled races reflect what is considered newsworthy in Old Crow. The articles also record a way of life that is gradually being changed by contact with the outside world.

LaFlesche, Francis, *The Middle Five: Indian Schoolboys of the Omaha Tribe*. University of Wisconsin Press, 1963; gr. 4-up (Omaha).
This reprint of a 1900 edition describes LaFlesche's experiences at the Presbyterian Mission School in Bellevue, Nebraska, during the 1860s.

LaPointe, Frank, *The Sioux Today*. Macmillan, 1972; gr. 7-up (Lakota).
Vignettes of the lives of Lakota people today, based on the author's own reservation experience, tell about Chuck, who decides to let his hair grow and is called a "militant"; Louis, who does not want to admit to being a Lakota; Shirley, who at 14 serves as mother to five; and Betty, a "new Indian," who refuses to be called a "squaw." Excellent.

Lyons, Oren, *Dog Story*. Holiday House, 1973; gr. k-1 (Onondaga).
Lyons writes of his boyhood on the Onondaga Reservation in upstate New York and of his dog, Smudgie. This is a touching story of how a boy and a dog meet and of the deep friendship that develops between them.

Markoosie, *Harpoon of the Hunter*. McGill-Queen's University Press, 1970; gr. 7-up (Inuit).
The hero of this story, young Kamik, tracks down a wounded polar bear and makes a long journey home alone after his companions have been killed. Life in the Canadian Arctic is depicted as an unrelenting, brutal, often fatal, struggle for survival.

Mayokok, Robert, (1406 Twining Avenue, Anchorage, AL 99504) (Inuit).
Mayokok, a well-known artist, has written and illustrated five paperbound booklets: *The Alaskan Eskimo* contains information on Inuit food, Native clothing, hunting and fishing. *Eskimo Customs* tells of such customs as piercing lips and tattooing and also has information on the language. *Eskimo Life* tells about oogrook, hunting, catching birds and arctic hare. *Eskimo Stories* is a selection of traditional tales. *True Eskimo Stories* tells about the hair seal, seal hunting, how the seal is used, dog teams, walrus and driftwood.

McGaa, Ed, *Red Cloud: The Story of an American Indian*. Dillon Press, 1971; gr. 8-up (Lakota).
Red Cloud, an Oglala leader, struggled during the second half of the 19th century to save his people from cultural and physical destruction. This great leader emerges as a vigorous man whose incisive mind enables him to state his case with sharp wit and sly humor. Written by a member of the Oglala Nation, this biography contains information about Lakota culture.

McNickle, D'Arcy, *Indian Tribes of the United States: Ethnic and Cultural Survival*. Oxford University Press, 1962; gr. 8-up (Flathead).
A discussion of American Indian attempts to adjust to Anglo-American culture and why the efforts have failed.

McNickle, D'Arcy, *Runner in the Sun: A Story of Indian Maize.* Holt, Rinehart, Winston, 1954; gr. 7-up (Flathead).
An adventure story as well as the history of a town settled centuries before Columbus set sail from Spain, this novel is a scholarly reconstruction of the life, customs and beliefs of the ancient cliff-dwelling settlements of the southwestern United States. Salt, a teenage boy, is chosen to make a hazardous journey to Mexico in search of a hardier strain of corn and a better life for the people of his village.

Monture, Ethel Brant, *Famous Indians: Canadian Portraits.* Clarke, Irwin, 1960; gr. 10-up (Mohawk).
The life stories of Joseph Brant (1742-1806), a Mohawk; Crowfoot (1821-1889), Blackfeet; and Oronhyatekha (1841-1907), a Mohawk; are set against the background of their times. These concisely written biographies contain a great deal of historical and cultural information.

Mountain Wolf Woman, *Mountain Wolf Woman: Sister of Crashing Thunder*, ed. by Nancy Oestreich Lurie. University of Michigan Press, 1961; gr. 10-up (Winnebago).
An unusually candid and authentic account of Indian life—told from a woman's point of view. In this narrative, recorded on tape and then translated into English, Mountain Wolf Woman, at the age of 75, describes her wandering childhood days in Wisconsin, her brief stay at a mission school, the marriage arranged against her will, the death of her chosen husband, and the misfortunes of her children.

Nez Percé Tribe, *Ne Mee Poom Tit Wah Tit (Nez Percé Legends).* 1972; gr. 7-up (Nez Percé).
Coyote, the principal character in these legends, is known as a trickster-transformer. Sometimes a man, sometimes an animal, he possesses supernatural powers and can change himself, other animals, people, and objects in various ways. He is a silly, clumsy, stupid, laughable rascal who gets into one scrape after another but he is also a cheerful, happy creature who is in no way evil. By acting out people's socially disruptive drives, Coyote reveals in these stories the results of violating conventional Nez Percé mores. Stories of Coyote's exploits are used to teach Nez Percé children how to behave properly and to instill in children values which will help them become good people. This book, sponsored and edited by the Nez Percé Tribe, is the first of a three-phase project on the history and culture of these people. Good for reading and telling.

Nuligak, *I, Nuligak*, translated from the Inuit by Maurice Metayer. Peter Martin, 1968; gr. 7-up (Inuit).
This autobiography of a member of the Kitigariukmeut tribe of Canadian Inuit spans the years from 1895 to 1966. It is simply told and reveals the gaiety, laughter and warmth of Inuit community life as well as the physical hardship and privations of life in the harsh Arctic environment.

Parker, Arthur C., *Skunny Wundy: Seneca Indian Tales.* Albert Whitman, 1970; gr. 5-up (Seneca).
Different animals take on different traits in these tales: Fox and Raccoon are clever, while Rabbit is often easily fooled; Bear is brave but not very smart, and Wolf is frequently a villain. Originally published in 1926, these stories are good for reading aloud.

Plenty-Coups, *Plenty-Coups, Chief of the Crows*, ed. by Frank Bird Linderman. University of Nebraska Press, 1962; gr. 10-up (Crow).
Eighty-year-old Chief Plenty-Coups discusses his boyhood, how he became a chief, and describes his participation in Crow culture. This book was originally published in 1930 as *American, the Life Story of a Great Indian, Plenty-Coups, Chief of the Crows.*

Senungetuk, Joseph E., *Give or Take a Century: An Eskimo Chronicle*. Indian Historian Press, 1970; gr. 10-up (Inuit).
The author tells the history of his family in Alaska as they move from a century filled with customs, traditions and lifeways of an ancient time into a new century in which they are confronted and confused by the mores, social life, and technology of a different culture.

Shaw, Anna Moore, *Pima Indian Legends*. University of Arizona Press, 1968; gr. 6-up (Pima).
Shaw relates stories heard from her parents and grandparents, and combines ancient Pima history with more current happenings.

Silook, Roger, *...In the Beginning*. Helen A. White, 1970; gr. 6-up (Inuit).
This is the story of people in pre-historic Alaska as told by two Alaskan Inuits in simple words and drawings. Order from: Helen A. White, 7323 Duben Ave., Anchorage, Alaska 99504. It will be a surprise to some to learn that Alaska was once "warm all 365 days a year."

Sneve, Virginia Driving Hawk, *High Elk's Treasure*. Holiday House, 1972; gr. 3-6 (Lakota).
This story about the High Elk family, a contemporary Lakota family, has many dimensions. It is an adventure story with an element of mystery regarding the contents of an old rawhide bundle discovered in a cave where young Joe High Elk takes refuge from a storm. It is also a story about Lakota reservation life.

Sneve, Virginia Driving Hawk, *Jimmy Yellow Hawk*. Holiday House, 1972; gr. 3-6 (Lakota).
This story about a contemporary Lakota boy living on a reservation in South Dakota tells of the excitement of a rodeo, a search for a lost mare in a dangerous storm, the pageantry of a dance contest, and learning to trap animals properly.

Stands in Timber, John, *Cheyenne Memories*. Yale University Press, 1967; gr. 11-up (Cheyenne).
Stands in Timber offers a record of Cheyenne life from legendary times to life on the Northern Plains Cheyenne Reservation in Montana.

Tall Bull, Henry, *Cheyenne Fire Fighters*. Montana Reading Publications, 1971; gr. 4-up (Cheyenne).
This is about a crew of Cheyenne who fight forest fires. The story opens with the sighting of smoke on the horizon by a forest ranger, describes how forest fires behave, and details modern methods used to contain and control forest fires.

Tall Bull, Henry, *Grandfather and the Popping Machine*. Montana Reading Publications, 1970; gr. 4-8 (Cheyenne).
Humorous stories current among the Northern Cheyenne.

Tall Bull, Henry, *The Spotted Horse*. Montana Reading Publications, 1970; gr. 4-8 (Cheyenne).
Little Thunder breaks in his first horse, saves the camp's horse herd, and participates in a buffalo hunt.

Tall Bull, Henry, *The Winter Hunt*. Montana Reading Publications, 1971; gr. 5-8 (Cheyenne).
In the first story, Little Thunder and Spotted Horse search for badly needed food. In "Snake Medicine," Little Fawn is bitten by a rattlesnake while she and her mother are picking Juneberries. Black Hair treats the bite and saves her life. In the third story, two women, Good Feather and Red Tassel, make it possible for the men of the camp to capture seven horses.

Toineeta, Joy Yellowtail, *Indian Tales of the Northern Plains*, with Sally Old Coyote. Montana Reading Publications, 1972; gr. 2-4 (Crow).
The authors present a rich collection of Blackfeet, Lakota, Cheyenne, Crow, Flathead and Arapahoe "how and why" stories.

Toineeta, Joy Yellowtail, *Indian Tales of the Northern Rockies*, with Sally Old Coyote. Montana Reading Publications, gr. 1-4 (Crow).
This volume recounts folk tales from the Blackfeet, Flathead, Gros Ventre, Nez Percé and Shoshone peoples.

Two Leggings, *Two Leggings: The Making of a Crow Warrior*, ed. by Peter Nabokov. Crowell, 1967; gr. 10-up (Crow).
This is a first-person account of the everyday life of a 19th century Crow man. Two Leggings describes the process of becoming a Crow warrior and gives a great deal of information on the religious and social values of his people.

Velarde, Pablita, *Old Father, the Story Teller*. Sale Stuart King; 1960; gr. 7-up (Tewa).
A Tewa artist writes the stories and legends she heard from her grandfather and great-grandfather.

Webb, George, *A Pima Remembers*. University of Arizona Press, 1959; gr. 7-up (Pima).
Webb wrote this book to acquaint young Pimas with some of the background and traditions of their own people. He describes in short-story form the old ways, a rabbit hunt, Pima games, his own school days, a horse roundup, and includes some Pima legends. He describes Pima life before and after a dam was built across the Gila River upstream of the Pimas.

Welch, James, *Riding the Earthboy 40*. World, 1971; gr. 9-up (Siksika/Blackfeet).
These 46 poems, rich in the imagery of the land and life, are moving comments on the human experience and one person's search for meaning in a difficult world. His first collection of poems, *Earthboy* immediately establishes Welch in the forefront of younger American poets.

Wooden Leg, *Wooden Leg: A Warrior Who Fought Custer*, as told to Thomas B. Marquis. University of Nebraska Press, 1962; gr. 10-up (Cheyenne).
This reprint of a 1931 edition is the narrative of a Cheyenne warrior who fought against Custer at the Battle of the Little Big Horn. It includes observations on Cheyenne daily life and customs.

Yellow Robe, Rosebud, (Lacotawin), *An Album of the American Indian*. Franklin Watts, 1969; gr. 5-up (Lakota).
Paintings, drawings, and photographs, accompanied by a brief text, serve to illustrate various facets of American Indian cultures and history from past to present. Although designed primarily for young adults, this album will be of interest to all ages.

Zuni Pueblo, *The Zunis: Self-Portrayals, by the Zuni People*, translated by Alvina Quam. Univerisity of New Mexico Press, 1972; gr. 6-up (Zuni).
 Here, for the first time in print, are 46 stories from the great oral literature of the Zunis of New Mexico. The creation story, rituals of masked dances, farming and hunting practices, battles, fables, and history are all recorded in this book. There are tales of ghosts and personified animals, as well as fables told to discipline children or to warn them against foolhardy bravery and braggadocio. Some of the stories are simply for entertainment and some deal directly with the problems of modern society. In his introduction, Robert E. Lewis, Governor of the Pueblo, says, "We are proud to present this, the first volume of stories told by the oldest members of my Zuni people, for your reading enjoyment—old and young, in classroom or home."

Miscellaneous

Photographs and Poems by Sioux Children. Tipi Shop, Inc., 1971; gr. 6-up (Lakota).
 Thirteen teenage students of the Porcupine Day School on the Pine Ridge Reservation in South Dakota took the photographs presented in this exhibition catalog. The photos are accompanied by poems written by the student photographers and their classmates. The photographs explore many aspects of life and the natural environment of the Porcupine community, and document western rural life during the winter season of 1969-70. The poems are an extension of the photographic themes. Order from: Tipi Shop, Inc., P.O. Box 1270, Rapid City, SD 57701.

Tales from the Longhouse. Gray's Publishing Ltd., 1973; gr. 6-up (Northwest Coast Nations).
 Students living on Vancouver Island and in the village of Kingcome Inlet on the British Columbia coast gathered these stories and legends from older relatives over a six-year period. The stories are from the various bands in British Columbia, and are arranged under such headings as origins, power, nature, crafts, customs, animals, birds, and legends.

Tales of Eskimo Alaska. Alaska Methodist University Press, 1971; all grades (Inuit).
 This collection of tales and legends from four areas of Alaska includes legends of the supernatural, a story about mischievous children, a porcupine hunt, a tale of war, and stories about the past.

The Weewish Tree, a magazine of Indian America for young people. The Indian Historian Press; gr. 1-up (all Nations).
 Written and illustrated by Native people, young and old, this magazine contains stories, poems, games, history, legends, illustrations, and cultural articles written for young people.

The Whispering Winds: Poetry by Young American Indians, ed. by Terry Allen. Doubleday, 1972; gr. 8-up (various Nations).
 A collection of poems written by students at the Institute of American Indian Arts in Santa Fe, New Mexico, a combined academic high school and art institute. The poetry covers such varied themes as Indian lore, the Vietnam War, childhood memories, thirst, and loneliness. A brief biography of the poet precedes their poems.

Contributors' Notes

Beth Brant is a Bay of Quinte Mohawk from Theyindenaga Mohawk Territory. She is the editor of *A Gathering of Spirit*, a collection of writing and art by North American Indian Women (Ithaca, New York: Firebrand Books, 1988). She is also the author of *Mohawk Trail* (Firebrand Books, 1985). She is 48, lives in Detroit with her lover, Denise, and is a mother and grandmother. She is working on a collection of short stories and a personal journey-narrative about her long illness and the recuperative powers of nature.

Joseph Bruchac is of Abenaki, Slovak, and English ancestry. A storyteller and writer whose books include *Survival This Way, Interviews with American Indian Poets* (University of Arizona), and *The Faithful Hunter* (Bowman Books), he lives with his wife, Carol, and their two sons in Greenfield Center, New York, in the same house he was raised in by his Abenaki Grandfather.

Mary Gloyne Byler is an enrolled member of the Eastern Band of Cherokee Nations in North Carolina, and a longtime associate of the Association on American Indian Affairs and the Council on Interracial Books for Children. She lives and works in Washington, D.C.

Hooty Croy is a 35-year-old Shasta/Kuruk artist, who wants to learn more and teach about his experiences in the school, welfare, and prison systems, in order to make this world better for his three children and future generations of Native children.

Michael Dorris, who is Modoc, is a professor of Native Studies at Dartmouth College and author of *Native Americans: 500 Years After* (Crowell), *A Yellow Raft in Blue Water* (Holt), and *The Broken Cord* (Harper & Row). He lives with his wife, novelist Louise Erdrich, and their six children in Cornish Flat, New Hampshire.

Rosemary Gonzales is Ojibway and white. A poet who uses Native imagery in portraits of people who have influenced her life, Rosemary works with the Urban Indian Child Resource Center in Oakland, California. She and her two young children live in El Cerrito, California.

Sharol Graves is Shawnee, Chippewa, and Sisseton. She has worked as an instructor in silkscreen, beadwork, and maskmaking at the American Indian Arts Workshop and the Indian Education Program of the San Francisco Unified School District, where she encouraged Native children to reclaim their cultural, spiritual, and historical heritage through art. Sharol, whose prints and drawings have been shown throughout the country, works in her San Francisco studio, where she synthesizes electronic graphic imagery with Native design, form, and legend. She also creates sculptural forms of parfleches in mixed media on paper and in ceramics.

Kahionhes (John Fadden) was born into the Turtle Clan of the Mohawk Nation at Akwesasne. Kahionhes is an artist, art teacher and the illustrator of more than 20 books dealing with Native peoples. He lives with his partner, Eva Thompson Fadden, and their three sons in the Adirondacks. A collection of his drawings, *Visions in Ink*, was published in 1984 by Strawberry Press.

Lenore Keeshig-Tobias is an Ojibway storyteller, writer, and activist. A founding member of the Committee to Re-establish the Trickster, organized to reclaim the Native voice in literature, and the pro-tem chair of the Committee on Racism in Writing and Publishing, Lenore, with her daughter, Polly, has just written *Bird Talk*, a children's book about the racism experienced by a first-grade student. She lives with her four daughters and infant son, and her partner, David McLaren, who works on land claims for the Saugeen Ojibway in Ontario.

Cení Myles is a 20-year-old Navajo/Mohegan/Pequot woman who is attending Pomona College. She plans to study business and/or law and put these skills to work for her people. She still thinks about the past, and wonders how to take real experiences and make them into stories. Cení wrote *Fiery Red* during her senior year of high school.

Doris Seale, who is Santee, Cree, English, and French, is a children's librarian and writer. Her work includes articles and book reviews for the Council on Interracial Books for Children *Bulletin*; contributions to *Fireweed* and *A Gathering of Spirit*, two anthologies of writings by Native women; and *Blood Salt*, number one in the University of Arkansas' series of chapbooks of Native writing published by the American Native Press Archives. Doris is ma and grandma to a number of Indian children in the greater Boston area, and lives with two cats in Everett. She loves pow-wows, fry bread, and kids—not necessarily in that order.

Beverly Slapin is a poet, writer, teacher, and single mother. She has been known to refer to herself as a "pain-in-the-neck-social-activist parent." Her work includes *Books Without Bias: A Guide to Evaluating Children's Literature for Handicapism* and *Books Without Bias: A Multicultural Bibliography*. Her passion for justice is tempered by a good sense of the ridiculous. She not only "gets" Indian jokes, she even thinks they're funny. Beverly lives with her 13-year-old son, Carlos, in Berkeley, California.

Index